WO[MEN]
A Fe[minis]
Jo C[...]

WOMEN IN SOCIETY
A Feminist List edited by
Jo Campling

Published

Sheila Allen and Carol Wolkowitz **Homeworking: myths and realities**
Jenny Beale **Women in Ireland: voices of change**
Angela Coyle and Jane Skinner (*editors*) **Women and Work: positive action for change**
Gillian Dalley **Ideologies of Caring: rethinking community and collectivism**
Leonore Davidoff and Belinda Westover (*editors*) **Our Work, Our Lives, Our Words: women's history and women's work**
Emily Driver and Audrey Droisen (*editors*) **Child Sexual Abuse: feminist perspectives**
Diana Gittins **The Family in Question: changing households and familiar ideologies**
Frances Heidensohn **Women and Crime**
Ursula King **Women and Spirituality: voices of protest and promise**
Muthoni Likimani (*Introductory Essay by Jean O'Barr*) **Passbook Number F.47927: women and Mau Mau in Kenya**
Jo Little, Linda Peake and Pat Richardson (*editors*) **Women in Cities: gender and the urban environment**
Sharon Macdonald, Pat Holden and Shirley Ardener (*editors*) **Images of Women in Peace and War: cross-cultural and historical perspectives**
Shelley Pennington and Belinda Westover **A Hidden Workforce: homeworkers in England, 1850–1985**
Vicky Randall **Women and Politics: an international perspective** (2nd edn)
Rosemary Ridd and Helen Callaway (*editors*) **Caught Up in Conflict: women's responses to political strife**
Patricia Spallone **Beyond Conception: the new politics of reproduction**
Taking Liberties Collective **Learning the Hard Way: women's oppression in men's education**
Clare Ungerson (*editor*) **Women and Social Policy: a reader**
Ann Woodhouse **Fantastic Women: sex, gender and transvestism**

Forthcoming

Eileen Aird and Judy Lown **Education for Autonomy: processes of change in women's education**
Niamh Baker **Happily Ever After? Women's fiction in post-war Britain**
Jennifer Breen **Women and Fiction**
Maria Brenton **Women and Old Age**
Joan Busfield **Women and Mental Health**
Ruth Carter and Gill Kirkup **Women in Engineering**
Lesley Ferris **Acting Women: images of women in theatre**
Tuula Gordon **Feminist Mothers**
Frances Gray **Women and Laughter**
Eileen Green, Diana Woodward and Sandra Hebron **Women's Leisure, What Leisure?**
Jennifer Hargreaves **Women and Sport**
Annie Hudson **Troublesome Girls: adolescence, femininity and the state**
Susan Lonsdale **Women and Disability**
Mavis Maclean **Surviving Divorce: women's resources after separation**
Lesley Rimmer **Women's Family Lives: changes and choices**
Susan Sellers **Language and Sexual Difference: feminist writing in France**
Deborah Valenze **The Other Victorian Women**
Janet Wolff **The Art of Women**

Learning the Hard Way

Women's Oppression in Men's Education

Taking Liberties Collective

Lorraine Biddlecombe
Julie Browne
Berni Charlton
Helena Dowden
Carmen Northcott
Jane Onslow
Judith Priestley
Jane Thompson

MACMILLAN

First published 1989

Published by
MACMILLAN EDUCATION LTD
Houndmills, Basingstoke, Hampshire RG21 2XS
and London
Companies and representatives
throughout the world

Typeset by Vine & Gorfin Ltd
Exmouth, Devon

Printed in China

British Library Cataloguing in Publication Data
Learning the hard way: women's oppression in
men's education. — (Women in Society)
1. Great Britain. Women. Education
I. Taking Liberties Collective II. Series
376′. 941
ISBN 0–333–43283–5 (hardcover)
ISBN 0–333–43284–3 (paperback)

Series Standing Order

If you would like to receive future titles in this series as they are
published, you can make use of our standing order facility. To place a
standing order please contact your bookseller or, in case of difficulty,
write to us at the address below with your name and address and the
name of the series. Please state with which title you wish to begin
your standing order. (If you live outside the United Kingdom we may
not have the rights for your area, in which case we will forward your
order to the publisher concerned.)

Customer Services Department, Macmillan Distribution Ltd
Houndmills, Basingstoke, Hampshire, RG21 2XS, England.

Contents

Acknowledgements   vi

Preface   vii

Introduction by Jo Campling   xi

1. **The truth about our lives**   1

2. **Prisoners of gender**   42

3. **The obstacle race**   65

4. **Deals and dilemmas**   110

5. **Worming into Women's Studies**   126

6. **Doing it for ourselves**   140

7. **Beware the backlash**   162

Acknowledgements

The women whose writing is included in this book are:

Thia Chay-Pong Andrews
Lorraine Biddlecombe
Julie Browne
Mary Caraher
Sue Carrol
Fran Carroll
Berni Charlton
Anji Clarke
Sharon Collins
Helena Dowden
Sue Ellis
Jane Frances
Sue Griffin
Trish Guerri
Marj Hales
Mary Haylett
Mary Hawkins
Sue High
Mary Hughes
Blue Joyce
Chris Kent
Chris Kibbey
Sandi Langridge
Carol Larter
Carol Lewis
Mandy Limbrick
Shirley Manzi
Rita Mulcahy
Carmen Northcott

Jane Unslow
Peggy O'Shea
June Ponsford
Pam Moore
Judith Priestley
Jill Radford
Barbara Rannigan
Linda Read
Betsy Reid
Pam Roberts
Pat Robson
Helen Rowan
Marcia Saitch
Mary Selwood
Catherine Smith
Chrissie Snell
Marian Stala
Audrey Stammers
Pat Stevens
Nesta Stocks
Sally Stubbs
Lin Tetlow
Jane Thompson
Christine Turnbull
Judy White
Rose Wiles
Judy Woodman
Karen Wyatt

Preface

Writing books isn't easy – even for those with a room in which to write, some peace and quiet in which to concentrate and the expectation that other people will take what you have to say seriously. On the whole, women like us don't write books. If we do, they don't get published. In this book we've included the writings of 57 women. All but one or two of us started life as working-class children. All but one or two of us are working-class women. A few of us are black and a few of us are lesbian. Most of us left school at 15 or 16 with no educational qualifications. Most of us live on very little money – courtesy of the DHSS – or on the low wages we, and sometimes our husbands, earn.

The kinds of jobs we were doing at the time of writing include nursing, factory work, waitressing and bar-work, teaching, crêche-work, home-work of various kinds, secretarial and shop work. Some of us are married, a few of us live with the women who are our lovers. All but a few of us have had children. Many of us are single parents with nobody very much to help us look after our children. Some of us have lost our children, to adoption agencies, to Social Services or to ex-husbands. Some of us have direct experience of sexual abuse, alcoholism, drug-abuse, domestic violence and prostitution. We are the women that books get written about. The experiences and ideas of lots of women like us have gone into the making of this book – women who have written for us, talked to us about their lives and shared the experiences we have included here.

The responsibilities for putting this book together has rested on a few – the Taking Liberties Collective – but we couldn't have done it without all the other women who have given us their words and their experiences to include among our own. We came together as a collective through our involvement over the years with a women's education course called *Second Chance for Women*, held at the Women's Education Centre in Southampton. This is a course for working-class women who want to give education a second chance.

In our collective, 7 out of 8 of us have had no previous experience of writing books, and have had to learn as we go along. During the 18 months we've taken to write the book we were all engaged in other work, paid and unpaid, so we could only set aside one day a week (during school hours and excluding school holidays) to work on the book. By the end of the year we had written four chapters. Three of us had got new jobs and two went on to do full-time courses. Some of the current *Second Chance* women stepped in to help finish the last two chapters. The circumstances of those of us in the collective were far from ideal – most of us were hard-up, two were in the process of getting divorced and two were in the middle of court cases.

While the stress and circumstances of our lives are precisely those which make it very difficult for women to write books, it seems as though they are also the reasons why we should persevere. We are fed up with experts writing about us as objects of research – and getting it wrong. We are fed up with experts writing about education, policies, theories and developments – without any reference to us and how we live our lives – and all contributing to the view that education is somehow separate from those lives. Also we want to put the record straight – to tell the truth about what the experience of 'being educated' did to us in the past and continues to do to us as women now. We want those who see themselves as 'educators' to listen, and try to learn, from those of us on the receiving end of education, as well as those women who like us might be tempted back into education to know what's at stake.

All of us working on this book acknowledge that we are feminists, but we have come to share the set of values and commitments that feminism represents via different routes, according to our own circumstances. At a time when life is hard for many of us, we take comfort in the growth of women's writing and publishing which is one of the achievements of the current wave of feminist activity. But all of us writing this book have at times felt alienated from the very books we have turned to for some reference or record of our lives – either because the experiences of working-class women have been ignored or else they have been expressed in the elitist language sometimes used by academic feminists.

The book which has inspired us the most to redress this balance is *Heart of the Race – Black Women's Lives in Britain*, which came out soon after we'd embarked on *Learning the Hard Way*. We found the personal testimonies of black women's experiences of racism and oppression extremely powerful. For those of us who are white they were also extremely challenging and made us determined to confront our own part in that oppression. We also felt encouraged by their example to continue with our own contribution to broadening the base of women's publishing.

We want more books to be published by women which unravel the complexities of our experiences, but they should be books that are also *for* women, women like us, rather than books *about* us, written in ways we don't understand. We suspect that not everyone who reads our book will agree with our arguments, but we hope they will, at least, undertstand them.

In writing this book we have written as women committed first and last to women. The arguments we have made have been checked out with each other, in the light of our own experiences, and while our ways of writing vary enormously, we have altered only those words and phrases in each other's contributions which seem confusing or unclear. To those of you reading this book who have been taught to gut and skim books for their main points and to discard the bits which seem like elaborations, we ask you to read our words carefully – all of them – and especially the poems and personal accounts. To those of you who'd never dream of behaving so thoughtlessly with our lives, we apologise for the previous instruction. It's just that having now had some experience of being 'educated' ourselves, we know the score and we know what gets read and what gets ignored.

Our method of working has been to meet together as a group once a week, and to work out together the kinds of arguments we wanted to make in each chapter, and the bits of personal writing we could do to illustrate those arguments. At this stage we asked other women to write too, and sometimes we taped discussions with women who felt easier about telling us their experiences·than writing them down. When we'd sorted out the ideas and the personal writing for each chapter, one or two women took responsibility for putting the draft of the chapter together, and different women agreed to work on different chapters. When each chapter was drafted, we checked it through together in the collective, to make sure we all agreed with what was being said and that the writing of it was clear and uncompromising.

By the time we got to the last chapter – 'Beware the Backlash' – we were in the middle of a backlash ourselves. Funding was being taken away from the *Second Chance* programme and we found ourselves in the midst of allegations, deputations and demonstrations. So serious was the attack on *Second Chance* that we seemed to be expending all our energies in resisting it, and we were getting well behind schedule with our writing. As much as any other chapter, therefore, this one is stamped with the authority of our own experience and we hope it will serve as a warning to those who imagine that women's liberation – or even decent women's education – can be secured easily and without much of a struggle. Women in similar circumstances to us will know precisely what we mean. We hope that others in the future won't – as we have done – have to learn it all the hard way.

Introduction

It is appropriate that *Learning the Hard Way* is included in the Women in Society list. It takes as its first principle the feminist maxim that 'the personal is political' and creates an analysis about women's oppression in men's education that is firmly rooted in the authority of women's own experience. In the contemporary literature of feminism it contributes a much-needed polemic, which is not absent in other, more literary approaches, but which often gets subsumed in academic feminism's concern to be scholarly. The Taking Liberties Collective write from a commitment which is *for* women rather than *about* women. However, they do not hesitate to draw conclusions and make generalisations about women's oppression in ways that represent the best tradition of women building their own knowledge and creating their own theories out of the validity of women's experience. *Learning the Hard Way* has been written by women whose words are usually never recorded.

Fifty-seven women participated in the writing of this book. Some are black, some are lesbian and most are working class. They came together through their involvement over a number of years on an adult education course at Southampton called 'Second Chance for Women'. They reflect considerable credit to a course which has focused consistently on women. They argue with great conviction about the need for women to be in control of their own learning and to define the kind of education necessary for women.

Yet *Learning the Hard Way* is about much more than education. It is about the realities of working-class life. It is about survival: survival on state benefits; survival against the violence and abuse of male power; survival against racism; survival in a political climate which takes children and jobs away from lesbians. If sexism makes life difficult for successful and aspiring women, it makes the quality of life available to poor and powerless women almost intolerable.

The fact that women do survive is a measure of our strength. The fact that women find the energy and conviction to resist is a measure of our courage. *Learning the Hard Way* reminds more privileged sisters that women's liberation will not be achieved as long as working-class and black women are getting poorer and their lives are becoming harder. It is an honest, provocative and inspiring book which everyone concerned about women's education and women's lives should read – and then read again.

JO CAMPLING

The truth about our lives

From a carriage in a train
I saw some women all in green
Working in the vilest place
That as a child I'd ever seen.
The train had rumbled to a halt
As if determined to proceed
Along the straight and narrow lines
With just the minumum of speed.
I stared in what I think was dread
At those who were my kind
And willed the train to travel fast
And leave it all behind.
One of the women stopped her work
And looked up at the train
Her face a sign I'd seen before
And would often see again.
Faces tense with anxiety
Warning that women were cheated
Shadows at the kitchen sink
Bent as if defeated.
The place was 'Aggie's Ropery'
Somewhere on the Tyne
The women seemed to get old quick
In nineteen forty-nine.
When I became a woman
And travelled with friends full-fare
Being a female became another barrier
That all of us would share.
It was always in the background
Though more distant on the trains
With our tickets to destinations
That never lived up to their claims.
We were restless and dissatisfied
With the same old situations
And half aware that settling down
Meant curtains and no more stations.

We had no real expectations
Just very spontaneous and young
The only certain thing we had
Was an instinct to fucking run.
Pleased yet sorry, leaving home
Glad to be out of the factories
Though catering was worse for money
They thought we ran on batteries.
Trains to hotels for caps and pinnies
To camps to work in bars
To hostels as shop assistants
And to houses as glorified chars.
A non-stop train to London
Waitressing night and day
Working our bloody arses off
Serving dinners to black suits and grey.
Saving to board the dreamers train
The one that went to the docks
Across to France to find the sun
And sand without any rocks.
Down there we found the students
And lots of friendly hippies
They said they couldn't place us
We told them we were skippies.
We learnt a lot about ourselves
Just watching how they accepted
The sun, the sea and lying around
We felt as if we'd defected.
Well the city died, as the weeks went by
We liked this paradise
We stretched the money with shitty jobs
And lived on bread and rice.
Some affluent men thought women alone
Just had to be looking for them
Women they would love to use
And would later love to condemn.
I remember three in particular
They'd hired a house to let
But they got it wrong with me and my friends
Five women they won't forget.
We all split up as the time went on
With different things to do
We'd meet up on the circuit
If nothing else came through.
When we came home it was Autumn time
And nothing much had changed
The Christmas cards were in the shops
With the wrapping all arranged.
Well, we carried on, but not the same

Then soon on separate trains
With 'Amen' like so many others
Closing doors with hidden chains.
And so the years went slipping by
With house-life and the kids
Then one way or another
I got landed on the skids.
I watched the men from a distance
And I didn't like what I saw
I began to ask some questions
That I'd never asked before.
I was near the track when I saw the train
Slowing in its pace
A child stared out from a window
I looked back and remembered a face.
And so I learnt the hard way truth
The kind that can't be bought
The kind that leads you to 'The Women'
When the lessons have been taught.

According to United Nations statistics, women make up half of the world's population, do two-thirds of the world's work, earn one-tenth of the world's wages and own one-hundreth of the world's wealth. This doesn't come as much of a surprise to us. It doesn't take official statistics to convince us about what we already know. Women work extremely hard and have very few resources to show for it compared to men. If men are poor, women are poorer. If women are rich it is either because they are among the few who, in the attempt to prove that equal opportunities exist, are allowed to work side-by-side with men and earn men's wages. Or their wealth is conditional upon the men who provide it. Women who are economically dependent on middle-class men may well enjoy a good deal of comfort and a high standard of living. Their affluence gives them choices and opportunities which are not so readily available to working-class and black women. But material well-being does not necessarily go hand-in-hand with emotional well-being, and is usually dependent upon good – that is dutiful – behaviour.

Like the rest of us who have little money in our own right, and few opportunities to earn a decent wage, the majority of women are just one man away from welfare. Nor do we assume that middle-class men are any more enlightened in their attitudes to women than other men. Indeed we know that they are not.

When I had to leave home with the children it was as if I changed overnight from being a reasonably well off, secure middle class woman with a comfortable home and always enough money in my purse – to being the sole financial support for three young children without any means of providing that support. There we were out on our ear, no home, no money in the bank, instant total insecurity. Even when I went to court for the house and maintenance for the children – he was allowed to stay in the house on his own while I had to pay £200 a month to rent a virtual slum, and the judge still only awarded £189 per month maintenance for the children. With child benefit we had £83 a month to live on – bills, food, everything. He was earning about £18,000 at the time.

My husband stayed in the home – a five bedroomed house – on his own for eight months before he agreed to move out. He refused to allow me to have anything out of the house apart from a few old sheets and a carrier bag of clothes for the kids. I still had a key and once I got my courage back I used to carry out day time raids when I knew he was away. I'd take things I thought he wouldn't notice – some toys, a few pieces of cutlery, and the odd plate. After a while I got more stroppy and lifted the duvets and food out of the freezer. Mind you, I got letters from his solicitors complaining.

The exercise of male power over women may vary in different classes and racial groups and may reveal itself in different ways. But it is a feature of all relationships between men and women in a society in which men as a group have power over women as a group, and have a vested interest in keeping it that way. Power is not just to do with access to money – although that's a big part of it. It's also about access to paid work and to the political process. Working men in trade unions have colluded with their employers since at least the Industrial Revolution to deny women craft skills, to fix the rates of pay for jobs that men do at a higher rate, to prevent women from competing for men's jobs, to confine women to low paid insecure employment and to claim for themselves a family wage with which to ensure women's economic dependency at home.

Because men have also had grievances against their employers and others of a more powerful class, they have organised their resistance politically in trade unions and the labour party. This – the labour movement, or what Beatrix Campbell calls the 'men's' movement – is rooted in male culture, male friendships and the defence of men's interests. Here women's concerns are not greatly reflected and women have never been welcome as equal partners. Of course women are held responsible for this: 'Oh, women aren't political – they won't come to meetings.' But with trade unions in their formative years officially closed to women; with political business conducted in bars and clubs at times when women are at home cooking meals and looking after children; with organisational structure, roles and terminology embedded in male pedantry and machination; with sexual harassment and disdain for women the most common form of address – it's not surprising that we have felt excluded.

Contrary to popular prejudice, it is not working-class heroes who are the true radicals. Nothing could be more conservative than the labour and trade union movement in its attitude to women. And whatever its opposition to the bosses might be, the labour movement has never been noticeably opposed to the bosses system which benefits enormously from the exploitation of women as a cheap labour force and from women's economic dependency on men at home.

Middle-class men also have their representatives in high places. It is impossible to think of any public institution which has a decisive influence on peoples' lives which has not been created, and which is not now controlled, by middle-class men. And while these institutions – like government, law, business, education, religion, science, culture and communications – may well promote the interests of their own class in preference to those of other classes, when it comes to the relationship between men and women they endorse men's power and predominance – whatever their class – at the expense of women's independence.

For example, men can't be convicted of raping their own wives, and in all matters to do with domestic violence the institutions of the state remain largely unconcerned about what happens between consenting adults of the opposite sex in the privacy of their own home. The fact that women don't willingly consent to physical and sexual abuse, but cannot often prevent it, is one of the most vociferous complaints of the women's movement and is the one that gets actively suppressed by men's indifference and reluctance to change. The systematic creation and circulation of ideas about women which confirms our dependency on men (that we're passive, helpless, hapless incompetents), which increase our availability to men (as sexual objects) and which define our status in relation to men (by ridiculing spinsters and hating lesbians) is a work of considerable persistence and achievement – undertaken by men's representatives in every institution of the state – on behalf of themselves and other men. Again, this is a way of strengthening the differences in power between men and women – even on behalf of men who don't have access to these institutions themselves and who might find it hard to establish such authority on their own. They are able to benefit none the less.

The creation of women as sex objects (by men) and the spread of images and messages to do with increasing women's sexual availability to men, means that any man, however insignificant and undesirable, can claim the right to make sexual judgements about women and sexual advances whether we want them to or not.

I was sitting in a pub with my women friends. Mistake number one. Never take up men's space – especially in large numbers. (There were three of us). And never approach the bar on your own.

At first the banter was innocuous and wildly original. 'Hello darling. Wot's a nice girl like you doing out on her own?' (Apparently my friends were invisible) 'Let's have a bit of service here. Isn't anyone going to serve the little lady?' (Is this the chivalry I've heard so much about?)

'Wot's the matter? Lost your voice? Thought you ladies didn't know how to keep your mouths shut' he laughs. 'Nice pair of knockers' (Another one joins in) 'Bet she could show us a thing or two'. A hand reaches for my breast, another clutches at my thigh.

'Fuck off you arseholes' I shout with some degree of terror and go back to my place at the table. Jenny gets the drinks by going next door into the lounge and standing by an old man with a stick, who looks harmless enough. He beams in on her breasts and allows his arm to brush against hers. Could be an accident. (Am I becoming paranoid?)

Meanwhile back in the bar Sir Lancelot (the 'chivalrous' one) and Neanderthal Eddie (his oppo) amble over to our table. By this time we are the centre of attention with every male eye in the pub fixed on the fun.

'Wot's the problem girls? We're only trying to be friendly. Wot you talking about? Maybe we might have a few thoughts on the matter.'

'Look – why don't you piss off' says Pam (who's braver than me) 'and leave us alone'.

'Leave you alone! I wouldn't touch you with a barge pole you ugly bitch! Cunt. Cow. Fucking lessie'.

The effects of exchanges like this – which are a common occurrence when women venture out and about without men – is to make us think twice about where we go, how we dress and whether or not we go out at all. It is still almost impossible for women to go into city pubs on our own, or with other women, without inciting sexual comment, unsolicited attention or aggression. And for women without cars – the majority of us – the streets and public transport are a nightmare. Merely to be out and to be a woman is to be 'asking for it' in a way which would never be applied to men. And every woman we know considers herself a target. The fear is not one of abstract violence, but of men. It's certainly not gangs of marauding women who make the streets dangerous and unsafe for children, young women, mothers pushing prams and women of all ages trying to go about their business.

If working-class and black lads feel themselves to be under continual surveillance and harassment from the police in inner city neighbourhoods, women feel like this almost all the time, everywhere, from men. For women, the fear of male violence is almost as effective as the actual experience of it. It has the same outcome, which is to control our behaviour. We know of women who never go out at night, of women who carry keys, umbrellas or a metal comb in the spirit of defence – as if a pin prick could deter a tiger. We know of women who wear clothes they hope won't draw attention to themselves. Women who think that pushing a baby in a pram will provide immunity. We did a survey about male violence in Southampton.

> I was putting my son in his push chair outside the Co-op and a man put his hand on my bum and then between my legs. It was a summer afternoon. I followed him into the shop and shouted at him 'How dare you touch me!' He just laughed. I knew there was no use telling the police.

Here are just a few of the tactics women of all ages said they used to avoid being hassled by men when they went out.

Stay in well-lit areas
Avoid underpasses
Avoid doorways
Walk in the middle of the pavement away from the gutters
Walk near the wall so they don't notice me
Walk quickly
Don't run
Walk purposefully – head up
Avoid eye contact – keep head down
Stare men out
Dress down – wear shoes I can run in
Dress up – if I look smart they might leave me alone
Don't talk to anyone
Answer back

Carry an umbrella
Carry a shoulder bag
Don't wear a scarf

We don't think men need to consider their appearance, modify their dress, plan their routes in advance, keep their heads down and their ears open for fear of women. For women such fear is a fact of life – not because we are neurotic, hysterical or weak, but because men have power over women and part of the exercise of that power is the continual possibility of violence.

When we tell the truth about our lives it is important to remember the context in which everything else must be understood. We live in a world in which sometime, long ago and far away, men grabbed power for themselves and used it over time to strengthen their grip on every aspect of public life, to control the ideas which form the basis of our behaviour and to reinforce the right of individual men to exercise authority over women should they choose to. And this is perhaps the greatest achievement of male power in the oppression of women. We are conscripted into individual relationships with our oppressors, distracted by the language of love, romance and desire, and very possibly by real feelings of affection, so that the power dimension in such relationships becomes obscured. Problems are explained away as incompatibility or the personal deficiencies of individuals who are ill-suited to each other. Because the power of men has even entered our heads, we often think the problem is within ourselves.

That is often what happens to working class women and girls. Everything around us is somehow geared to zoom into one half of our brain so that we can't think clearly. We then become prey to every kind of shit in the book. We get swept about like litter in the streets. We get to think we can't do anything right so we do nothing. Good thing they built all those nice factories for us to work in every day and all those nice other places like laundries and hotel kitchens and worse! What would we have done with ourselves if they hadn't?
    Working in a factory all day is real natural and right.
    Clock in to the din.
    Telling the truth about it is real unnatural and wrong.
    Clock out and shout.

Women's work

Most working-class women who go out to work are to be found in a limited number of jobs – factory work, shop work, catering, cleaning, office work and nursing. Most of us have children. Many of us work part-time to fit in with school hours and holidays. Lots of us are single parents with dependent children to support. The jobs we work in are the ones we can get.

Because I couldn't find a full-time job I worked part-time in three jobs after spending an horrendous year on the dole. From 10–1.00 Monday–Friday I was receptionist/typist/accounts clerk and coffee-maker for a Design Studio. From 2–5.00 I was a cleaner for a photographic agency and a detective agency for 9 hours a week. And from 6–2.00 in the evening 4 nights, I was a waitress in an Italian Restaurant.

Then the detective agency fired me for not being thorough enough about the toilets and the photographic agency no longer needed my services (there was really only ½ an hour's work to do so I just ended up making coffee and getting in the way). I found another job, filling up shelves with cakes and bread. I also went back at 1.00 to help serve in the shop for one hour. The pay was disgusting (the boss and his wife were extremely religious) so I helped myself to bread and cakes. Eventually I gave the job up, the early mornings were impossible after my late nights. One night I just didn't bother going to bed as by the time I'd unwound the sun was coming up, besides I'd only oversleep. For six months I was working approximately 56 hours a week for which I earned £58 in total.

Now that I have a child, part-time work is the only kind of work I can do. It's low pay, inconvenient hours, juggling baby sitters and child minders. Most of the time I end up feeling underpaid, undervalued and exhausted.

Our paid work is rarely a fulfilling and life-enriching experience.

What's the worst job you've ever had? Easy – working in the chip shop. Three nights a week – six o'clock to closing time Thursday, Friday and Saturday – with a free supper thrown in. What hits you straight away is that behind those shiny hot food displays and ceramic tiles is a subterranean world of filth. Grease, dirt, the sickening stench of mushy peas on the boil, inch thick potato water on the floor. You have to wear rubber flip-flops – any other shoes would rot in a week.

You're expected to be quick and efficient when it's busy – hard when you're slipping and sliding all over the place, you can't get two scoops of chips into those daft little bags and you keep burning yourself all the time on the fryers. Bad enough, but the quiet times are worse. You couldn't sit and relax, you had to keep wiping off the counter, tidying up the chip packets, watching the clock. I ate so many chips in the quiet times that I put on half a stone in the first week. And then I was so sick of the sight and smell of them that I couldn't eat the free supper when I got home. Who needs fish and chips at midnight anyway. You just have heartburn half the night and the smell of fish and chips never leaves you. At twelve o'clock I had no energy to take a bath and wash my hair and I had a young child to see to early in the morning and then college and housework. I just had stinky hair all the time.

Worst of all were the customers. Somehow because you're wearing a greasy overall, you're seen as the lowest of the low. There was one man who came in every evening and complained that his last nights supper was cold. It turned out he drove five miles to get it home so it was no wonder. The boss told me not to be rude to him even though he was extremely rude to me. The customer is always right. However little it was, we needed the money badly.

Job satisfaction isn't usually a consideration we can afford to take very seriously.

The hotel trade isn't the pleasantest to work in. One day there was a terrible stink coming from one of the bathrooms. I was horrified to find out why. Someone had plastered crap all over the walls, floor, toilet, everything and I was the one who had to clean it up. It was a Sunday morning, and the following week it happened again. Someone was going on a bender on Saturday night and coming in blind drunk. It took me a month to find out who was responsible by which time I was dreading Sunday mornings.

A lot of our time – apart from working unsocial hours in unsatisfactory conditions – is concerned with keeping clear of men.

Sperrings (my local newsagent/supermarket) was needing someone to work in the office. Well, I thought to myself, Sperrings, this is your lucky day. So I got me tobacco, rushed upstairs, lit up me breakfast and had a look in my expansive wardrobe – another pair of jeans. Still, not to be deterred, I spent the morning beautifying myself. I put me contact lenses in and make-up on and down I went to Sperrings.

By the time I got to the office door I was all but counting how much I was to earn. I braced meself and knocked. 'Come in' said a voice, so I took a deep breath, coughed and went in. There, sat at the desk, was what I later found out to be the Assistant Manager. 'I've come about the job' said I. 'Em', said he – talking to my tits. 'Yes' said I, folding my arms. 'Yes well', he coughed. 'Name' etc. The usual type of interview was conducted and then he explained that really the interview was just a formality as they were going to appoint one of the women already working in the store. All the time he was talking to me I think he looked at my face twice. He was obviously one of those men who suffer from vertigo if they have to look higher than your bust and apoplexy if they have to look lower than your fanny. 'Being a divorced woman' said fat gut sympathetically, 'I'm sure you must get lonely, not to mention' – peels of laughter – 'frustrated'.

There I sat, while he proceeded to give me a resumé of his latest exploits, which I'm sure gave him much more pleasure to talk about than to actually perform. I don't know why but I find other people's sex lives about as interesting as the contents of a manure heap.

It always rains at night – well most of the time when I was doing night work it did. I worked in a large car factory filling the vending machines and I had to walk around the place – full of men – on my own. I would often choose to walk outside rather than put up with the stares and whistling and crude remarks. That's why I know it always rains at night.

The worst place I had to go was the tool room and the offices. Office staff don't work at night and the tool room was in a separate building away from the main production line. I was always worried about the men. Sometimes one of them would corner me in the dark, out of the way places. I don't know why because I always used to make a point of wearing frumpy clothes even when I was pregnant. It didn't seem to make any difference. I'm glad I had that bunch of keys.

I need my job for the money and for my sanity. Every woman should have the opportunity to have something outside the home – although it seems at times when I go to work that I am escaping from one prison to enter another one.

I am 28 years old, married 10 years with two children. I work part-time as a bookkeeper/secretary for a local businessman who owns two petrol stations. The amount of work involved probably takes about 20 hours a week but because of the children I only get into the office two days a week for about 4 or 5 hours – the rest of the work I do at home. However because of this my boss's attitude is that as I attend work for less than 16 hours a week I do not have any employment rights such as paid holidays, bank holidays, maternity leave etc. When my 2 year-old was born I was in the office the day before getting all my work up to date. A week after the birth my boss brought round to my house that weeks work for me to do so that I wouldn't fall too far behind. (He is very thoughtful) I know my rights – I am entitled to all these employment rights but there is no way I could stand up for them and keep my job. I have learned through experience to put up and shut up. He can make life very difficult for me if he chooses (a) just by being very unpleasant and downright rude and (b) an old favourite is to phone me up and tell me that he must have certain figures urgently for the bank the next morning. I work frantically until 2 or 3 o'clock in the morning to produce them only to find the lot in the bin the next day. He knows that I know it's all a game but he's proved his point. He's won and I conform and behave. Despite frequent advances I don't sleep with my boss. He tells me that this is because I am not yet a mature woman and I am frigid. He constantly reminds me that I am very lucky to have a job at all in my circumstances (having young children) and that he has an endless list of women waiting to take over from me at any time.

You have to be careful what you say when you're a waitress. Never use phrases like 'Would you like a roll?' 'Would you like some more?' 'Are you ready?' 'Would you like some cream?' 'Can I help you?' Often simple questions like these can lead to sexual innuendo.

The worst job I had was in a nightclub. If it was quiet in the restaurant I had to go down onto the dancefloor area to serve drinks and collect glasses. It was always packed with drunken slobs and you were lucky to get through without being groped and verbally abused. I remember one of the barmaids threw a drink over a man because of what he said to her. The boss sacked her on the spot. I preferred to stay behind the bar because at least you can shut yourself in.

Because the summer holidays were on the way and I had no one to look after the kids, I decided to work the 11pm to 7am shift at the local motorway services station. With a couple of exceptions it was all married women who worked there.

Getting a good regular sleep was always a problem. We'd all go home in the morning, get the family up and off to school/work, do a bit of housework, shopping, and then prepare the evening meal. I'd go to bed till everyone got in and then get up and go to work. It was worse at weekends and when the summer holidays arrived. I'd sometimes snatch only a couple of hours sleep on a Friday morning and then not go to bed again until Sunday. During the week I dozed when the kids went out and snapped at them the rest of the time because I was so tired.

Police patrols used to drop in during the night to check that we were OK but they were only concerned with 'real' emergencies. Much more frequent was the gangs of guys returning from the Bournemouth discos – full of the 'all boys together' syndrome and a fair amount of booze. As soon as I saw them heading in my direction I'd find a trolley of dirty crockery that needed washing or something else preferable to actually having to be there and put up with them.

For most women the idea that we work part-time is a joke. What it means is that we work part of the time outside of the home and the rest of the time inside the home.

Sometimes I feel that there are not enough hours in a day – or is it that some days I seem to be always working? Like many women I have to work to support the family because my husband's income is insufficient. Even though my job is important and responsible – I am a manageress in a restaurant – because it is part time and because I am a women it is not seen as being of any value except to get me out of the house.

Like most women whose job is part-time, I have to put up with all sorts of bad conditions and low wages that men would never tolerate. Because I have children, work has to fit in with school hours and my husband's job. I am still dependent on him and I need his approval – although I don't often get his help. I can't imagine a man having to ask his wife if it's alright for him to work or arrange his hours to fit in with family life. I am forever being asked if my husband minds me working or being told at least it gets me out of the house.

A typical day for me begins at 7-30 – I get up. Wake the children. Give them breakfast. Wash up. Make the beds. 8.45 take them to school. Come home 9.05. Clean the house. Do the washing. Go shopping. See to any bills etc. 11 o'clock go to work. Come home 3.30. Collect the children from school. Make tea. Do the ironing. Prepare dinner. Eat dinner. Wash up. Go to work again at 7pm. Come home from work between 11.30pm and 1am depending on how busy we are. Tidy away all the mess left by my family. Wash the dishes left lying around from evening snacks. Make sandwiches for their packed lunches tomorrow. Go to bed.

Arriving home with the place in a state seems like the last straw. According to my husband the housework is my responsibility. His work finishes when he gets home from work. He's tired and he needs to relax.

Perhaps it's not surprising that women are rarely thought of as 'unemployed' – because we're not. The reason why you don't see women hanging around on street corners, or playing pool in the local Drop In Centre for the unemployed, is because we're getting on with our other work at home. You don't hear too much about massive redundancies among houseworkers, or women being laid off because of the introduction of new technologies in the home. Contract workers are never wheeled into families to undercut the housewives – although 'community care' is a term which has been slipped in recently to explain what we now do 'for love', now that we've lost our jobs as home helps, dinner ladies, in hospitals, old peoples' homes, day centres and special schools.

Since 1975 unemployment among men has nearly trebled, but for women it has gone up more than four times. Women don't show up in the unemployment figures because most of us don't sign on because we aren't entitled to any benefit. We return home to the place where most people think we should have stayed all along, to do the work we've always done and watch programmes about unemployment on television showing working-class men with their hopes for the future smashed into smithereens. Of course, soccer violence and street riots also get put down to unemployment and seem to justify the speed with which the British police force is becoming armed to the teeth in the defence of law and order. But whether it's 'marauding hooligans' or disposable craftsmen with sons 'robbed of their inheritance', the images of unemployment are almost invariably male.

The rare occasions in which women are mentioned are usually in the context of taking men's jobs. It seems unlikely to us that the reason why women don't show up in the unemployment statistics is because we're all down the coal mines, or in the steel mills or driving bus loads of women to work on the production line in car factories. It's more likely to be the other way round. Now that some people can make more money and a career out of senior nursing and becoming head teachers in infant schools, men are moving into the jobs which have long been associated with women. And it's young men rather than married women who are increasingly getting the jobs as shop assistants in high street stores and at supermarket checkouts. When jobs are scarce it's white people rather than black who get them, and men rather than women. So much for our chances of becoming economically self-sufficient.

We understand that Socialists and Marxists like to put the blame for all of this on capitalism. But none of them has properly explained to us why capitalism needs men to dominate women and not the other way round. Why, if there has to be a division of labour between production and domestic work, is this based on sexual division? Why is childbirth automatically associated with childcare, and why is it assumed that women must do both? And why, if someone is needed to dish out beefburgers and chips in the works canteen, and scrub out the men's urinals to keep the workers happy, are these tasks automatically reserved for women? We don't think that even those who put it all down to biology can prove that women are genetically more suited to cleaning out toilets.

The problem with Socialist/Marxist arguments is that everything is put down to production, to peoples' relationship to production and to the growth of capitalism. Not very much is put down to men. So far as we can tell, men had power over women long before capitalism appeared on the scene – which became just one more way of exercising it. And while Socialist and Marxist revolutions in other countries may have worked wonders in providing an economic alternative to capitalism, we don't see much evidence of 'liberty, fraternity and equality' having made a contribution to women's rights or the reduction of men's power over women.

This kind of contribution becomes even more desirous when you look at what happens on the home front. We do vast amounts of domestic labour which keeps up the supply of new recruits. We make sure they grow up fit and strong – to the best of our ability – and if there are men in our lives who have work to go to, we do all the domestic management which allows them to make it their priority. In this way we do unpaid work for a number of men – our husbands/lovers, their employers, the state and, if we have a part-time job, our own bosses too. What is worse – we're judged badly if we don't complete these tasks with competence and enthusiasm.

> Today, this day of rest, Sunday,
> Spent in obeisance to the great god housework.
> Kneeling at the foot of the stair
> Brush in hand
> Paying penance for all those grubby feet
> That walk roughshod over your life's endeavours.
>
> Today, this day of rest, Sunday,
> Spent appeasing friends, neighbours, relatives,
> Social workers, health visitors
> All those who sit and judge you
> By your ability to keep a clean house.
> They watch over you in a body,
> Eyes criticial as the dust piles up.
> Beat your breast you slattern,
> Beat your breasts and clean.
>
> Today, this day of rest, Sunday,
> Spent praying my tormentors would take brush in hand,
> And in a righteous frenzy
> Wash themselves away.

Although no government would ever seriously consider paying wages for housework when they've got nuclear weapons to buy – and guess who'd never get let out of the kitchen if they did – attempts to quantify the hours women work at home (including twenty-four hour childcare and all the emotional shitwork that goes into trying to keep everybody happy) would run up the kind of wage which, even if it was paid at the lowest rate, could put us in a much stronger position financially. But of course there is no way in which men's interests can be served by making us less financially dependent upon them. If women didn't have to stay with men for reasons of poverty, a whole lot more of us might choose not to. And why pay women for labour which centuries of conditioning, and the shaping of society by men, has persuaded us is our natural responsibility anyway? Persuasion is a much more efficient means of social control than brute force. With a little friendly persuasion we consent to policing ourselves.

Our sense of duty and responsibility to those we love is a powerful sentiment which is carefully nurtured and encouraged by those who need us to take care of them. It's also why women who have kids put up with intolerable treatment from men – for the sake of the children. This is not to say that 'caring' is wrong. If it was the kind of quality which ruled the world as well as rocked the cradle, the world might be a very different place. 'Caring' is part of our strength as women, but it is also a product of our oppression. It is a quality which is encouraged in girl children and demanded of women in ways that would never apply to men and boys. And for the most part, except in sentimental terms, it goes unrecognised. It is not rewarded in the same way as society rewards everything else which is highly prized – with money, authority and power. It is sustained by a good deal of concentration on guilt and duty – two other emotions which are uncommon in the behaviour of men. These emotions get passed about from woman to woman and mother to daughter; resuscitated now and again by men's reproachful silences or anger when they look like evaporating and are dumped all over the place in an effort to escape from their control. Like nuclear waste, they are impossible to get rid of.

Although women put so much effort and energy into 'caring', and although everyone on the receiving end benefits enormously as a consequence, most of it is taken for granted. Invisible. Only commented upon when, for some reason, it is withdrawn. Like housework – the only time anyone notices it is when you haven't done it. It's not that as women we want to be continually thanked and praised for what we do, but it would feel better if it was acknowledged for the hard labour it is.

A lot of excuses are made for men – some of them by women because they've put their ideas inside our heads – about men 'being the strong and silent type', 'they can't show emotion', 'no-one's taught them how to care', 'they're victims of their conditioning', etc. But you don't need to have a bleeding heart, and wear it on your sleeve, to prove by your behaviour that you think more of others than yourself. Unfortunately, it is more likely to be women who put others – everyone – before ourselves, and whose self-esteem suffers in direct proportion. Women who don't think and behave like this are called 'selfish'. Just the kind of label guaranteed to trigger guilt. Men, on the other hand, are led to believe that they are made in God's image and will inherit the earth. So most of them behave accordingly. And when it comes to the crunch there's often not a lot to choose between those who 'do' and those who 'don't' like to consider themselves 'enlightened'.

For a long time now I've been more than a bit suspicious of the family as a way of life – yet still felt all tied up with old loyalties. Now I know better. Say the wrong thing a couple of times and you soon find out . . . testing . . . testing . . . Easy to say. What I need is practice.

I'm writing this because of my own feelings and because of the things other women have told me about their brothers. And because I probably knew their brothers anyway, because other women's brothers are everywhere. It seems to me that the control which brothers have over sisters is often masked by a form of friendliness, unequal physical strength, and of course protection from other women's brothers and sons.

Many women have brothers who are pro-feminist now, and many women go out with other women's pro-feminist brothers.

I expect lots of women are fond of their brothers. It's all tied up, no doubt, with the business of sharing the same parents, same background of struggle or whatever . . . I would even say that some of my brothers and some of my friend's brothers could possibly be grouped with some of the best pro-feminists around me (male that is). I would also accept that a change of terms must be sought with the male and that my brothers and some of my friend's brothers would be good material for all that. (You have to use what's about.) But at the end of the day, I still know what I know about them (in my guts). And that's why I find myself wanting to say to all feminist women who go out with other women's pro-feminist brothers – 'You must be joking!'

I suspect that a lot of brothers (especially those with single parent sisters) know very well that 'the game is up' when it comes to their sisters. They really expect you to get involved with another man – but if you don't, they still don't really worry all that much, because they don't expect anyone to hear you. Mind you – they will rally round in a dire emergency and make a big song and dance about it – not seeming to know that most women on the breadline (and off it sometimes) live close to a state of emergency most of the time. And being told by people (who care as much about the starving as they do about you) to 'get up and go' makes women feel crazy. They expect you to keep your knowledge and truth to yourself, keep up appearances, stay loyal regardless, keep the peace at all costs, and then tell you what you are trying to say, about anything that matters to you.

According to one of my single parent friends, her brothers would rather pour booze down their throats than give her any real help. She thinks they see her as a sort of substitute 'Mum' even tho' they've gone on with their own ideas. It's like they must have someone a bit immobile sitting somewhere. Dawn also has three little boys and her pro-feminist brothers have given her no real support – no *physical help* whatsoever and shown no interest in the boys. They did help her move into the maisonette tho' – big deal! She did the place up on her own (no offers of help came from the big strapping brothers). She suffers from nerves and depression and her pro-feminist brothers are far from hard up. They are also not deliberately callous. They have just been taught from a very early age not to really think about the way it might be for women, and to know they can get away with not doing anything if it suits them. Just as we have been taught from a very early age that 'men know more!' And as Dawn would say 'it's not that you really want their help, because in the end you know you *don't*' – but it does make you wonder what some of these pro-feminist men are all about. I have a friend in Ireland and she says they're all about bullshit! And I'm beginning to think she's right – iron fists in velvet gloves – though I know you can't really generalise can you?

Sometimes I think my brothers are fantastic until I remember my own truth in their world, and their partial truth in mine. And none of this means I don't see the class struggle the way I always have. I still know that the working man's dirt goes down the same plug hole as the working class woman's. It's just that I don't see men in the same way and I believe there must be a sort of line – even a very thin one. But once it snaps I think men know. Which makes you realise that they know 'the game is up'. Which means they have known all along that a game was going on.

The politics of everyday life

The other problem with 'caring', when it isn't appreciated or valued and when it rests on a basis of powerlessness, is that it can all too easily be associated with servility and used as another weapon in the arsenal of male control. Cleaning the toilet is one thing and scrubbing dirty underpants is another. Being made to feel it's all you're fit for is something else. Waiting on another adult hand and foot, at his convenience and according to his instructions, is a kind of slavery. Picking a good moment to broach something you know he won't like; judging his mood before saying what you want to say; working out what you'll have to do in return for the favour you're about to ask; recognising that when you stay in, you stay in, and when he stays in, he's babysitting; knowing that having sex is not necessarily the same thing as making love and doesn't usually satisfy the same needs. All of these are the responses of the powerless. They get described as 'using feminine guile' or 'knowing how to get your own way', but they are not the tactics of anyone who enjoys the experience of equality. Nor are they necessarily an indication of a 'bad marriage'. They are a feature of what almost every woman knows about in her negotiations with a man in a relationship between unequals. Talking about it is called 'moaning' and 'nagging' by men. For women it is a vital discussion about the Politics of everyday life.

> I was brought up to believe that life is never easy and that a good marriage has to be worked at, but I seem to have been doing most of the work – physically and emotionally. I began to suspect all was not well the day I found myself on all fours, heavily pregnant, mopping up a large puddle of water which had come through the roof – while my husband lay in bed and watched me. It's an example of the sort of indifference which to me sums it all up. I find it hard to imagine a woman behaving like that, but men do it all the time. Being thoughtful or caring isn't a necessary attribute for a man, although it's considered essential for a woman.
>
> My husband was very excited about the birth of our first child and was the typical proud father, but once the novelty had worn off he continued his life exactly as before (he didn't even wake at night when the baby cried) and left me to it.
>
> I felt lonely and scared and out of my depth, but when I looked to my husband for support he was quite incapable or unwilling to give it although he still expected as much from me.
>
> My dream turned into a nightmare and I just didn't understand why – I still don't fully understand how the man I loved and the man who loved me would cut himself off the way he did then, and still does now, when I most need him.
>
> Like most women I kept going – managing to avoid the valium if not the nicotine in my efforts to survive. I eventually adapted to motherhood and learned to enjoy it, but my husband feels to me like an outsider most of the time – I dish up his dinners, buy his new underpants, supply the minimum of sexual gratification and he in return takes the kids swimming on Sundays.
>
> > You earn your money,
> > Me?
> > I make your tea and toast,
> > Your bed, your love,
> > I wash the children's faces,
> > Your excuses whiter,
> > Your pots and pans.
> > I watch your television,
> > Your clock for your return,
> > Your face.

I meet your friends,
Your bills and your demands.
You spend your money.

But sometimes in the dead of night
I turn my face into your downy back
And shed *my* tears.

I suppose there had to be a price to pay for the hour I took for myself. I went to play netball. I suppose I'm lucky. Lots of women can't even get an hour on their own. It happens every week. I get the dinner ready so all they have to do is sit down and eat it. Then I rush out the door so I can run round a netball court and wear myself out even more. I must be mad.

Anyway, last night I mentioned the fact the kids need a bath. (He wouldn't notice that for himself). I might as well not have bothered because when I got in they were still running around and the dishes, minus some of the food, were still on the table. I started to scrape the cold congealed remains of the meal off the plates when my little boy reminded me I had to test him on his spelling for school tomorrow.

I dump the plates in the sink to do later and go back in to the dining room to sit at the table to read out the list of words. I find the rest of the dinner I had cooked on the carpet. The carpet I vacuumed that afternoon. I don't know why I bother.

Conveniently for him my husband had to make a telephone call which lasted at least an hour. It couldn't wait until after the kids were in bed.

My daughter decides her doll needs her hair brushing 'right now'. So I brush the doll's hair whilst at the same time trying to decipher my son's writing.

My husband starts making signs to me that he wants a cigarette. I get one for him.

Then my daughter wants to sit on my lap for a cuddle and then she wants to test my son on his spelling whilst I brush the doll's hair. I hate dolls.

I brush the doll's hair, read out the list of words for my daughter to repeat, give her a cuddle and repeat the words again, because my son doesn't understand what she's saying.

My husband wants an ashtray. I get one for him. I arrange myself back under the kids with daughter, son, doll and spelling test. The kids start to argue and the cat decides she wants to sit on my lap as well.

I've had enough and I realise that I'm going to have to bath the kids myself. So we troop upstairs, both children crying because they don't want to go to bed.

My husband tells me to keep them quiet. I try to console them. The bath takes time and they are both going too late to bed again, which means they won't get up in the morning and getting them off to school will be a hassle. My daughter loses her toothbrush down the plughole and my son gets soap in his eyes.

I get them into bed and read them a quick story, Sleeping Beauty. I hate that story.

I come downstairs just as my husband is putting the phone down. He collapses in the chair muttering about being knackered and asks me to make him a cup of tea when I've finished the dishes. No wonder women like me don't often write books about our lives for publishers like Macmillan.

> So I rely on you for
> Bricks, chairs, tampax,
> A new eyeliner, half a pound of carrots,
> A pair of tights and heat to cook with.
> You bring your filthy lucre,
> And boring conversations on
> Model ships and army operations
> And how you would have liked to
> Be a train driver.
> (But only in the golden age of steam!)
> You supply my sexual needs,
> Well, almost, and most important,
> Let me scream and
> Wipe my tears away
> (But only at your own convenience)
>
> And in return,
> I do the shopping, washing,
> Sewing, cleaning, servicing, flattering,
> Mothering, until I feel
> I've almost lost the person
> You say you fell in love with,
> Me, the real flesh and spirit
> Who loves the smell of dusty hedges
> In the summer haze, and
> Reading poetry in the twilight
> Cuddling my babies soft warm skin
> And trying to unravel some of the
> Complexities of this existence:
> This me needs air and laughter
> Dancing and strength
> But most of all
> My own approval

Expressed more cruelly, men's use of women as servants and sex objects reduces the marriage contract to what it so frequently becomes – the exchange of sex and services in return for money and a roof over your head and a stake in the normal world. But it also underlines the imbalance of power which characterises relationships between men and women and the violence which can be called into play to back it up when persuasion isn't enough, or just when they feel like it.

Don't bite the hand that hits you,
For it will hit you harder.
Don't get up,
Don't lie still,
Don't breathe, don't cry, don't laugh
Please die, for me.
Plot revenge in the dead of night,
While waiting in fear for his return.
Key in door,
Foot on stair,
Quilt thrown back,
Announcing your loved one's return.
Let him be tired and fall into a deep sleep.
(Never to awaken)
Evil thought go away.
But you know you excite him,
In strange and violent ways.
However sour you appear to look,
It's never off-putting, just turns him on.
Makes him bristle with anger,
And delighting in his own anger,
He mistakes it for lust.
But horror, you don't make a sound
So he hits you, you cry,
Wrong sound.
So he hits you again, to shut you up.
Can't stop crying,
Can't stop hitting
How dare you cry
My mistress moans in pleasure, he spitefully adds.
How odd I feel,
Unclean after my loved one's love-making.
In books I should feel the earth's moved.
It has,
It's burying me, brown and cloying,
Alive.
Wishing I was a better woman
Must try harder, but then it's so hard
When I'm tired through the fear.
Leave him – for a week – or two.
Get rested, think up new ways to please him.
He needs, wants and desires you.
Pushed home, you slowly die within.

I had gone to bed early to try to get rid of a headache. The front door opened with a bang. I lay there pretending to be asleep. He stamped up the stairs and into the bedroom over to the bed. I felt the bedcovers being pulled and then I was on the floor. I stood up and faced him. I didn't smile (it might irritate him). I didn't cry (it might irritate him). I didn't look straight at him (it might irritate him). I just stood there. He started shouting at me asking why I was in bed early. I tried to explain about my headache. He wouldn't listen. He wanted something to eat. So I turned to go out of the bedroom and downstairs into the kitchen. He grabbed me at the top of the stairs yelling that I wasn't to walk away while he was talking to me. I tried to go downstairs. He pushed me. The stairs had two bends. I hit my head on the wall and rolled half-way down. Before I could stand up he kicked me. I went the rest of the way down to the bottom. Now I stood up. It was a mistake. He punched me on the side of my head. I fell down again and he kicked me. This time I stayed down. He walked into the kitchen and filled the kettle, lit the gas and put the kettle on the cooker. Slowly I stood up and walked towards the bathroom. Then I felt him behind me. In panic I opened the front door and ran out of the house. I ran down the road to the corner then I had to stop because I couldn't breathe. Leaning on the fence I looked at myself. My nose was bleeding, my head was ringing and I was sure I wasn't able to hear properly, but above all was the pain in my chest. Every time I drew breath I had a stabbing pain. I remember thinking 'Oh Christ, he's cracked a rib'. I realised I was only wearing a cotton nightdress. I had nothing on my feet. I leaned against the fence trying to make sense of what had just happened. Vowing not to go back into the house because now he was going to be angry. At least the kids had been asleep. The kids! I had forgotten the kids, I had to go back, there was no telling what he would do to them if I didn't. He had never hit them before but I lived in terror that he might one day. There was nowhere to go. My parents were long dead. There were no refuges I could go to and my neighbours didn't want to know. So fully aware that when I got back inside the house he was going to hit me again, I turned and walked back into the house. Hating myself for being such a coward, for not being able to make my marriage work. For in some way being responsible for the beating I was about to receive. 'Oh God, don't let him hit me where it shows, my face is going to take some explaining already.'

He was standing at the front door waiting for me. I walked towards him. I didn't cry (it might irritate him). I didn't smile (it might irritate him). I didn't look straight at him (it might irritate him). I walked under his arm and into the house.

The next day I tried to commit suicide with a razor blade.

I failed at that as well.

For women, male violence is the base line in our oppression. It isn't something that women like to talk about – incest, rape, domestic violence – it is the less acceptable face of family life. It feels like a disgrace – like shame – something we must somehow be responsible for. Usually we don't tell the police, often we don't tell anyone. It's like all the other emergencies women face in isolation, cut off from each other by closed doors and privet hedges, by tunnels and lifts that smell of urine, and streets that smell of fear. It's not an accident of planning. It's part of the grand design. Divide and Rule. Keep us separate. Keep us quiet. Keep us under control.

> Solid armchair near the door
> holding me forever more
> feel so scared and insecure
> I'll be alright – must adapt
> got to stop crying
> I am not trapped,
> Get the baby, go for a walk,
> ask for directions
> got to talk.
> Precious baby in the pram
> shouldn't feel so lost
> should know where I am
> Others cope – it must be me
> don't cry out here
> what's wrong with me?
> Can't be common – would have heard.
> Other women
> would have spread the word.

Children aren't the problem

It's easier to feel angry and resentful about men's indifference and cruelty and about housework than it is about children. In fact it's forbidden for women to feel resentful about children – 'they don't ask to be born', 'they're our responsibility', 'if we can't cope it's because we're bad mothers'. If anything happens to children – from nits to delinquency – 'it's because we're bad mothers'. If we want anything for ourselves – like education, a job or some privacy – it's because we're bad mothers'.

The control of women through guilt and through responsibility for children is enormous. In the end it's the reason why so many of us settle for circumstances we would not otherwise choose. But in one respect at least, the pious moralisers about the 'joys of motherhood' are right. Children are not the problem. (Neither are we.) They are exhausting, relentless and insatiable in their demands, and terrifying a lot of the time. When you are trapped in tiny flats and houses with little money and little practical help, with nights without sleeping and days stretching ahead as an endless invasion of mind and space and body, children can become the focus for our anger or despair.

> The stairgate stands in its Mothercare glory,
> A little battered perhaps, but steady –
> But then the ideal – 2.2 kids,
> Stands also a little ragged round the edges.
> Once, it was the guardian of my peace,
> Separating my uneasy solitude
> From Ryan's persistent needs,
> But too soon its intricacies
> Unravelled by chubby fingers
> Yielded up my precious time
> And left me open and resentful.
>
> Outside – the cold, the long steps
> Down to Simon's day.
> Inside – the clutter of unwashed clothes
> And smeary faces.
> My children cling to its strength
> Excitedly anticipating their hero's return,
> Whilst I give up my flesh
> To its cold steel,
> Massaging the fingerprints away
> From tired legs.
>
> Sometimes I flick a duster
> Contemptuously over its elegant form –
> It seems to taunt me – standing there –
> Well, go on, pick them up
> And watch their tiny bodies
> Tumbling, tumbling down the steep stairs
> To lie twisted amongst the broken glass –
> An exclamation of my power.
> It seems to me, it marks
> The boundaries of my sanity.

But it's not children that are the problem, it's the circumstances under which and in which we take care of them. Because men can't have children themselves, and because a random ejaculation is of relatively small significance in the whole mystery and magic of childbirth, it has been important to men historically to keep control of mothers and children, and to make sure that father-rights are properly recognised legally and rewarded socially. Just as the male medical profession has gained control of how and when we have children – at the expense of women's rights to choose, midwifery as a profession and natural childbirth as a serious option – our childrens' fathers continue to supervise the conditions in which we take care of them.

Usually the supervision is undertaken somewhere a long way away from the front line – a bit like at the battle of the Somme. 'Can't you keep the kids quiet?' 'You get up and feed the baby – I have to go to work tomorrow.' 'I'm not changing shitty nappies/cleaning up sick – that's your job.' Most working-class men would rather be at work doing overtime than be at home with the kids, and although middle-class men might like to think of themselves as being more involved in childcare, there's usually a price to be paid when they take their responsibilities seriously.

Beware the anti-sexist man – the caring, involved father you've all seen pushing a trolley around Sainsburys with a small baby strapped to his chest like a medal awarded, no doubt, for services over and above the call of duty. Back in the 1970s when many of us bright young things – who thought we'd invented Women's Lib – turned broody, and exchanged our independent incomes and job satisfaction for shitty nappies and annual prescriptions for valium, we were sure that we'd be able to 'break down the traditional division of labour' and involve men in the joys of parenting. With our consciousness raised sky high as our personal horizons plummetted, we turned with zeal to the task of transforming last year's action man into this year's model father. We prided ourselves on 'what he could do' (when he put his mind to it), 'what he didn't mind doing' (nappy changing when we were too ill to get out of bed) and even 'what he could do better' than us (bring up wind, rock baby to sleep, especially in front of an audience of friends, neighbours, relatives and health visitors who lost no opportunity to remind us how 'lucky' we were to have such 'helpful husbands'). At the time it would have seemed like a betrayal of our feminist ideals, and certainly a personal failure, to admit that these paragons of anti-sexist virtues would only do these tasks when it suited them and that they regarded them not as their responsibility but as a personal favour for which there would usually be a price to pay. For me, the price turned out to be too high and six years after the birth of my first child, and two more children later, I decided to get a divorce.

During divorce proceedings he used his involvement in child care, and the evidence of witnesses who had occasionally seen him with the kids, to present himself as 'the only responsible parent' making up for my alleged 'deficiencies as a mother' and being 'forced to take time off work himself

himself because of my galivanting'. I'd gone on my annual overnight trip to Nottingham to a work meeting – the only time I ever left the children in his charge. He's a university lecturer – he worked in another town and he was always off on conferences of one kind or another, sometimes for days on end.

What started off as a genuine, if naive, attempt 'to do things differently', and which involved my exaggerated praise for the little he did in an effort to get him to do more, rebounded on me dramatically when it came to the divorce. If he had persevered with his claims, as well as the allegations of feminism which he also used against me, he would have got custody of the children I'm sure. But in the event, the prospect of having to do what he claimed he always did, for 24 hours a day, without me to take the lion's share, was more than he could contemplate. He took a well-paid job abroad instead – the sort you always seem to get when you're stuck at home with kids and up to your eyes in dirty nappies!

It's not that long ago (the 1950s and 1960s) that a woman's adultery was enough to lose her custody of her children. In the most recent divorce laws (1984) our conduct (bad behaviour) is directly related to the amount of maintenance we can expect to forgo. It was only in 1973 that women were given the same rights as men in matters of custody and upbringing of children, but if there is any suggestion that women are lesbians, it is extremely unlikely that these rights will apply. The vast majority of lesbians caught up in battles over custody stand to lose their children. In our own experience we know about the courts' extreme prejudice against lesbians and their lovers – just one more example of the ways in which so called 'neutral institutions' support men's interests when their power base in the family is under threat.

In divorce most women are granted custody of their children because, consistent with popular ideology, there is a 'natural' bond between a mother and her children stemming from some innate maternal instinct that makes her automatically the best carer. Except when she's a lesbian. Then it seems the 'natural' bond between a mother and her children becomes a problem and has to be severed because, consistent with popular ideology, a lesbian mother is judged to be an 'unnatural' one. So it doesn't matter that you've always done the things that 'real' mothers are supposed to do; it doesn't matter that you'd have thought that having children made you an automatic member of the motherhood – your eligibility is now under review, you are defined 'unfit', your subscription is cancelled and your membership revoked.

Fathers going for custody claim to be concerned about the 'normal' development of their children and the courts uphold this concern. It is claimed that our influence will subvert the 'natural' distinction between the sexes by diverting girls from their feminine nature (compliant, narcissistic, submissive) and boys from their masculine one (forceful, competitive, egocentric). Inevitably, they are particularly concerned to protect their sons. Once in court, we find that gross stereotypes, prejudice and downright lies about lesbians are accorded the status of established facts and used as 'evidence' against us.

In my own case it was claimed I had 'placed particular emphasis in dressing the son in girl's clothing. He has frequently been dressed in girl's knickers and nighties and girl's hairstyles together with the accessories of a little girl. This "dressing up" was not part of a special play activity, rather than the petitioner's attempt to introduce this into his normal wear, and she has in the past sent him from the house dressed as a girl. As a result of the petitioner's bizarre indoctrination of the children the boy has in the past described his penis as "my clitoris".'

However, if I could be persuaded to give up my 'unnatural and homosexual behaviour', my 'obsessive involvement in sundry political and feminist organisations' and return to the heterosexual fold, I could both avoid getting beaten up and be certified a fit mother again. 'If the petitioner were to cease to behave in such a manner, and if she were to terminate her homosexual relationship, the respondent (the father) would not be therefore provoked by her to striking her and the petitioner could thereafter be reasonably expected to live with the respondent and the children.' As that didn't persuade me, the judge then decided to order me to terminate my 'cancerous relationship' by placing an order prohibiting me from having any further contact with my lover – either meeting or by phone or letter. When the father managed to redirect my mail to his address, and opened a letter from my lover to me, he was able to take me back to court for contempt. I was in the ludicrous situation of having committed no crime but of being threatened with imprisonment because my lover wrote a letter to me which I never received!

There can be no doubt about the threat to male esteem, masculinity and male power itself, which women loving each other presents. Sitting in successive court rooms, I have repeatedly witnessed the unlikely alliance between men of different classes, races, beliefs and generations, united in their intention to prevent us, by giving us the impossible choice – cease to love women or lose your children.

When women separate from men and the custody of children is in dispute, the issue is not usually to do with day-to-day care. On the whole men don't want to look after children themselves. They may want to take them away from lesbians as a punishment for daring to remove ourselves from men's control: in which case another woman – a new wife, a mother, a sister, or a housekeeper – will be brought in to do the work. We know of one father who took his children on a tour of children's homes, not wishing to be responsible for them himself, but preferring local authority care to allowing them to stay with their mother. In most heterosexual divorces as long as women and children can still be controlled by men – by men having joint custody recognition, by giving or withholding maintenance and by using access as a means of interfering – most men settle for the control without worrying too much over the care. For women the arrangement merely exchanges one form of poverty for another.

I've been poor all my life, my parents were poor and I haven't done any better. I had a supposedly 'good' education, mainly due to passing the 11-plus and going to Grammar school, but that didn't get me very far. At 23, after a series of grotty office jobs and worse bedsits, I married an accountant, actually my boss. I thought I was escaping, and so did my parents, judging from their delighted reaction. But I never did get any richer – oh, we had a car (*he* had a car), we bought our own house, I went to dinner dances with him, wearing long frocks, but to keep all of that going I lived on fish fingers, especially when my son was small. I had a variety of part-time jobs to keep myself in cigarettes, clothes, and self-respect; all his money went on bills, his precious car, his 3 piece suits. So I worked evenings in a chip shop, sold 'Avon', worked as a VDU operator on Saturdays. Somehow it's alright for an accountant's wife to do all of that for 'pin money'. He never let me know how much money we had; I was always scared of getting into debt so I scrimped on all the bits that didn't show, like food for me and Gregory. Then he would come home with a new portable TV so he could watch Match of the Day, in bed.

When we separated I was poorer. He took 'our' car, 'our' portable TV with him. I studied for four years on a student grant, still taking fish fingers, but somehow it felt a lot better. At least I could occasionally have something new, go out for a drink without feeling his freezing disapproval. I was in control of the money – OK, terrible things did happen, like once I didn't pay the rates and only stalled the bailiffs by paying up at the eleventh hour. But students are meant to be poor, it didn't seem so bad, and I felt optimistic about the future then.

My husband fought me in court over a difference of £5 a week maintenance – he's doing well now, promotion, 2 good salaries coming into his household, no other children to support. I know his squash club subscriptions must work out at more than a fiver a week, but why should he keep a parasite like me in luxury when he's struggling to run 2 new cars and a £50,000 house? And he obviously needs even more 3 piece suits.

I'm very afraid these days; I get Gregory to fetch the post for me. I hate those brown envelopes that come every month wanting impossible sums of money for gas, rates etc. I don't have insurance, MOT or tax on my moped, and I always park it carefully very close to a wall so the old tax disc isn't too obvious. I'm terrified of getting a fine I can't pay. Sometimes I get really brave and open bank statements when they're only a few weeks old, but mostly I file them, and I put my hand over the display panel when I get money out of the Bank's cash dispenser. The truth about my bank balance is just too depressing and frightening most of the time.

When the weather was really cold some of the pipes froze; I was scared to death they'd burst, so I lagged them with socks and cut up plastic bags hoping it won't happen again. The whole house is furnished from car boot and jumble sales, handouts and bits that were left by the previous owners. I can't afford to heat more than one room at a time, and still have bare floorboards in my bedroom. Gregory, the cat and I all sleep in the same bed with 2 quilts, socks, T shirts and a hot water bottle in the cold weather. Neither of us had a pair of shoes that didn't let in the water until the January sales. His father spent £25 on leather kickers for Gregory, but keeps them at his place and only lets him wear them on access weekends, making Gregory change back into his holey trainers on Sunday afternoons when he brings him back. If I complain, his father says £20 a week maintenance buys a lot of pairs of shoes, so what am I spending the money on for God's sake?

What frightens me the most is the difference in lifestyle Gregory has at weekends. When he's with them, he's in a smart new house, centrally heated, with fitted carpets, colour TV, video, never having to walk anywhere, taken out for meals and treats and bought expensive presents which he's never allowed to bring back with him. His father fought for custody of Gregory; Gregory's not daft, he can see how comfortable and easy life would be with them. How long before he wants to stay there? If this is the best I can do by working and taking in a lodger, how do other women manage on their own? The truth is, we're not meant to; we're supposed to get another man to support us. Mind you, doing that didn't keep me out of poverty the first time, did it?

Because of the belief created by men, and upheld in law, about father's rights, and because of women's poverty and economic dependency, even men who have no legal rights to children can still exercise considerable power, and do considerable damage.

The children's father arrives an hour late and we leave the flat immediately, to visit my mother. On the way I ask him if he could have the children on Sundays, so that I could have a break and they could have a break too. I hurry on, telling that he would have more influence on their upbringing and how good it would be to spend more time with his children, without me to interfere. I scold myself inwardly for feeling the need to justify my request and then curse him because he says he is going to London next weekend. It is no good trying to pin him down regarding the following weekend, as he has forgotten his diary. I don't need a diary to tell me if I'll be free next weekend!

At my Mum's we play happy families, or at least, we try to. I spend as much time as possible in the garden but the rain keeps chasing me in. The children try to get their Dad to leave his typewriter because they want to show him some snails. I wander into another room and listen in on the conversation.

I wonder if I dare remind Mum that she has again served the men their cups of tea first. I get the same answer as I always get and my tea is delivered last and almost cold.

We are all tired when we get home and I snap at Dave, the children's Dad, he shouts at me and leaves. I put the children to bed amid the usual squabbles about who stands on the stool first to clean their teeth. Mark wants three kisses and his dog wants one too. Sharon shyly says she loves me and I reassure her that I love her. The door is closed. Freedom? No, I'd better pick up their clothes and wash the dinner things. At last, I sink into a warm bath with a book and stay there until it is nearly cold. Thank goodness I don't have to be the seductive mistress tonight!

I know when Emma was conceived. I remember the night because it was the only time I had sex that year. Had sex – not made love. A catholic upbringing meant I stumbled on an organisation called Life. Didn't realise when I went to them for the test. Just can't look into it too deeply now or I'll go mad. Now I am stuck with a man who should have seen his last days with me years ago. We don't live together but I'm still not sure who's pulling the strings. I can never be myself when he's around. 'He must see the child.' I try to make it when I'm out. Use the time to my advantage. Babysitting. He's got a car. He can choose his nights – I have a part-time job. The unspoken contract is drawn up. Still there's a price. I wish very much to undo the ties with the past. But how can I do it now? From one who was indifferent there is suddenly this emotionally keen father who's delighted with his little girl. If I had the money – there'd be no choice. Sometimes I hear him shouting at her – but I'm watching you mate, you destroy her confidence and I'll destroy yours. No holds barred. Brave words – but he still turns up.

Because our resources are so few and the responsibilities so enormous, the prospect of taking children away from men can be terrifying.

> Come little children leave your home,
> Leave your toys, your friends,
> And leave your school,
> Come join me in uncertainty.
> And the children came,
> Eyes alive with anticipation,
> Hearts aflutter, tingling with fear,
> Crowding to their mother's side,
> Trusting her warmth and judgement.
> The blind leading the innocent.
> 'We've escaped' she softly breathes,
> And the children dance in glee.
> Watchful eyes as she packs,
> Is she taking us?
> 'Don't forget us Mummy, we're part of you.'

And standing in the cold,
Belongings scattered at their feet,
Rain drizzling down on unprotected heads,
Their mother's face, set and grim,
They pick up feelings of insecurity.
But they stay close and prepare themselves.
Then forward into the future go the family.

Survival and resistance

But then the price of staying with men is also frequently quite enormous, so that looking after children on our own can seem like a blessed relief. Part of men's power over women is to persuade us and make us believe that we can't manage without them, that we won't be able to cope on our own. As experts in the art of crap detecting when it comes to man-made myths, we're happy to report that this is another much publicised inaccuracy. Not only do thousands of women and children cope very well on their own, but the phenomenon appears to be contagious.

'6.30 when Daddy comes home' used to be the magic time of day. That started when I was at home with three children under 3½. It certainly wasn't because action man zoomed in ready to make the tea, bath the kids, iron the washing – all whilst mixing me a dry martini. It was more to do with a sense of relief that another adult was around. So that just in case the chaos, noise and shit finally proved fatal there would be someone else reasonably capable to take over.

If you begin to rely on someone being there you also begin to believe you can't manage without them. Despite the evidence that you do for most of the day every day, week in week out, month after month. Almost as much as financial dependency it kept me in the marriage – how could I go? I'd never manage the kids on my own.

In the event I had to and I'm not saying it was easy to start with, the kids were in a state and so was I. But despite all the difficulties the kids became more settled and I felt immensely grateful they trusted me and relied on me to cope. Then came a time when I realised that not only was I coping on my own, I was actually enjoying it. No rows about who does what. I had to do it all, so I did it and I felt stronger and better about myself as a result.

I don't want to be a martyr or get off on being superwoman. I'll accept any offers of help any friends care to make now but I think it was important to prove to myself that I could cope on my own and feel strengthened, not weakened, by doing so.

We were some of the casualties of marriage, only roaming free because the psychiatrists, psychotherapists and psychoanalysts hadn't got their hands on us yet. All of us are mad in our own different ways, driven to it by incarceration with small children for years, overdosed with nappy changing, shit shovelling and watching Houseparty and Pebble Mill. Brains rotting with misuse, sentence construction blown away with conversations punctuated by 'get down Gregory', 'Stop it David'. All independent thought quenched by men who 'Knew Better' – from political opinions to the best way of not wallpapering the bathroom again this spring. Thoughts addled by reading the instructions on fish finger packets, having conversations that began 'how was your day dear?' through newspapers and Match of the Day, listening to endless lectures about what Smiths in Accounts said, who scored which home goal, what's wrong with its 'big end', and being expected to know when tea will be ready.

I used to come over all funny in supermarkets and have to cling onto the trolley to get to the door of Tescos, ears buzzing, heart pounding, knees shaking. Another woman couldn't get home without making frequent stops in telephone boxes waiting for the panic to subside. Another kept sweeping up leaves on the lawn at midnight so that the garden would be as tidy as the house. We can all laugh at how we were – and frequently do hysterically. But it's really only funny when you're quite sure it can't happen to you again because you ain't married no more. And it's not funny at all when you think of all the women who are.

We're learning a new kind of independence.

I opened up to you once
Let you into my body – into my mind
Depending on you to be understanding and kind
Instead you took my body and stole my mind
I depended on you to always be there
To be my friend with my troubles to share
To understand my problems and fears
But you weren't around to dry my tears.
Depending on you has hurt me too much
So now I depend on only one person
That's me.
My body's my own. My mind is free.

The price of freedom is not without its costs however. The woman who wrote this poem spent two years in a hostel, in a room and a kitchen with her daughter sleeping in the kitchen, because she no longer wanted to be married and because she had no money of her own. Another woman lived in a hostel for four years with her four teenage children. She was not a council priority because her husband's drinking got the family into debt, leading to rent arrears. She left the family home because of his violence and was only rehoused when it was discovered she had terminal cancer. The social services thought it might be easier to move someone into a house to look after the kids than split them up. Seventeen years of marriage, the debts of an alcoholic husband, domestic violence and four years in a hostel probably caused the cancer. 'She was a good mother and very involved with her children', the social worker said. A lot of good it did her!

If the state continues to have its way, single parenthood will never be allowed to become an easy option. The chances of women managing without men have to be minimised so that marriage can be protected from women's increasing tendency to defect in the face of the enemy. Two major strategies are used – poverty and gross interference. The only good thing to be said about dependency on the state is that your pittance is your own and at least you don't have to sleep with the Social. In every other respect it's like exchanging one form of interference and control for another.

> To claim Social Security [now Income Support] you must have little or no other source of income, therefore to put it bluntly, you have to be desperate.
>
> As desperate as you might be though, don't for goodness sake bank on receiving a DHSS giro cheque on time – they have a notorious habit of arriving late. So what you have to do is tell your children 'We cannot eat today – but with a little luck we may eat tomorrow'.
>
> You might be lucky to have family or friends who can help out whilst you're waiting on money. If not you might panic, and find yourself with a screwdriver and a pair of pliers messing around with your electric meter, trying to outwit it, to get some free electricity, or ripping off your friendly neighbourhood supermarket.
>
> Panic is not the answer of course. Do try and keep your head together. If your cheque hasn't arrived at the proper time and you are skint, you could always go along to the Social Security Officer, create a fuss, and maybe come away with an emergency payment – providing of course you can raise the bus fare to get there in the first place. If you can raise the bus fare, you might find yourself resisting the temptation to waste your time, because if you come away with nothing, your bus fares are down the chute and you could have used them to buy a loaf of bread and three pounds of potatoes. When you are claiming Social Security it is very useful to know where you can buy wallpaper at 95p a roll and shoes for £4 a pair. Don't panic! If there is a sale on at Dodge City or UKAY you might find some oddments – though not in the same shade – and as for the kids shoes there is a 'Nearly New' shop in Foundry Lane which might

have something to almost fit. (It might come hard when you first start on Social Security to put second hand shoes on your children's feet, but don't worry, the guilt wears off after a while. After a while you'll be thankful they've got anything on their feet.)

If you do have children it might be difficult to go out to work. But if you can manage a part-time job without the Social finding out, you might not have to sell all your luxuries – like the television – to get by. If you are one of these 'shameful creatures' who has a lover, remember that, unlike prostitution, when you're on Welfare it is not illegal to sell sex for money. Indeed it is assumed that you do. If he stays more often than three nights on the trot the DHSS will take your book away, stop your money and ask questions later. It always pays to be discreet with lovers. Ask him to leave by the back door at crack of dawn disguised as a woman. When the Visiting Officer comes to call, make sure none of his belongings are lying around. The sight of anything that looks like it belongs to a man could start a full scale inquisition. I do hope all of this hasn't put you off claiming Social Security. After all, they have to watch out for scroungers – and if you'd stayed with your husband you'd probably be in even worse trouble.

June 18th (Baby due today)
Today I received a letter from the council saying my application for housing had been refused and would I go and see them. I didn't fancy the trip much but I thought it might liven the place up a bit if I went into labour. When I arrived the offices were packed and it was a boiling hot day. The drinks machine had given up on cold drinks and the water in the taps was sickly warm. I waited for 2½ hours before being seen. The interview cubicles are only screened from the waiting area by a waist high partition, so there's no real privacy. The interviewer took out my file and said in none too quiet a voice that I didn't qualify to be added to their list because I was still married and therefore still had a marital home to go to. I tried to pull my chair closer to the table to avoid the interviewer telling the masses of people still waiting about anymore of my personal details, but my very large bump wouldn't let me and the chair was too high to be able to tuck it under the table. I explained that I had been separated for almost two years and had lived with someone else for the past year or more whose baby I was due to have any day. I was now living in Bed and Breakfast accommodation. The interviewer didn't seem to understand 'but you have a right to live in the marital home – you are still married'. I asked how many husbands would take back their estranged wife plus someone else's baby. The interviewer didn't seem to hear. 'You'd better re-apply when you're divorced.' I can't do anything about a divorce until December because I wasn't married long and you have to wait three years before applying.

April
Oh happy day. Today I received my decree absolute. To celebrate I thought I'd take it to the Council Offices and put my name on their list.

My daughter Karla is nearly ten months old and we're still in the grotty dark room at the B&B. I managed to persuade the landlady to remove a chest of drawers to make room for the cot – for her first five months Karla slept in a moses basket on the floor. I now keep our clothes in suitcases under the cot. We are not allowed cooking facilities in our room tho' where I'd put a sandwich toaster even, beats me. I have a kettle but I keep it in the wardrobe so the dragon won't see it, along with the milk which stands in a bucket of water to keep it cool. I'm not allowed to use the kitchen.

At the Council Offices the man handed me a form to fill in. I showed him my divorce papers. I signed on the X and handed back the form. He placed it in the file and stood up as if to leave. He'd hardly said ten words. I was a bit dumbstruck but managed an 'excuse me'. He looked quite amazed as if no one had ever said that to him before. I asked him how long he thought I'd have to wait. Quite casually he said 'the waiting list is at present between 2½–3 years – more likely 3, there's a lot of remodernising work going on and we like to keep a few properties empty for reasons of flexibility'. I came home in tears. How could I go on living here for another 3 years? Karla would be 4 and there's no room for another bed.

Three years later
When I moved into my flat it was completely bare. It was so new the paint was still wet in the bathroom. I had lived in a Bed and Breakfast for more than three years with my young daughter in a 12 foot square room with no cooking facilities. I had no furniture or carpets. I had managed to save a little money but I knew it wouldn't go far.

I wrote to the DHSS asking if they could help with furniture, carpets etc. They wrote back asking me to compile a list of the individual items I needed. I only listed the major things as I thought it would be scrounging to ask for cups, saucers and plates – although I didn't have any. I was really astonished by their reply. I couldn't claim for carpets because we had a concrete floor with tiles which counted as floor covering. Neither could I claim for a fridge because it's not a necessity – food can be bought daily. I had to obtain three quotes for cookers from second hand dealers and send them to the DHSS. I could only have a table and two chairs, two armchairs, two single beds, six sheets and four blankets, two pillows and two wardrobes – all second hand of course. I was allowed £12 for curtains which was a joke, it cost me almost that for the living room alone. As it happened luck was on my side. A friend of my mum's was re-marrying to someone who had also been married before – the result being they had two of almost everything. They gave me their suite and my auntie offered me a cooker for £20. I managed to buy a carpet with the money I saved, but if I hadn't been lucky I wouldn't have any carpet at all.

For most working-class women any kind of real alternative to marriage, or living on benefits, seems like an impossible dream. Our lack of choice is of course no coincidence. The system which men have made over time, and which they benefit from enormously as individuals and as a group, needs to be continually re-created and sustained.

Men's monopoly of the world's resources; their control of every single institution of the state; their preferential treatment when it comes to legal rights, job opportunities and education; the control they have established over ideas so that their definitions of the world have become regarded as reality, are all forms of power which men are reluctant to give up. To give up that power, or to share it with women on a fifty-fifty basis, would change the world as they know it. It is also the power which influences inter-personal relationships. The power men have in society at large is just a bigger version of the power they exercise at home. It is usually maintained by a mixture of persuasion and tradition and a sense of how things are. For women, men are a fact of life. And when all else fails – the silly songs about romance, the daft advertisements for instant happiness and pre-packed drudgery, Mills and Boon romantic novels, the active incitement to develop a low sense of self-esteem – there is always the threat of violence to keep us in our place. Stepping out of line invites trouble and encourages reprisals.

When all of this becomes clear it seems increasingly hard to count on anything. It certainly feels difficult to go on believing that the relationships between men and women are based on mutual respect or equality. The feelings about women which excuse sexual abuse and domestic violence, which expect servility, which rely on bullying, which deny significance, and which create silence, are more to do with women-hating than anything that sounds like love. And when everything from Andy Capp to the pin-up on page 3 of the Sun newspaper serves to remind us that women, more than anyone else, are the main focus for men's derision and degradation, we should not be surprised that men don't like it when we begin to fight back.

Stepping out of line can be a flamboyant affair. Like deciding to love women, or joining the Women's Liberation Movement, or going to Greenham Common. All of these are flagrant disobedi-ences to the rule of men and invite serious reprisals. Women choosing to be lesbian can expect to lose our children, our jobs and our community support as a punishment, in an attempt to drag us back into line and to deter others from making the same error of judgement.

The personal is political.
Yet why are my politics so personal?
Locked in my head by an intolerant society.
Lived out behind closed doors,
Hidden
In the dark.
Straight women who understand say
'Come out, who cares these days.'
But a straight face fits.
It doesn't get the hate and fear of time
Thrown at it in the shape of
Lost children, jobs, lives.
The stone that hit my head
Was not aimed at me personally
I force myself to think.
That was a political stone,
So it's okay to throw it,
For in democracy everyone is valid,
Except me.
But then in this society
My actions are not my politics,
Just the product of a sick
And sorry mind.

Women who go to Greenham can expect to have our words struck off the historical record and need to be brave in the face of increasing punishment.

Since we have taken back our voices we are asking a lot of very awkward questions. Those questions have to be 'unasked', those words, 'unsaid'. The lies, the horror covered up again. And that can best be done by just pretending it was never said or by simply changing the words. Sometimes, more importantly, by changing who is saying them. They can't really have 'ordinary women' standing up and challenging NATO defence policy both with facts and figures and statistics, and weapon movement details – with a simple gut knowledge that something totally insane and indefensible is happening. So they distort what we're saying and deny who we are. Leaders are manufactured – 'respectable concerned women', and muddy lesbians are divided off. And if at all possible they'll talk to a nice conventional and reasonable MAN from CND with a few 'genuine worries' but no panic, no sense of emergency, and definitely no ANGER.

That anger makes a lot of difference. It separates us off somehow, puts us on the line, makes our behaviour, our words, our actions – unacceptable. Our will to live is too fierce for comfort, too loud, too raucous, too insistent – it puts us outside, it makes us something 'other' – living without men, without guilt, without respect for the law of the powerful, without shame, and mostly without a proper sense of helplessness. It really grates, and what grates most of all is that we're not frightened anymore, not in comparison to our fear of what will happen. Our lives are on the line anyway – everyday. What I mean is, once they've done the worst they can, at present – prison, some violence, harassment – and we've come through it, and they haven't changed our minds, they haven't got power over us anymore. They can only do it over again, maybe a bit longer, a bit nastier. But it doesn't actually make us think they're right – so it's meaningless. It's unpleasant, terrifying sometimes, but compared to what's inevitable if we don't carry on, it's nothing.

Women joining with other women to change the world have to admit that achieving women's liberation from men never has been, and never will be, easy.

> Look at these words and what they mean,
> Feminist, sexist, racist, ageist.
> Well, angry words,
> The product of angry minds.
> Angry women.
> Woman, are you angry enough
> To be in the front line
> Of a long line of angry women?
> Will you stay the course?
> Can you be angry for a lifetime?
> Mellow woman of time,
> Pick her up and teach her
> How to be angry,
> For dear child it does not come to us
> Like the baby to breast,
> And men in their wisdom
> Take our daughters and say
> How tired you'll be all the time,
> How unfeminine
> How you'll hurt us
> Bring us to our knees.
> We'll love you peaceful, tame and quiet,
> Put you on the precipice
> Of love and wonderment.
> Some women fall from the pedestal of love,
> Angry women jump.
> How many broken women do you see?
> The jump was high
> Broken by divorce, custody, treachery and beatings.
> How many broken women do you see?

> None sister, none.
> Anger heals the wounds
> And dizzy with the new atmosphere,
> Lungs filled with the woman's song,
> Hearts filled with the woman's touch
> March forth.
> Sisterhood feeding on anger, draining,
> Draining.
> How many campaign-weary women do you see?
> Woman, find a mirror.

But lots of women step out of line all the time. Our resistance is not just about making the grand gesture – although this is not to underestimate the courage of lesbian, feminist and peace women. But you don't have to go to Holloway to be a 'right on feminist'. Most of the women in Holloway are there for much the same reasons really.

> If we don't accept a criminal record as a disgrace, or prison as a punishment, then they're not. We can even use the time in prison against them too. It brings us together with all kinds of other women in struggle – against racism and poverty and oppression and violence. There's nothing to do in prison except talk, and learn from each other, and share our different struggles for survival. If you've decided that 'crime' is about not having enough money, enough chances, that it's about being pushed outside society in some way – then we're all political prisoners, we're all there for a reason, for choices we've made, or been forced to make. For not fitting in.

The woman who leaves home, who refuses to give in, who knows what's wrong, who speaks out inside and who survives despite everything is resisting the beliefs and behaviour which men would have us adopt. We know of women coming to our Women's Education Centre who have had as big a fight with men to establish their right to be there, as the women on the wire at Greenham. It's all part of the same struggle, the same resistance. It invites the same sort of penalties.

It also gives lie to the usual analysis of all of this – that women are the victims or our own inadequacy. Victims we surely are – of men's power and organisation against us – but not of our own failure. We are not 'our own worst enemies'. We are our own best friends. The ones who know better than anyone else what the odds are against us, and how little space we have in which to manoeuvre. We might have learned from men to call this 'inadequacy' or 'lack of confidence' – but it's none of these.

We have also learned to call it 'class', which is nearer to the truth. But class doesn't explain what justifies working-class men's behaviour towards us. The root cause is powerlessness – a condition we share with other women and with which we live as a fact of our inequality. But in this sense we are also survivors. We are the daughters of women who for centuries have lived against the odds and survived the stupidities and cruelties of men. And we have our own knowledge and truth and anger about it which men haven't been able to destroy.

We also know that survival is only half the battle. However, the real concern is to change the circumstances in our lives that make survival a daily struggle – which means reclaiming some kind of control over our lives from men. Women's education is just one way – possibly – of beginning to do that. But first we need to remember what education has done to us in the past and how the seeds of our powerlessness, passed off as 'inadequacy', have been watered and nourished by a system designed to advance the interests of white, middle-class men.

2

Prisoners of gender

When most of us were serving our time at school, sexism was a word still to be invented. We all suffered from it, it shaped and constrained our lives in all the ways we now understand in hindsight, but there wasn't a word to describe it, a concept with which to analyse it. We suffered from sexism in the curriculum – learning about male ideas and male achievements – when we were lucky enough to be allowed to take the same subjects as boys.

Most of us were at school before there was any pretence at equality of opportunity for boys and girls; when it wasn't questioned that we should do domestic subjects rather than science and technical subjects, even sports; when careers advice openly directed girls into 'female' jobs (shop work, secretarial and office work) if we were considered worthy of careers advice at all. We learned either about male knowledge, or about how to be the women men wanted us to be, in secondary schools that had Headmasters and male Heads of Department, female cleaning staff and dinner ladies, which were saturated with the male values that rule the world. We learnt our place in their hierarchy. We experienced being pushed to one side, as boys took up all the space and had the teacher's time and attention, and put us in our place if we had the nerve to try and stand up for ourselves. Sexual harassment was another term which hadn't been invented when most of us were at school, but we knew by vulgar comments, bullying put-downs and physical mistreatment from boys what it meant. Now there is a name for it and it's still hard. Then it felt impossible to speak out against it.

During the time we were at school there did begin to be debates about equality of opportunity and increasing concern about the way the IQ tests and the 11-plus disadvantaged working-class children and a concern that what the Grammar/Secondary Modern system was doing was more or less sorting out middle-class and working-class children into two different kinds of education. Liberals discovered that the education system was reinforcing the class system. However the problem was seen only in terms of class, concern was focused around the under-achievement of some working-class children whose IQ levels were under-rated. Race was rarely mentioned.

The creation of the Comprehensive system was heralded as a great leap forward in providing equality of opportunity – an attempt to answer some of the criticisms about the kind of deal working-class children were getting from state education. We know in practice the class system has survived, as has racism, and arguments to do with the role of education in providing preferential treatment for white, middle-class children continues. However, nobody at this time had much to say about the education of girls and the way in which we were at a disadvantage whatever the educational system.

It took the re-emergence of feminism in the late 1960s before anyone thought to ask questions specifically about girls' education, before anyone thought to look at why girls ended up doing less well than boys despite the promise we had shown in primary school. Why girls were consistently under-achieving in secondary schools. Why girls with the same qualifications as boys left school earlier, with less varied and less promising job opportunities than boys, in a system that was holding out the promise of equality of education for all. It took feminism to put these questions on the agenda.

Feminist teachers and researchers have had a great deal to say about what happens to girls in the education system. There is now a wealth of studies on the subject which we don't intend to repeat here except to acknowledge the significance of what they say. An early and pioneering book by Eileen Byrne called *Women and Education*, explains the problem in terms of 'inequality of opportunity' and provides useful evidence of the discrimination experienced by girls and women in the education system. In *Women and Schooling* Rosemary Deem looks at education in terms of how it functions for capitalism. She argues that schools are in the business of turning out the future labour force (male) and the domestic workers (female). To do this schools have to teach boys and girls the behaviour appropriate to these two different roles.

Dale Spender takes this analysis a stage further and argues that the education system exists to benefit boys whatever their social class. In both *Learning to Lose* and *Invisible Women* she describes how knowledge is man-made, and how the experiences of women are deliberately left off the record. She argues that in achieving less in school, due to the sexism of the curriculum and of teachers, girls start to show boys in a better light. In other words, the academic success of boys is achieved at the expense of girls in mixed schools.

For black girls the problems of class discrimination and sexism are additional to another formidable oppression – racism. The black women writing about their education in *The Heart of the Race* had already been consigned to inferior schools, bad teaching and gross ignorance on the part of whites and racial prejudice, before the additional burden of sexism was added to their schooling.

Pat Mahony in *Schools for the Boys* concludes that the problem is not girls under-achieving or the 'system' discriminating against them, or even capitalism, but what she calls 'Social Maleness'. By this she means that to become men in our society boys have to learn to dominate and control girls. She argues that schools are the training ground for patriarchy, where boys learn that they will have power over women, and practise that power by intimidating, harassing and putting down the girls around them. Mixed schooling is therefore less to do with preparing girls for their future lives as battering them into submission to patriarchy. While all of these ideas are not taken seriously enough by those working in education, the criticisms about the treatment of girls in schools will continue to be made. We can add to this discussion by what we know from our own experience – by what it feels like to be on the receiving end of an education designed for and by middle-class men when you're a working-class girl.

All of us received our education during the 40-year period after the last war, at a time when we supposedly had more opportunities than at any other in history. However, we all look back on what were supposed to be the 'happiest days of our lives' with a good deal of cynicism about what was offered. Some of us had parents who really believed in the promises that education held out to us, who really thought it would be the 'way out' for working-class children.

My parents started out with the feeling that teachers were experts and knew what they were doing, and were not to be questioned or interfered with – by the time they had seen all 3 of their children through the educational system they were sadly disillusioned. They were always keen for us to do well, especially as we had more opportunities than they had when young, but they never really got involved themselves.

These were parents who felt they'd 'missed the boat' themselves but who thought we could make it in ways they hadn't, if we only worked hard enough, listened to what the teachers said, behaved ourselves, did our homework and passed our exams. They encouraged us, pushed us to succeed, went without themselves to buy the uniforms, believing that if we could only make full use of the wonderful opportunities now open to us, we could make our lives dramatically different from theirs.

Of course they were misled. Everyone always expects more from education than it is ever intended to achieve. The providers and controllers of education never intended that we should all succeed, whether we worked hard and paid attention or not. Certainly education could provide opportunities for some – the one or two working-class children identified as exceptionally bright or talented, who were permitted to get on and succeed as individuals. It was never intended that we would *all* make it, or even that great numbers of working-class children should be allowed out from under, just a few of us, to keep us buying the promises.

But those of our parents who wanted us to do well, also wanted it both ways. They might have encouraged us to do well at school, but not at the expense of our sexual destiny. The promise of decent jobs and a good living was all alright so long as we also found a nice husband and produced some grandchildren. Perhaps we might aspire to better jobs before marriage, make 'good' marriages with men whose prospects would seem to offer us a better lifestyle, aspire to very different lives from those of our parents. But that we might choose a career over marriage wasn't seen as a possibility, and when we had brothers any ambitions on our behalf were secondary to theirs.

> The only interest my parents showed in their childrens' education was when my younger brother – the only boy in the family – was starting to take 'O' levels and they panicked about his future. Suddenly things were taken seriously, even my brother who had never bothered about schoolwork and who had never been considered as bright as his sisters, made an effort and consequently left school with better qualifications than either of us and now has a well paid job in the engineering industry. It is impossible for me not to compare my brother's experience with that of myself and my sister. Although my parents wanted their girls 'to be happy', a decent job was only considered essential for their son.

And our schooling, however 'bright' we might have been, didn't question these assumptions about our futures either.

Others of us had parents who, perhaps more wisely, had no such belief in education as the key to advancement. They had never benefitted from it themselves and knew no-one else who had either. They had no unrealistic expectations of what it could do for their children. Without any such illusions they saw school as a necessary evil, a sentence to be served between infancy and joining the real world of adulthood and work. For them, education filled in the time until boys got jobs and girls got married and had babies. It's not surprising really, given the way in which many teachers think about the destiny and abilities of working-class children. For such teachers our background, our parents' jobs, our houses and lifestyles marked most of us out as failures from the start of our school careers, rarely worthy of their time and attention.

> When I was younger my reports were generally quite good – I was a dreamer or a chatterbox but 'tried hard'. As I got older the reports went downhill and I was 'lazy and insolent' and 'could do better if I tried'. I also remember attracting a lot of sarcasm from the teachers – the feeling was mutual. I was probably a pain in the neck but it wasn't intentional. If I had had some sense of purpose, perhaps I could have been more interested in what I was doing. I got the distinct impression that we were being fed into the system at one end as not bright enough to do much with our lives, kept busy for five years, and churned out the other end as shop girls, typists and filing clerks who would all be married within a couple of years – why should we want more?

> The only things I learned at school were negative and unimportant to my life then and now. I heard one teacher say that we could all end up with half a dozen kids and a husband who knocks us about. When I talk about my school days it is with reference to my secondary school because I was a very sickly child and never went to school very much, so in consequence had a lot of catching up to do and spent little time having a social life so I was left out where friends were concerned. I was always a loner and very quiet so no-one ever took any notice of me.
> I managed to get up to CSE standard without any help from my teachers. I know it sounds big-headed but I did very well although I had so many problems. I remember reading my school reports – all anyone could say about me was that I was average or I was holding my own which used to make me see red. I always did more homework than anyone else and had to struggle to do it; everyone used to criticise my spelling but no one thought of asking me why. There were some boys in my class who had similar problems to mine but because they were noisy and aggressive they all got special help – I just faded into the background.

Only the most exceptional teachers had any expectations of us or of what we might achieve. Most seemed to see their role as 'caretaking'. Stuck with us in their classes, they saw their duty as keeping us occupied and out of trouble. So long as we kept our mouths shut and looked busy, all was well.

I was never absent in the seniors at all except for sickness because I was too scared to do anything else. I was scared of my teachers and of my father. My school reports mostly said 'not trying enough' or 'tends to dream a lot'. I can remember day-dreaming a lot, my attention didn't seem held for long in the Seniors, my behaviour was always O.K. if that means 'doing as you're told'.

The worst school I went to was just unbelievable, bizarre, disgraceful, you name it. No decent facilities at all, the girls used to trail a mile or so to another school for cookery and that stopped after a while. I was there for 3 terms and we read a book called 'The Prisoner of Zenda' 3 times and we learnt to sing parts of the Mass backwards in Latin. I used to bring books into school with me and read them under my desk when it was 'Prisoner of Zenda' time, and at other times as well. I can remember the Headmaster and his wife quite well. I was sent to him on more than one occasion to be caned. Because, he explained to me, I was a wayward monkey and must learn not to contradict. One time I didn't go to him when sent, just waited a bit then went back to the class, no-one seemed any the wiser so that was that.

When our boredom became more visible the reprisals were extreme.

The rules were very strict – school uniform complete with beret, gymslip, tie, lace-up shoes, stockings and gloves. One very strict rule was no eating on the bus – instant dismissal was the punishment – so at the age of five, before most of my friends had even started school, I was expelled. My step-parents were furious. I shall never forget the beating I had – no education learnt and expelled already.

I was then sent to a boarding school because they reckoned I was uncontrollable. I hated it. Every morning up at six, wash, make our beds – 2 or 3 times if the nuns who taught us thought they were not made properly. After this we had to go and pray every single day, then we were allowed breakfast. If we spoke while eating it we were allowed none the following day. About 8 o'clock a loud bell would ring – this meant time for assembly, more prayers and then to our classroom. First lesson was, believe it or not, religious instruction. That went on all morning till lunch time. After this we would have needlework and music for the rest of the afternoon till tea-time. When tea was finished, which was about 5 o'clock, we would have an hour of Maths and English. We would then be allowed an hour of recreation which consisted of reading and homework before it was bed and lights out. I stuck this for five years before I cracked. I punched one of the nuns straight in the stomach. Of course this meant once again I was dismissed from school. I left school when I was 14½, not really knowing much, wanting to know more but never able because, to most of my teachers, I was a pain in the ass, and they only had time for the kids who in their minds had halos round their heads or wings growing from their shoulders. My schooling never really taught me the way of going out into the world.

Other teachers, having written many of us off as 'no-hopers' seemed prepared to collude in our not being there at all. If you talk to those who had the benefits of a middle-class education, who were viewed as bright sparks or who had middle-class parents that visited the school, bunking off and skiving were capital offences – as were not doing your homework, working Saturdays, having a social life even. Heavy pressure was applied to make them give their all to school-work. Not so for working-class children. Once you'd been identified as a loser, your absence could make life a lot easier for the teachers.

Money I saw was a way out of the life I had grown up with and I intended to hold on to it. About this time my absence at school increased. Always at the shop they welcomed any extra time I could put in and were well used to my excuses for not going to school, claiming it was sports day, or a special holiday etc. Of course they knew but nothing was said. Excuses for school purposes were easy. My sister Pat would write out pages of different excuses including illnesses of all types. All I had to do was select one and fill in the appropriate date. All made easy by the fact Mum could not read or write – even her own name. She had never attended school herself, scrubbing doorsteps at the age of eight was her start to the hard, manual working life ahead of her. Being able to read and write were in themselves huge achievements to her. No teachers ever confronted me about my absence from school. Just a sneery remark about a bulgy register. What did I leave behind there in that classroom, compared with the scar left on me?

The one school I did like was Catholic. I was there for about six months. The Headmaster was nice and our teacher was really good, he had a sense of humour and seemed to get everyone interested in everything. He never used to hit us, didn't mind when you asked questions and he called us all by our first names. When it closed all the seniors went from there to a big convent school, it was well equipped, the best I'd seen, but I hated it. I started playing truant there for the first time, just now and again by myself. I went to the pictures one afternoon, it was an 'A' film so I had to ask a woman in the queue to take me in. The film was 'Carmen Jones'.

I remember some teachers taking a liking to me but as I got older they got fewer. I was always 'average' at school, I didn't feel anyone really noticed me most of the time. In my last year at school I was very unhappy and played truant almost continuously, yet I was never once asked to explain my absences.

Not that the futility of the whole exercise made teachers less likely to humiliate and browbeat us when we were in their clutches. Many of us felt we were wasting our time in school, and the teachers clearly agreed in many cases, but that didn't inspire many of them to make serving our sentence any easier or pleasanter for us. For many of us the most lasting impression of our schooldays is bullying teachers, of feeling mortified by their attempts at bashing something into our heads while we were there.

I choose a seat near the back of the class, behind Mary Scott. I won't be seen behind her. I curl up tightly clutching my book, 'David Copperfield', opened at the appropriate page. The lesson begins. The teacher reads from the page we finished on last time. Her acting ability as she portrays the characters in the book remains with me now. At random she chooses a different girl to continue reading out loud. 'I think I've made it' – a quick glance up at the clock shows the English period nearly over and she hasn't chosen me yet. 'God, she's looking in my direction'. I lower my head still further, till my nose is nearly touching the book. 'Is that you, Josephine, at the back?' I gradually uncurl my back and look up at her. 'Er, Yes Miss'. 'Continue please', she says. Silence descends again in anticipation of my virtuoso performance. She scolds me for having lost the place, but I haven't. The girl next to me points out to where we are now, but my eyes are focussed already on that spot. It's just that nothing will come out. Gradually words do stumble from my mouth. My legs no longer part of me, seem to be back to front and my heart thumps loudly in competition with the spoken words. The bell goes, followed by the snap shut of other girls' books in readiness for the next lesson. I look up waiting to be put out of my misery, but I'm to continue to the end of the page. The girls in the corridor waiting impatiently to enter the classroom for their English period chatter loudly. Then I sigh as my book can be closed. The affliction of stammering, and literally shaking when reading aloud stayed with me for years after leaving school. It was only reading aloud to my children from their books that a gradual flow developed and indeed it has become a pleasure, not the horror I remembered.

Unfortunately for me I followed my sister through school, who is only 13 months older than me. I say unfortunately because she was very bright and I don't think they could believe at times that I wasn't as bright as Helen and I had to constantly show my 'bad' work to Helen in the next classroom. I found this most embarrassing in front of the whole of Helen's class, it was also excruciating for Helen. It was peculiar that most of the teachers had this practice of embarrassing us. They would lead me into the class and I had to walk up to Helen's desk and say, 'Look at this terrible work I've done'.

One hot summer afternoon I'd been asked to carry a food tray over to a boarder who was unwell. On my way up the steps I tripped, spilling the bowl of salt. Sister Peter who was walking quietly meditating dropped her Rosary beads and demanded that I lick the salt up. I told her it was an accident but she insisted. I did as I was told but I never spoke to her or looked at her again.

Clearly treatment like this was not aimed at getting the best out of us, rather it reinforced the message of failure and humiliation, making the experience of school so painful and alienating that for many of us the most sensible ambition was to leave as soon as possible. Being treated as unruly, ignorant children by teachers was adding insult to injury for most of us. Teachers knew little about our lives outside of school, and cared less. At best, for most of us, school was just irrelevant.

Secondary school was for girls only. I thought this would be different, but as far as I can remember there were no real career discussions, or indeed any relevance to the world outside. I mean, when you're all walking around in grey dowdy uniforms all day, whatever happened in 1066 doesn't seem to be of any great importance. My first school report was very encouraging, but my mother left home soon afterwards and from then on any absence, lack of homework or work in class was put down to this and eventually ignored. My grades dropped immediately. I just couldn't see the point. There I was cooking, cleaning and virtually my own boss at home, and yet still having to ask to use the toilet at school.

My parents were all for me to do well, but when it came to homework it was a bit difficult. There was no heating in the rest of the house, so in winter we had to do our homework in the living room with the telly on. My parents both worked hard and did not always have the energy to support us.

My strongest feeling about school, especially secondary school, was that it had nothing to do with my home life or the outside world. I certainly never linked the work I did in the classroom to earning a living – how could you use algebra when you were a shop assistant or a typist? Even the domestic subjects were a nonsense – I could make a dress at home in a few hours, at school it took weeks.

My school days were not the best days of my life. I found that school had no relevance to my life at the time, at home I was expected to be an adult and help look after my brothers and my sisters, at school I was treated as a child and had to do as I was told.

By our mid-teens most of us were viewed as young women in other areas of our lives, expected to at least earn our own spending money, help out at home, even contribute financially and look after brothers and sisters. Schooling was by now just an irritating charade that still had to be gone through, completely irrelevant to the real problems of our lives.

'Congratulations Josephine, you've managed to complete a week's attendance since the start of term.' She slams shut the bulgy register she'd previously complained was full of my excuses-for-absence notes. I look down at the desk, a pretence at oblivion to the heads that turn in my direction. School – how I hated it! I suppose that's the only memorable thought I have of those latter years spent at secondary school. 'Has the ability but does not try'. This repeated comment was the basis of remarks against each subject, only different handwriting signifying different teachers, but the same opinion. Distinction for religious knowledge my notable exception. What the hell (sorry God) should I try for – wasn't I for factory fodder? I'm being unfair here, for wasn't it my decision? Ambivalence now is best left forgotten. Was it money that turned me to the doors of Mullards factory? True I would earn approximately twice the amount Mum earned as a canteen assistant in Mays, but it was in earlier years that the seeds were sown.

I was nearing 14 when I got my first part-time job in Jenkins fruit and veg. shop. No more wearing my sister's holey tights which I bunged up with nail varnish (usually red) to stop the ladders. No more cutting open the toothpaste tube, the crevices an untapped source of supply (an addiction however that I was unable to kick). No more wondering if the S.T.s would last me out. Every evening after school and all day Saturday I worked. Sweeping the floor, filling the bins and making the display stacks. True when I opened the brown envelopes containing £2 and 10 shillings my joy was not complete until at home I spread it over my bed and counted it several times.

The sting in the tail, however, was the contribution to be deducted for Mum. Negotiations started on a vocally high pitch with Mum wanting half. The out-come was I should pay my school dinner money, uniform, clothes and give her 10 shillings. Resentment and bitterness was short lived, for soon my money increased to take account of the time worked in holidays etc. but my contributions remained the same. Besides there was not room for compassion when I filled any flicker of misgiving I may have felt with the injustices of MY LIFE. I had not asked to be born was a worn-out classic. Besides Mum smoked – if she was that hard up she should give up and I told her so.

I started Secondary school in September 1963. The journey to school was very long. I had to leave at 7.30 in the morning, to catch a bus to Hamble and then a train to St Denys where I changed trains and caught another to Swaythling, school was then 10 minutes walk away. I used to get home about 5.30, even later if I had been kept after school in detention or if I missed the train connection or bus.

The first two years at school I got on quite well, I was in the 'O' level class and was in 9th and 11th position in exams. My reports said that 'I had settled down and worked well'. However I knew that I could do better if I was encouraged and given the incentive. My memories of subjects are that it all seemed boring and didn't relate to my life. If I asked a question in lessons I would be told off for not paying attention or given extra work. The teachers were mainly interested in the really bright children and that they assumed was mainly boys. Life seemed as bad at school as it was at home, no one seemed interested in what I did or cared about my needs. Home meant keeping house as my Mum worked. My father was Polish and didn't like us to mix with English people. I could never bring my friends home and we only mixed with other Polish families, at home we spoke in Polish all the time and I never seemed to belong to either culture. My friends were always suspicious of the way Polish families behaved and I was always being made fun of.

Mum and Dad were not happy and sometimes would not speak for weeks. They took their unhappiness out on me and my brother and things were very difficult at home. When I was 13 Mum left home and so I had to look after Dad and brother and keep house. I became very depressed and rebellious at school. My school work deteriorated and my reports were bad. Now they said, 'It is a pity when a pupil who can do well makes no attempt to use her talents and sets a bad example when she could be an influence for good'. 'The ability is there but her absences and the seemingly uncontrollable urge to gossip cannot enhance her chances'. 'She did not give herself a fair chance owing to her many absences and her need to gossip'. 'It is a pity that so much ability is so little used'. None of the teachers were bothered to ask me what was wrong. My need to talk to someone, because there was no one at home to talk to, was seen as gossiping.

My father used to sign the reports but he could not read much English and certainly not the teachers' handwriting. Nobody at school ever contacted him about my work or many absences, and so I realised that I was alone, no-one cared at school and home was miserable.

I became independent and stubborn. I was always in trouble at school. I mixed with girls from the lower streams and was always being caught smoking or 'bunking off'. School had nothing to offer me in relation to how my life was. The subjects were boring. At home I had a great deal of responsibility. When I was 14 I started working in a chemist shop when they were open late on Saturdays, eventually I worked in school holidays. The pharmacist used to show me how to mix up the medicine and creams. I served in the shop and checked stock. After a time, I used to make up the prescriptions. Gradually I spent less and less time at school. I worked whenever I could or just stayed home, because I felt I was just a faceless person who was only noticed when I stood out because I wasn't behaving how they wanted.

I decided that I wanted to be a Pharmacist but discovered that I couldn't because I had not done physics at school. Only the boys did this. What was the point, I thought? I didn't bother to revise for my exams and only gained 4 CSEs.

Rarely did teachers know or care about the often grim realities of our lives outside school. Not only did many of us find it difficult to make time and space for homework, most were expected to help out at home, some running households. Many had part-time jobs out of financial necessity and a whole range of other difficulties that teachers took little account of. Some of us went home to circumstances that couldn't possibly have been spoken about to teachers or to any other adults. It is only very recently that there has been any recognition of the abuses that go on in the 'normal' nuclear family and it has been the anger of the Women's Movement which has helped to expose the prevalence of male violence on the home front. At the time most of us were at school the existence of incest, sexual abuse, wife and child battering went either unacknowledged or taken for granted. So far as 'professional opinion' was concerned, they were the problem of 'a tiny minority' of very deviant families.

My father was an alcoholic, he beat my mother without mercy every weekend, as far back as I can remember. My gran had moved in with us the day I was born, she told me years later that when she came to see me that day my father was drunk and screaming at my mother to get up and cook his meal. My gran took over and never left us. I shared a room with my gran, my brother who was five years older had a room of his own. Friday and Saturday nights were a ritual, we locked ourselves in our rooms for protection against my father, he would never beat me, my gran promised, and I felt safe. My mother was continuously beaten. When my father was through with her, he would go on the rampage, he would beat his fists on the door and shout abuse, and could keep this up for hours, but the door stayed locked. The times that our door was unlocked stand out clear in my memory.

When I was about eight years old, my brother was then thirteen, he had unlocked his door in a bid to save my mother any more punishment. When we ran out my brother was being kicked around the room like a rag doll, we dragged him away. It was the first time I had witnessed my father's cruelty. When I was ten, the crashing and thuds woke us up, we unlocked the door, my mother was unconscious, my father kneeling over her, his hands around her throat. We pulled him away, he fell into a drunken sleep on the floor, we couldn't bring my mother round, my gran was sobbing to me, your mother may be dead. She recovered, but only to go through it all again. From the age of about twelve I begged my mother to leave him, but she said there was nowhere else to go. So it went on.

I was sixteen the night I called for an ambulance, my mother was beaten unconscious, she was bleeding internally and underwent an operation. My mother had become a human punchbag. Something had to be done before he killed her. I cried myself to sleep, endlessly wondering where to turn to for help, there wasn't any. When she came home from hospital, my mother moved into our room, her body couldn't take any more punishment. Now the three of us were locked up together at weekends. For me this went on another four years.

It's hard to see how anyone could have concentrated on schoolwork, or paid it any attention, with abuses like this going on at home. Not that telling the teachers would have necessarily helped us. Experience shows us that if working-class children are thought to come from 'problem' families, such as single parent families, or where there is unemployment or male violence, we are frequently labelled at school and even less is expected of us in terms of educational achievement. Frequently teachers use such knowledge to justify further abdication of their responsibililty for the educational 'failure' of working-class children.

It has to be said, however, that not all of us were written off as failures at school. Most of us did go to Secondary Modern schools, or the Catholic equivalent, but there always had to be the token 'successes' to justify the system to everyone else, a few working-class children picked out as being especially bright and worthy of greater things. Some of us went to Grammar schools, legitimising for everyone else the claims of equality and opportunity in education. We were viewed as having 'made it'. For us the job of schooling was to separate us from our class backgrounds, our class loyalties. If we were to make it we had to take on the values and assumptions of the middle classes, learn to play the game their way.

Our behaviour, both inside and outside the school, was policed mercilessly, and the most trivial of misdemeanours were given the significance of cardinal sins. We were not safe from the supervisory control of teachers even on Saturdays. If we were spotted working, or smoking, or behaving in an 'unladylike' way it would be the cause for retribution the following Monday. Girls who looked different and spoke differently, and who came from the wrong side of the tracks, were still utterly visible, despite the invisibility of school uniform. We did not call it class at 11 or 14 or 17 but we knew what it was. Those of us who survived were either good at games, like me, or persuaded to relinquish their working-class loyalties.

I think the Headmistress of Newbury Girls Grammar School thought she was running a finishing school – we were constantly reminded that we should be ladylike at all times. Only 'common' girls (like me) worked in Woolies on Saturdays, went into the Circle cafe after school. Some of my chief memories of school are the hassles I got about school uniform, the most expensive shop in town sold the correct uniform the school insisted on, but my mum just couldn't afford it, so I never looked right in my homemade stuff, just that alone made my life a misery for most of my time there.

I left school at 18, with a passable number of 'O' and 'A' levels, but mainly with an overwhelming sense of inferiority. Not because I was stupid – I always did alright at lessons, but my school reports were the most mediocre you're ever likely to read – 'works fairly well', 'has attained a reasonable standard'. The inferiority was because I didn't look right, wasn't ladylike enough to have a posture girdle or be a monitor. I always felt I was there on sufferance because of a slight accident, a slip of the pen at 11, which lumbered them with me. They would have liked me to do the decent thing, leave at 16 to do shorthand and typing at Tech. college – as it was I left at 18 having had no sensible careers advice and fired with no ambition, further than burning my boater. The school would always have claimed that it was about high academic achievement, but only, of course, if you fitted in and that meant being from the right sort of background. Even I knew it wasn't a coincidence that the girls who had posture girdles and were also monitors, prefects and went on to University were the same girls whose mums were there on Speech Day wearing hats and gloves and who lived in the big houses on the outskirts of town.

These were hard and painful lessons for us and for our parents, who tried pathetically hard to meet the demands of the school, believing that we had been offered a golden opportunity and must make the best possible use of it, whatever that meant in terms of their own sacrifices and humiliation.

My parents supported the school to the hilt. They went without a holiday, Christmas presents and clothes for themselves to pay for the uniform. They revered every view and value the school transmitted and carried out every instruction and request that was demanded of them – except attending school functions which made them feel intimidated and self-critical. My mother said she couldn't come to things because she was at work – which was partly true – but it was more to do with taking me on the bus the first morning and catching sight of the other mothers – the clothes they wore and the size of the cars they arrived in. My father's one visit to the school was because I persuaded him to play in the father's team against us at cricket. He had taught me to play cricket long before I went to school and used to practice with me in the evenings and weekends. We went on our bikes. Already a big crowd of parents and girls were gathering. When the fathers' team came out onto the field my Dad was the only one not wearing whites and proper cricket boots. He hated every minute of it and never came anywhere near the school again.

Our parents probably wouldn't have wanted to know about the petty humiliations we suffered every day at school, to tell them would only have added to their burdens. Not only the humiliations inflicted on us by the school because we didn't fit in – because we were 'common', not quite what was wanted – but from other kids, ex-friends even, who saw us as snobs, to be ridiculed because we wore school hats, boaters or berets. We were marked out in their eyes as 'toffee-nosed swots'.

I'd get on the bus at one end of town to the jeers of kids I'd grown up with for wearing a school uniform and going to the snob's school and get off at the other end to be ridiculed for being common and coming from the wrong side of the tracks. It felt like moving in two different worlds and being accepted in neither.

Within months I was a nervous wreck because I didn't have any friends. The doctor gave me tranquillizers and my mum kept me at home. I didn't fit in because I wasn't the same as them, they spoke differently and they lived in the big houses, by the common, where we used to go and play in the holidays so my mum could get some sleep – she worked the night shift in a factory canteen. We lived on the council estate on the other side of a main road from the big houses which was a clear dividing line between us and them. It was when I was in the third year that I realised if I could make the girls in my class laugh, by challenging the teacher, I became more acceptable to them – at least that's what I thought at the time. I just disrupted most lessons in an effort to get more friends. I can remember an English teacher telling me I have given up any chance of getting a decent English qualification and she refused to have me in her class.

In truth we belonged to neither world – a personal conflict that had to be resolved either by isolation from and rejection of our roots, or by resisting the new middle-class culture school represented. Some of us, in our attempts to stick with what seemed to be our own culture, rebelled against school by getting heavily into clothes, make-up, boys and going out. Unfortunately it was a protest that in the end did us more harm than good, providing us with another set of constraints that weren't really in our interests either. We were simply reverting to traditional female roles and aspirations.

I went through my local Grammar school 3 years behind my brother. He was top of his class right through school and I had the misfortune to be taught by the same teachers. They constantly compared me with him and asked why I wasn't like him. I don't remember finding anything interesting at school at all and I channelled my 'obvious ability' into breaking school rules and getting away with it. By the time I was 15 I was pretty good at forgery and bribery – I could sign my mum's name on sick notes better than she could and frequently bribed the class prefect to mark me in the Register when I was in the local coffee bar.

I slid down the streams as I went through the school and ended up taking only 3 'O' levels. I passed the English Language and Art because they came easily to me but I failed the English Literature – I don't think I even read the course books. The night before the exam there was probably a good band on up the Locarno and I expect I drank too many Ponies.

During my final year at school my best mate was called Margaret – I don't remember where I met her but she had been to Comprehensive school, left at 15 and was working in an office. She always had plenty of money and paid for me to go out and bought the Woodbines. I don't think we had much in common except that we both looked how girls were supposed to look then. If you were into boys and discos in the way that we were, you needed a good looking mate so that his mate didn't complain at getting the ugly one. Margaret always looked stunning and it tended to be me who got the spotty one and we had many an argument in the loo when I refused to go home with his friend, especially if he was the one with the car. Anyway, my last year at school was spent trying to keep up with Margaret and waiting to leave to get money for clothes and going out. This was in the Sixties, and jobs were ten a penny, and being at school just seemed a waste of time. Having a proper career never crossed my mind – I knew I could get a job and there was always the assumption that marriage and kids would follow. It was quite soon after leaving school when I used to visit my brother at University that suddenly his life seemed quite attractive – he spent his summers on Greek Islands and then got a job that took him to Africa and Sri Lanka – and meanwhile I got married and had kids, lived in a council house, and was lucky to get a weekend in Weymouth – maybe they had something after all!

So for the few of us who were seen as 'able', the price of making it was cutting ourselves off from our working-class roots. If we couldn't or wouldn't do that our opportunities turned out to be only marginally better than the majority who went to Secondary Modern schools or the Catholic version of them (usually all-girls schools with women teachers). But it couldn't be said that such schools provided a positive atmosphere for girls, or that they were inspired by any feminist ideas. What we received was a domestic education, one that prepared us for marriage and child-rearing, with the expectation that we would work as factory or shop girls for a while before we got on with the real business of producing and servicing the male labour force.

> Because I went to an all girls school the range of subjects was very limited – as was the careers advice. I don't remember feeling that anyone was interested in me or what I might do with my life – I was certainly never asked, perhaps they thought it was obvious! I found school so uninspiring that by the time I was 14 I couldn't wait to leave, get married and have a baby – it was the height of my ambition.

Certainly the part class played in our experience of schooling and education was a negative and destructive one. Being working-class marked most of us out from the start as being automatic failures. But we all paid the price of being girls as well, whether we went to co-educational or single sex schools. In mixed schools we learned the appropriate social roles for men and women perhaps a little earlier. Sexist attitudes in school taught us very clearly the future roles we would be expected to play.

> School instilled the feeling that not so much was expected of girls as of boys. Even the lessons meant segregation. Girls had needlework whilst boys did Technical Drawing. Girls had domestic science whilst boys did metalwork or woodwork. Girls only had biology, whilst boys could do Physics or Chemistry. None of us questioned this at the time. Then it seemed important to know how to cut a tomato into the shape of a water lily or rose and how to sew a dress that resembled a sack with holes. If you didn't actually enjoy doing this you would be told off for being lazy and not trying.
>   After cookery lessons the boys would hang around the classroom door waiting for culinary handouts. They preferred samples from those whose cooking was best, so even cookery lessons became a test or competition for their benefit. The better you could cook the more the boys would ask for some.
>
>   On returning to the fourth year I found that part of my timetable was allocated to cookery and home management. I hadn't chosed to do either of these subjects, I felt really insulted. Home management was in a classroom made to look like a flat, complete with a plastic doll in a crib. You were taught how to hoover, sweep, dust, make beds, change the

plastic doll in the crib's nappy, and learn how to open a tin of baby food. Home management wasn't on the boys' timetable, but they could take cookery if they wanted to. I didn't mind cookery, I quite enjoyed it in those days, but at the time I fancied doing woodwork much more than cookery. I did that at home anyway and I'd always liked the look of the bookshelves and three-legged stools that you saw the boys taking home at the end of term. So I approached the form teacher, proposing to take woodwork instead of cookery, they were on at the same time, but he told me 'Girls don't do woodwork in this school'. I said, 'Jimmy McKay's doing cookery, so why can't I do woodwork?'
'That's different, he's going to be a chef', he said.
'But I want to be a carpenter', I said, although I had only just thought of it.
'You can't, you're a girl', was his answer.

In my secondary school I chose physics in my third year. A few other girls did too, but I was put into a class on my own with 15–20 boys. I hated it. I couldn't say anything because the boys would take the piss out of me, if I was getting it right I got a hard time and if I was getting it wrong I got a hard time. More and more as time progressed I felt I couldn't ask about anything and so I got further and further behind. My self-confidence was considerably reduced by this experience, and added to the fact that my family weren't really into me doing well at school, I went into a general decline which I never really came out of. Even tho' I was moved eventually to the other physics class with the other girls it was too late, by now I believed that I couldn't do it, so I didn't bother applying myself anymore.

I was brought up in a slum area in an industrial town. My father was an alcoholic and a violent man – the weekly rituals of his brutality and wife-beating were commonplace in the area we lived in. My mother seemed to have little control over what was happening to her. She worked long hours in the laundry to feed and clothe us and we really only saw her at weekends.
   Education standards were low, because of the area we lived in we were allocated to one school. The teachers spent a lot of their energy controlling, bullying and breaking up fights. On the academic side being female was a distinct disadvantage. We were separated from the boys after reaching a certain standard in maths, for example, we had to concentrate on domestic skills while they went on to learn geometry and algebra and things of which we knew nothing. Due to overcrowding in the school we had to share the classroom at times. The boys would have half of the classroom with their teacher and we would have the other half and sit quietly and sew. Many times I would be smacked across the knuckles with a ruler for listening to the boys' maths lessons.

I went to ten different schools between the age of five and fourteen, always in mixed classes. But as I recall girls usually sat on one side of the room. Once the class had commenced every morning during my senior period, it was a girl's duty to go around the different classes to collect the dinner money and milk money. This chore meant missing half the maths lesson each day and was never given to a boy. I can remember doing it frequently, but in spite of this I managed to keep up with my arithmetic. But in retrospect I think it was most unfair. Needlework, cookery, washing, ironing, even knitting were included in the girls' curriculum at the schools I attended.

The subjects I was allowed to choose were mainly to do with Homemaking, once I was in the lower stream of the school, it was considered that would be the best for me. The thing I became annoyed about is the fact that they told me it was my option. In practice it was their decision, not mine.

For most of us our life at home relayed the same kind of messages, especially if we had brothers.

This inequality wasn't only confined to school life. I remember at home after my domestic chores were finished having to do things like polishing my brother's boots while he did his homework. At times I would get angry and say, 'Why can't he polish his own boots or take a turn to polish mine' and everyone would laugh but I still had to get on and finish them.

Even with our home circumstances and surroundings my brother did well at school. He always had a place to study, his own room, and was encouraged to do so. I shared a room with my Gran and my parents slept in the living room so there was no place to work anyway. Girls didn't have much homework, we had domestic chores to do. There was never any real interest in my school work from teachers, or at home, nothing was expected of me and I learned very little. I ended up with no qualifications at all. On leaving school my brother went on to do an engineering course and I attended night school. I got a job in the laundry where my mother worked. I'm not saying my brother didn't work hard for his qualifications, he did, I'm just saying that being a girl I was treated differently.

But it was not only the sexism of the schools, the attitudes of teachers and the subjects we learned that put constraints upon us. From an early age, even in Infants school, boys are practising their role of dominance, and the ways to exert power over girls. Sexual harassment has been named by feminists as not only a feature of women's everyday dealings with men, but as a form of power that boys use against girls from a very early age, to keep us in our place and to humiliate and degrade us. The manifestations of woman-hating began for most of us while we were still learning our ABC.

My grandparents had bought me a new sundress – pink and white stripes, a gathered skirt with straps over the shoulders crossing at the back down to the waist. In cooler weather I wore it with a blouse under the straps, but on the first hot day I wore it to school just on its own. I was seven. I can still feel the heat rising in my cheeks now, 30 years later, remembering first the giggles, then the pointing and jeering from the boys, as it dawned on me that I was on the receiving end of all this unwelcome attention, or rather my seven-year-old nipples were inadequately covered by the little straps. I spent the rest of the day in acute embarrassment, shoulders hunched and hands desperately trying to hold the straps over the offending areas. Needless to say I never wore the sundress to school again and never forgot just how those boys had made me feel. I worked hard at being anonymous, blending in with the background, for the rest of my time in that mixed junior school.

I started at the village primary at about 8, previous to that we had moved around a lot, my dad being in the army. My mum worked full-time, and had to leave for work really early, so my little sister and I used to have to go to school ages before anyone else, or so it seemed. We just used to hang aroung the buildings which were all locked. An older gang of boys often used to be the next to arrive, the ring leader being Badger Burgess, an illiterate thug who smelt and was enormous – really overgrown for his age or perhaps he was older and stayed on, I'm not sure). He and his merry band used to terrorise us, me particularly because I was older, I suppose, and more female looking than my sister. They used to insist we played kiss chase with them and Badger (I can't remember his real name) used to single me out and catch me. I hated it. I hated him. Going to school was a nightmare.

Boys and girls didn't play together unless it was kiss chase in which case the boys decided which girls could join in and which couldn't.

I wasn't particularly 'developed' for my age, and found the boys ridiculed me for that. The size of your breasts seemed to determine whether you were given some sort of 'respect' from boys, or pointed at and whispered about behind their hands. The girls were asked if they were virgins by the boys. I was asked and I didn't know what virgin meant, so I thought it must be something rude and said, 'No, I'm not'. There followed peals of laughter and I never lived it down.

Coming from a girls' school where we were encouraged to participate in class, it was very difficult for me to learn the lesson that, as a girl in a mixed school, I shouldn't have a mind of my own, let alone use it. Girls who dared to open their mouths soon got put in their place. During one lesson, a boy shouted across to me, 'Why don't you shut up. You've got more mouth than a cow's got cunt'. The (male) teacher told him off for shouting in class, not for what he said.

Rarely did teachers attempt to stop boys from brutalising girls in this fashion. On the contrary, we were frequently seen as the source of trouble, especially if we attempted to stand up for ourselves.

> On my first day it seemed as though I was the novelty 'new girl' to the boys, they kept coming up and touching me, touching my breasts all the time. I was still having to wear my old uniform, complete with green ankle socks and I was teased all the time about it. I was with a group of girls on the field at lunch time and the boys were coming up and touching us, saying things like "I like girls wearing stockings', or 'Are the flags flying?' (Meaning did we have our periods.) One boy, a big fat slob, kept continually touching me up, slobbering over me, grabbing me, saying 'Give us a kiss'. When I told him to go away, he and his friends surrounded me, all jostling and mauling me. When I screamed at them, they answered 'What's the matter with you, don't you like it? Are you frigid, or queer or what?' I was really terrified by now, they just wouldn't stop. I happened to have a pair of compasses with me in my bag, and in sheer panic I got them out and jabbed the fat slob in the shoulder with them. The headmaster accused me of over-reacting, telling me that because I hadn't been around boys for a couple of years, I just didn't know how to handle them. So on my first day at my new school I was in serious trouble – I got let off because it was my first day, and warned severely not to let it happen again. Nothing was done about the boys, the Headmaster's only comment to them was that they could have been nicer to a new girl.

> Going to assembly was like running the gauntlet, the boys squeezing against you, touching and pinching – it was a regular game. You'd try and get into the hall before they got you, and you had to listen to them talking about tits, virgins, bragging about their sexual exploits all the time. They were clever enough, they did it in such a way that the teachers hardly saw it, but even if they did, the worst that happened was the teachers just told us all to stop messing about.

Some teachers not only excused the boys but also made assaults of their own.

> The geography teacher was definitely interested in girls. So interested that all girls had to sit in the front row in his lessons. There was quite a scandal when a mirror was discovered under his desk, angled to look straight up our skirts. They didn't know how long it had been there. But he left soon after that.

Those of us who went to single sex schools escaped this kind of treatment, at least while we were at school. But that isn't to say that all-girl schools automatically encourage strength, independence or autonomy. Most of them were run on the same lines as boys schools. We learned male values, had to conform to male models of behaviour, and emerged believing that it was men who were important, and that our futures would be measured against them. Many a contemporary 'career woman' is a tragic testimony to this kind of early grooming. What we were learning was disloyalty to our sex, and the proper respect for and defence to maleness.

> Our school motto was in Latin and our school song was borrowed from one of the older (boys) public schools in which we had to think of ourselves as a male sports team (or army):
>
>> 'Follow up, follow up, follow up!
>> 'Til the field ring again and again
>> with the tramp of the twenty two men!'
>
> The fact that all of us, and 99% of the teachers, were female made not a wit of impression upon the curriculum, and the ways in which we were taught – by intimidation, competition, derision and fear – would have done justice to the best boys school in the land. Even the prefects, prizes and pecking order was straight out of boys public schools. As school Games Captain I had my second year fag to clean my hockey boots and carry my games bag. I didn't beat her of course but I had power to issue detentions to younger girls. By the time I got to University – although I had hardly had a serious conversation with a boy ever – I was under no illusions that women were boring and men were by far the most interesting sex.

Looking back on our school days, for most of us it was a painful and destructive experience, particularly for those of us who had expected something more, who believed that education could give us wider opportunities, a route to achieving a better life. For those of us wise enough to expect nothing, our expectations were amply fulfilled for nothing was what we got. However, most of us left feeling like personal failures, in a system that required the failure of most of us. School was a sentence to be got through, an exercise in meaninglessness and futility, cynically perpetrated upon us by teachers whose roles amounted to little more than caretaking, wanting as little aggravation from us as possible, writing most of us off as a waste of their time.

> I think a lot of the schools at that time were just like overcrowded shelters, where the buses came at the end of the year and carted us all off. Away to work in the factories and shops, laundries and building sites and all the other delightful places.

I remember the whole school having to clap because one girl who was leaving had got a job in an office. As I see it now it's all a bit obvious, because if everyone had received a proper education they would have learnt to expect more. Where, then, would the labour force come from – all those thousands of people that are used to do all the lousy jobs? What girl or boy, with a real choice, would have wanted to spend the best years of their life wearing themselves out, doing long hours in shitty places for joke wages? – they wouldn't and that's all there is to it. What a farce it all is, what an insult to ordinary men and women. Yet still those in high places go on pretending that all will be well if we just work harder, manage on less and place our trust in them. They're still telling kids in school that life is what you make it – at the kitchen sink, on the dole, in the inner cities, in the ghost towns – and there's room at the top for us all.

3

The obstacle race

It don't come easy, this life
for those of us with nothing.
At 27 with the mental age of an adolescent housewife
worrying round Tescos
pushing my dreams in a shopping trolley.
Life's ambition – an automatic washing machine.
Every spin dryer, every twin tub
a cheap imitation of my goal.
And now, every word I write
stares at me mocking, with sing song voices
this won't get you to college, no degree for you today
save your energy for the washing that's piling up,
like your past – a mountain of smelly clothes
breathing down my neck.
And like my past,
there's always one old sock left lingering, forgotten,
lurking in the dark
ready to pounce
and keep me in my place –
here, now, housewife, mother,
bore, drudge, plank.
Heart lackey to the literary dream,
sold out – to the nearest hot and cold fill,
self cleaning, self spinning,
automatic soul destroying,
wash my life's ambitions clean.

When experiences of schooling have left many of us feeling inferior and unimportant, it seems unlikely that we would be encouraged to give education a second chance. But a few years on, moving rapidly towards the skids, it can seem like the only way to improve our situations. In reality, the odds are stacked against working-class or black women re-entering formal education and surmounting all the obstacles to win the glittering prizes. But if we're on the beam end of our uppers we often feel it's worth a try.

One of six kids brought up in a typically working class family where money was always tight, the first one up in the morning was inevitably the best dressed and the term 'further education' was unheard of – nothing could have been more alien to my upbringing than becoming a university student. However times change and aspirations rise which probably explains why at the age of 32 I was embarking on a three year degree course in Sociology and Social Administration.

Times change and so do circumstances. For some it might be the end of a marriage which makes us take stock of our lives.

Conditioned to believe that as a women I would leave school, marry and have children clouded my judgement in terms of a career and economic independence. It was at the age of 28, with a failing marriage and a child to care for, that I re-evaluated my role as a woman. If I, and many other women were continuing in that traditional role that was set for us long before our birth, why were we beset with so many conflicting and contradictory values and beliefs? For this reason I jumped at the chance to return to education.

We imagine that a qualification will be a passport to the world of well paid, satisfying employment and, like many migrants, it is as much the hardship and oppression we wish to leave behind, as the milk and honey we hope to find, that spurs us on.

Previous jobs had paid me very little and were demeaning, I was only qualified for the servicing trades which carry very little recognition and seemed to be associated only with women: barmaid, nursing, counter assistant, mother and wife.

I had numerous unskilled jobs, factory work, petrol pump attendant, anything. I had my son when I was 19 and apart from a couple of factory jobs and a bit of bar work I didn't work. Most of the time I was at home.

I couldn't get a job. Well I might have been able to get a job in Woolies, but that wasn't the sort of job I wanted, so I thought I'd retrain. I had a part-time job three years ago, just before I came to University, at the telephone exchange. It was such an awful job I thought God, if I'm condemned to this sort of work for life, I've got to do something different.

For some women the decision to enter higher education has been born out of sheer despair at the self-denial required of women in a world where we are often seen only in the context of our relationship to others.

I was walking the walls, – that was about it. I went through a lot of depression. I was really fed up, no meaning to my life at all. You know, feeling useless and wishing for something more. I kept thinking, there must be more to life than this . . . something for me . . . I'd done nothing to stretch my mind since leaving school.

I think the prime thing in coming to University was to stop 'playing wife', to become a person. It was a conscious way of changing my role.

Others, working with women in refuges, in community groups and in campaigns against pornography, have turned to education to acquire the qualifications and skills to help us develop our own political work and give us a wider perspective to supplement what we already know from our own experience. We've believed that our lack of education has contributed to a lack of control over our lives, and that acquiring knowledge will somehow make us less vulnerable to that control and more able to take an active part in shaping the conditions which structure the world.

Now all this might seem like a narrow, instrumental attitude to education. Whatever happened to learning for its own sake, to the pursuit of excellence? For most of us that's a luxury we can't afford. But even so, those of us who've returned to study have usually done so with a sense of anticipation, eager to engage with new ideas. But for some of us, the intellectual excitement we thought we'd discover has been hard to find.

We couldn't imagine what it would be like mixing with all those bright students, taking part in intellectual discussions, listening to inspired brilliant lecturers and soaking up really important ideas. After being mothers and housewives for years, the whole idea of University was intoxicating. However, we were in for a big disappointment. Lectures were often boring, as were many of the books. When we learned to decipher the jargon and complicated language, the ideas often seemed obvious, and measured by my experience, pretty irrelevant too.

But whatever our reasons – to escape poverty, to seek personal fulfilment or to transform the world for women – some of us have decided, as mature students, to give education a second chance.

Home base

Returning to study is probably never as easy for mature students, whether women or men, as it is for younger ones. Rather than concentrate on any experience or wisdom we might have gained along the way, those who vet us and coach us draw attention to our lack of formal certificates, the length of time spent out of studying or the possible effects of ageing on the old grey matter. As a result we feel less able or equipped for the cut and thrust of intellectual exchange than the younger and fitter contestants. As mature women students, without wives of our own to help with the training or to masssage our fragile egos, we can feel nobbled before we start. Meanwhile, back at the home base, it's likely to be business as usual.

> When you get home the dinner has to be cooked, the children played with – they must not suffer because of a whim of yours. Eventually the children are in bed but your husband is watching the television and asks what he's supposed to do if the TV is switched off so you can concentrate and there is no other room you can go in the house, except the bedroom with only the bed in it, which is fatal because it's been a long day. So you sit at the table listening to Coronation Street, the news and then the film and hope you'll manage to write the essay that you feel sure is beyond your capabilities. After God knows how many sheets of paper and three hours later you decide to go to bed and leave it till tomorrow – do some of the reading in bed perhaps. You miss the next hurdle altogether because one of the kids is ill and it's your responsibility to look after them.

The reality of most women's lives under the present system handicaps us before we start. We have to bear the main responsibility of domestic and childcare labour, regardless of whether we are studying or not. We also spend vast amounts of energy doing the emotional and caring labour that is required, both in family life and increasingly in the wider community. We can't automatically rely on the kind of emotional and practical support for our own studies that we would expect to receive if we were men.

> In principle he is really quite supportive, when he talks about it to other people you'd think it was all his idea and he thinks it's terrific. I think he likes telling people what I'm doing, but in our day to day life I honestly can't say he's supportive at all. He resents the time I spend with my books and not with him, he resents anything at all that's changed, that affects him – you know, I can do what I like so long as it doesn't affect him. Of course it has affected him, it's bound to, it's a completely different way of life and he doesn't consider writing essays or reading books to be work and I do, and I think he just feels neglected.

We can't rely on any interest being shown in what we do.

> He just walks away, he gets a glazed look in his eye if I start talking about it and wanders off. He's just not interested, academic work has never interested him anyway, he thinks I'm crazy to want to do it, it's the last thing he'd want to do anyway. He's always been a bit like that, he never wanted to listen while I was working either.

Studying isn't considered to be real 'work'.

> He works for money to keep the family, that's the way he looks at it. He thinks that what I'm doing I'm doing because I want to do it, it really hasn't got anything to do with real life. For him there's this vague idea that sometime at the end of it I might get a decent job. My elder daughter is more interested in what I'm doing, you know, sometimes after you've had a really good lecture and you want to talk about it to someone, she'll talk about it, but my husband won't.

It's not only lack of interest and practical support that handicap us, many women also have to find the stamina and courage to survive the hurdle of direct, systematic opposition and abuse.

> My husband tried a whole range of tactics to prevent me returning to education. The first was money – even when I started Second Chance he made it plain he wouldn't give a penny towards anything. It was the same when I applied to the Poly. Right from the start he refused to sign the grant forms. He did eventually when he realised I was going to anyway. Then his tack was 'You can do it as long as it doesn't affect me'. But of course it did. So he had to then try something else. Because I used to drive to Portsmouth, the obvious target was my car. His way of finishing arguments was to hide my car keys or physically stop me from leaving the house. He once even took the rotor arm out of the car. His anger and frustration at not being able to stop me created a constant underlying tension at home. This meant I was uncomfortable doing work when he was around because he'd pick arguments if I was working and the dinner wasn't cooked or the house was in a mess. A couple of occasions he swept all my books off the table and once he ripped up a couple of my essays. This meant that I could never leave books or work lying around, so I always had to make sure I put them all away and out of sight when he was due home. From then on I wouldn't work at home until he'd gone to bed and then I'd work through the night.
>   Because he would never discuss anything I was doing or learning I felt I was existing in two different worlds – one college, one home and they could never overlap with each other.
>   During my final year, (although things didn't get any better as regards working at home) things weren't so bad perhaps because he could see an

end in sight. He would sometimes say that although he still didn't like me doing it, he could understand why I wanted to. When I got my degree he actually took credit for it. He maintained that he was a great help to me because without the constant fight to go, I'd have given up and left in the first year! But the decision to do another year's study to become a teacher brought things to a head again. We had constant rows: as far as he was concerned I had to 'get off my fat backside and get a job' to bring some money into the house, as well as 'repay my debt to society instead of sponging off taxpayers anymore'. Yet again he refused to sign my grant forms – but this time I just forged his signature. We separated a few months later. I feel very angry about it all – if I'd known we were going to split up over this, I'd have done it years ago.

If we are wives our financial dependency on men is reinforced by a grant system that requires husbands to give their signed consent to women studying before the money is released. One woman we know had to send a solicitor's letter threatening divorce before her husband would agree to sign. Other men have used the requirement to emphasise their financial control and to demand our gratitude for being allowed 'to do what we want'.

We also know of women who've come home from classes to find their books on a bonfire in the back garden, or the house windows broken in by husbands who find the idea of wives doing something for themselves far too threatening. As past mistresses in the art of emotional management, we're used to spending a lot of time soothing and smoothing over the conflict caused when we direct some of our attention outside the home, in a manner which doesn't necessarily have an immediate and obvious pay-off for husbands and children. It's rather like the advice medical experts are fond of giving us after the birth of a baby: 'Don't forget your husband. He may feel a little jealous of baby if you're neglecting him. Try to remember to pay him some attention and cook his favourite meals . . . ' Except that all this takes time, energy and will away from what we've set out to do. One woman, in order to be able to apply to a polytechnic herself, also arranged an interview for her husband so that 'he wouldn't feel threatened'. The problem came, of course, when she was accepted and he was not. Although she did start the course it wasn't long before trouble at home forced her to give it up.

It seems to be a common phenomenon – one well known by university tutors. When one woman went to see her personal tutor about her husband stopping the maintenance and threatening to go for custody of her children just before her exams, the tutor told her:

'Oh, it's classic. They always play up before the exams, throw a wobbler before the finals, we get it every year.'

We don't find it consoling to know that it's 'normal' for men who feel they've been moved ever so slightly off-centre to jostle their way back into the front line at women's expense. It makes us feel angry. But individually, when we're lining up for the race and there's problems at home, it can be guilt that brings us to our knees.

> The biggest disadvantage for me personally is the way I feel. I don't feel I have the right to apply myself one hundred per cent wholeheartedly to what I am doing for myself because I am not independent; I am a member of a family and I am the mainstay of my family, I always have been. I feel that my time isn't my own, I'm taking time out for myself but I still feel guilty about it and it's the pressures of being pulled this way and that and hanging onto what I want to do. Several times this year it would have been ever so easy to give up, just let go and say 'what am I bothering for, I'm a wife and mother and that's it'. I think it's time and the pressures of the children wanting one thing and husband wanting another and the wider family too, mother and sisters. Men tend to see their jobs as their first consideration, for some of them their last consideration too, but I think just being a woman it's difficult for me to do that.

We're no strangers to guilt. We find it hard to justify doing anything for ourselves when the messages surrounding us from childhood have been to put others first. Even when we understand how guilt operates to constrain and control us, it's still hard to resist when those around us continue to heap the coals upon the fire. Even if we survive our own guilt, at the end of the day, our dependency on men can be reinforced in the very act of trying to become independent. We know of men who have moved jobs to another part of the country, just as their wives were embarking on a three year course, and even one who judged the time appropriate to resettle the family abroad. His arguments to justify it, though, were particularly pernicious.

> He said that Britain is too racist for a family like ours (he's white and I'm black) and that in fairness to our kids we should move somewhere more racially mixed. I asked him why he'd just decided this now. It never seemed to occur to him before – just when I'd been talking about going back to college.

It's ironic that we may work really hard to survive all the obstacles that home base presents, our emotional labour and physical caring oiling the wheels that keep our family lives running reasonably smoothly, only to find that this is used to disqualify us in another way. The solicitous enquiries about our home commitments from university interviewers whose hands look as if they've never scrubbed a floor or washed a nappy – make you feel that women like us shouldn't even consider doing anything other than housework and childcare.

> Firstly the automatic challenge 'are you sure you can spare the time and give the commitment to a degree course with all your family ties'. Well, my reply could only be honest. 'Of course I can.' If I now manage to hold down two jobs as well as run a house etc. etc. the course will offer me a reprieve. I can study and get a grant at the same time instead of two outside jobs, I can in a lot of instances read and write essays at home whilst cooking, cleaning and washing. In fact I'm so used to splitting myself ten ways it will be great to have that reduced to only eight – with the added advantage of achieving something I would never have believed possible until now.

> When I applied for the university I felt there was an underlying assumption on the part of the interviewer that I could not make it and if I did get accepted I would not manage the course. It appeared after I asked that they had very few mature students, especially women, let alone any single parents. They had known of one mature woman in the last eight years and she was married with no children. This is probably a reflection of my degree course in science. I feel they don't expect women as mature students, especially working class ones, to want to do it.

If we do a 'little job' to help the family budget, the view seems to be that we'd better not deprive the family by giving it up for the student life.

> I applied for the CQSW (Certificate of Qualification in Social Work) course at Southampton University. During the interview I was asked what my husband's salary was and when I told him he was most concerned whether or not we would be able to manage if I gave up my job. On reflection I should have lied about my husband's wage – maybe that would have made a difference.

But despite all this we should be finding time for voluntary work.

> For a start you have to do 'acceptable' voluntary work for at least a year before you'd be considered for the course. For a lot of working class women this just isn't possible if you've got a job. Of course all the

informal support we give each other, listening advising, accompanying each other to the DHSS doesn't count. Even support work we do in the women's movement around domestic violence, rape and divorce wouldn't be defined as 'acceptable'.

Social work courses in some places seem most reluctant to accept working-class women. Perhaps it's the spectre of all those 'latch key children' from 'deprived homes', where we spend the food money on booze and bingo, that makes them think we're getting above ourselves turning up as prospective colleagues rather than grateful clients. In fact, it's our experience at the hands of social work agencies that would make many of us good social workers if we ever got the chance.

> The chap from the CQSW was really blatant about it. He more or less said they don't accept working class women or single parents. They only accept mature women if their husbands can afford to pay for childminders and cleaners so that domestic responsibilities don't 'interfere' with the course. We gave him a hard time about it but it made no difference. He's in charge of selection and none of us were selected.

And so the objections of men at home are reinforced by the attitudes of men who guard the gates into academia. Far from getting approval for returning to study, we're more likely to meet opposition and obstruction on all fronts. Keeping the home fires burning, looking after children, doing domestic work and dealing with the opposition act as the preliminary heats designed to weed out all but the most dedicated. If we are determined to continue, despite these handicaps, there are still more qualifying rounds to endure before the big event.

Limbering up

It's not enough to know why we want to study, what we want to study and to move heaven and earth to make it possible. We have to jostle with all the other runners in the qualifying procedures. We may know which course we want to do but being allowed to do it is another matter. As we've seen, the reservations might be expressed in terms of our family commitments or they might be clothed in the language of academic inadequacy – 'the institution needs some proof of your capability'. We might be told we need a few 'A' levels or be directed towards one of the recently created Access courses. Before Access courses became fashionable, 'O' and 'A' levels have been the most common entry point and were usually taken at the local Tech. [In 1987 Ordinary Level General Certificate of Education (GCE 'O' Levels) were replaced by the General Certificate of Secondary Education (GCSE).]

After finishing the 2nd Chance for Women in June 1981, I enrolled in the September at Southampton Technical College to do three science GCE 'O' levels – Physics, Chemistry and Maths – and my fees were waived as I was on Supplementary Benefit. There were both day time and evening classes, but as I was a single parent, with one child at school and one under school age, and I was working part-time, I attended in the evening three times a week. My mother looked after the children for me – the classes were 6.15–9.15 and I certainly couldn't have afforded baby sitter's fees.

It was sometimes no mean feat getting there as the college is certainly not the most accessible of places – the buses stop in the city centre and this then meant a 15 minute walk past parks, pubs and down underpasses. I used to be able to go with another woman but she left before Christmas so eventually I was going on my own. I was often afraid doing this walk on my own as women have been attacked in the park.

Maths was a very mixed class as regards age and backgrounds; in September it was over twenty and by June the numbers were down to two. The lecturer was ex-army and suitably sexist. He thought that I couldn't expect to complete the course and pass the exam. The other tutors were quite patronising and cynical about whether I'd achieve my aim although they had quite a bit of respect for me trying. I didn't find the subjects hard and persistently asked questions as I felt, especially at the beginning with such large classes, that the lecturers focussed a lot of their attention on the boys and men in the class.

After I'd passed the three 'O' levels I was elated. I felt that I'd overcome a huge obstacle. I decided to do two 'A' levels next. I would have liked to have done a third but this would have meant I'd have had to enrol as a full-time student paying full-time fees, more than £200 in 1982.

The classes during the day amounted to a total of six hours a subject, some days these did not finish until 5pm so I had to arrange for a child minder to collect the children from school. This was expensive – about £5 a week, as well as tiring. It meant collecting them from the child minder and then walking home about 25 minutes. Bus fares amounted to about £4 a week as well. So about £10 a week was gone from my Supp. Benefit before I had even bought food or anything else. As some of the classes started at 9am I was invariable late. I was constantly broke, always rushing and usually tired. The work demand was great although I never found it hard. What did annoy me was that I couldn't spend more time doing it.

Somehow I had to fit it in with everything else and inevitably ended up completing something but knowing full well that I could have done much better. My tutor tried to console me with the fact that many mature students feel the same but it didn't console me. I don't find that thought very comforting.

I was having some problems financially so naively I applied to social security for help regarding my travelling expenses and childminding fees. If I had been working they would have paid towards this but as I was at college they didn't want to know. I was not working any longer and was totally dependent on Benefit which as it stands is completely inadequate. Some days I did not attend lectures because I did not have the bus fares and tried to put my time to better use by studying at home. Studying at home with children around however is a bit of an occupational hazard. Finding somewhere to study is not easy either. A room of your own is essential but in my household impossible. I have nowhere really quiet to work away from the telly and the children and have just a large room which all the family tend to use. Other practicalities, such as heating a room to study in, have to be overcome especially when you do not have the luxury of central heating, and as trivial as this may seem, some evenings it's a real problem.

I felt at the beginning when I was taking O and A levels that I was a 'part time' part time student. Even now that I'm doing a degree course, college life has to fit in with home life and not vice versa.

When I finally applied to University I was offered a place on condition that I got two Bs. I passed the two A levels but the grades were not good enough to get me to University so it meant resitting them and attending college for yet another year.

In order to get my maths beyond O level I had to enrol in an additional maths course. This was exclusively for mature students. Although it was an evening class which I couldn't attend, I managed to see the tutor briefly once a week during the day. This was not to my advantage as I didn't get the full amount of time spent on the subject in the evenings, but for most of the time I muddled through. This course and the certificate awarded on completion was recognised by the CNAA (The Council For National Academic Awards), but when I mentioned this at the University, they had never heard of it and were not really impressed at all – A levels were what they wanted.

In looking back I have spent six years studying to get where I am today, the beginning of a four year degree course in science and education. The route of taking O and A levels was painstaking and exhausting. (A levels I felt were the pits.) It was very difficult to find anyone to advise me of the best way to go about courses but I think there must be an easier way than the one I have described.

In these qualifying heats the obstacles can range from coping with the demands of home and children on an inadequate budget, to facing the sexism of teachers and sexist assumptions of institutions. It can mean doing courses which we think will qualify us for the big event, only to find that someone has altered the rules once the runners are under starter's orders. The effect of all this can make us feel that we are running on the spot or that the finishing line has been moved yet further down the track. Compared to all of this, recent developments in the provision of Access courses may seem like a simpler route into higher education.

At first sight there's something very attractive about the language of Access with its images of 'open doors' 'gateways' and 'new horizons'. But on closer examination the prospective student might be forgiven for thinking that Access does more to provide new opportunities for the colleges and institutions than for the students they set out to recruit.

The aim of an Access course is to provide those with no qualifications the opportunity to acquire them in the shortest possible time in order to gain entry into higher education. Put like this it sounds exactly what we want. Any device which allows us to cut through the qualifying rounds and gain swift access to a degree course sounds like a good idea.

How Access works is that a particular further education college gets together with a particular institution of higher education – a poly, university or college – to plan a one year course tailor-made to enable its students to get on to a specific degree course. Many of them are aimed at women because 'mature women do represent a relatively untapped market and a fresh source of student hours'.

Access courses claim to provide an alternative entry to higher education and are geared to the specific needs of mature students rather than the traditional 'O' and 'A' level route, designed with school pupils in mind. They avoid external examinations and sometimes provide discretionary grants to cover the cost. Otherwise the fees are quite high.

It sounds an attractive package, if you can afford it, but you might be disappointed when you discover what's really inside. For a start, because it's geared to one particular course it is not recognised anywhere else. So if you want to try for other courses, or if your husband moves his job to another area and you have to follow him, your Access course won't be worth the paper (lots of paper) that's been written about it.

Since Access is now 'big business', colleges are beginning to get more organised, which means standardisation, grading and, in some cases, even entry requirements.

Of course we'll need some evidence of students' ability to cope with the course. This is really difficult to assess when students have no acceptable evidence of their capabilities so, in practice, we'll be tending to look for an O level or two.

The logic of this would seem to be that if you can't be accepted on to an Access course to get qualifications, and you are without any qualifications in the first place, you'll have to go on another course (a pre-Access course or Access to Access) to get them!

Colleges providing Access courses are keen to convince the University or Poly to recognise their courses as entry qualifications and are therefore vulnerable to suggestions that students should come out at the end tested and graded.

We are moving towards setting some kind of standard by which to grade students' work and which will be acceptable to the University. There's even talk of a national system of validation. Many areas now have local consortiums deciding common modular syllabuses and setting common standards of grading.

If comments like this make you smell a rat you could be right, for it's hard to see how this differs from 'A' levels. But the guarantee of a place on a degree course might make it all seem worthwhile, until you discover that there is no such guarantee.

One college of Higher Education was particularly ruthless on this score. They contacted one F.E. College to provide them with an Access course but it was only later discovered that they'd also contacted nine other F.E. Colleges to do the same. The Higher Education College had been told by the Department of Education and Science (D.E.S.) to double its number of mature students to around 50 a year. So with 10 Access courses each with 20 places, that's 200 students looking for special access to that course. Well 150 of them are going to be disappointed.

Even when there's only one Access course, students aren't automatically entitled to places. 'It still depends on the competition for places that year and how well students fare on the Access course.' In fact, just like 'A' levels.

Getting a grant to do an Access course can seem like a big plus at the time, but it might put your future grant entitlement into jeopardy. Many colleges have been irresponsible in not pointing out to students that grants for mature students without formal qualifications to do degree courses are not mandatory, and that if you've had a grant already to do an Access course you may not get one to complete your degree.

Lifting the lid of Access is likely to reveal a can of worms, and surviving the course once you're on it takes a strong constitution.

Four women from the Second Chance programme decided to do a pre-degree course at the local tech. In some ways the idea seemed attractive to them. They felt they needed some more 'practice' before contemplating higher education. The course was twinned with the Polytechnic and promised a direct route into some of its most popular degree courses. An LEA grant was available which, although not a great deal, was an incentive to women without an independent income.

One of them decided to be quite instrumental about the whole experience. She read what she was told to read. She produced essays in the required way. She gauged the tone and politics of it all quite quickly and chose to keep her head down and her mouth shut rather than take issue. She completed the course successfully and is now training to be a social worker.

A second woman also completed the course successfully – but not without considerable distress. She felt the course was authoritarian and difficult in ways which she had not expected after Second Chance. The course requirements – three or four hundred years of British and European history, the study of innumerable literary texts, an introduction to sociology, politics, environmental science, maths and some instruction in the Russian language – were excessive and seemed to have been put together with no rhyme or reason other than they reflected the subject interests of the tutors involved. Rather than being critical of all of this, however, she felt intimidated and overwhelmed, and soon became convinced that she was stupid and that the problem was hers. She reacted angrily to what she considered to be patronising and insensitive behaviour on the part of the tutors, but was too afraid to make a public stand against them. Recently widowed, with three small children to support on a meagre pension, her determination to continue was enormous. But the year reduced her confidence and skills rather than enhancing them and at the end of it she was unable to get the place at the Poly which she had been led to expect. She was accepted at another college – further away from home – but found that the tiny grant which had accepted during her pre-degree year meant that she was not offered the discretionary grant she needed to continue her studies.

The other two women began the pre-degree course with a strong sense of working-class and feminist identity and were immediately critical of what they found. The course was a curious mixture of 'poor persons Oxbridge' with wine and cheese parties and sherry tutorials with tutors, and F.E authoritarianism – they had to 'sign on' at the college each day and provide written apologies for absence. When some students went on a field trip to France, those who couldn't afford to go had to sign in each day and do private study in the empty classrooms which their tutors and fellow students had vacated for the week.

It was clearly not expected that anyone might take issue with what the tutors were teaching. Most of the students were women and were the subject of much banter about women 'not being able to understand politics' and being 'more interested in housewifely pursuits'. Feminism was the subject of much derision with jokes about battered women, and Greenham freaks and lesbian libbers. In sociology they learned that poverty was relative and women's lives were improving. One of them, living in a tower block with a tiny child and complaining about claustrophobia was told 'the advantages of having a garden have not yet been established sociologically', which is fine – as long as you've got one. She never did find out why, on such a course, it was necessary to learn Russian when 'I can't even speak the same bleedin' English as them'. The other, who suffered from panic attacks and agrophobia periodically – and especially during her time at the college – was advised to come by bicycle so that she could get 'lots of air into her lungs'.

Both of them felt very strongly that they were the wrong sex and the wrong class in the wrong place, and the more they tried to speak out against the sexist jokes and class prejudice, the more they felt victimised by some of the lecturers and some of the students. Throughout their time on the course they both got consistently good grades for their essays – although most of them were completed in the small hours of the morning and to the detriment of their health and general well being. Both are mothers with domestic responsibilities and one also had to put up with continued obstruction from her husband. He made it very difficult for her to attend the course and would have been delighted to know that she wasn't enjoying it. It had taken a great deal of courage to establish her right to do it in the first place and it was a matter of continued argument between them. It would have been impossible to admit to him that it wasn't worth it.

At no time did they experience the social relevance of learning which they had come to expect on Second Chance, or find any serious attention paid to views which were contrary to the right-wing ethos of the lecturers. One decided to do her seminar session on the role of women in the family and was confronted by the men students arriving with inverted chamber pots on their heads inscribed with the letters MCP. It was all treated as a huge joke. Neither of the two felt she could continue after that. Both had to pay their grants back and one was threatened with legal action because she had difficulty in raising the money in the required time. Although she didn't complete the pre-degree course, she was offered a choice of two unconditional places at the Polytechnic, on the strength of her ability and her references from Second Chance – which was some consolation. Except that the experience of the previous few months had rekindled all the old alienation and hostility she felt during her school days and she concluded that education – apart from Second Chance – was definitely not for her.

As women at whom such courses are directed 'to develop our confidence', we feel more like the victims of yet another confidence trick. So far as we can tell, the real value of Access courses are not for us, but for those teaching and organising them. At a time when G.C.S.E. and 'A' level numbers are dwindling in F.E. colleges, Access provides the necessary boost to falling rolls and morale, and pushes up the number of student hours which colleges can claim. The funding such colleges receive from the D.E.S. is in direct relationship to the number of students they have and the number of hours they teach them. So money is a big consideration.

We feel like the pawns in a business strategy which seems to be taking over from educational ideals and principles. Having registered the declining profitability of established products, the education marketing men are wheeled in to identify a new market to take up the slack. The next step is to design a re-vamped product, cunningly disguised in brand new packaging. It only remains, to get together with the Admen to create a 'need' for the product for it to appear indispensible to the punters, who'll be persuaded to sign up in droves. Although we have to believe that outright deception is not the name of the game, the wide-boys of continuing education seem to be sailing pretty close.

Despite the effort spent telling us that we now have to do Access if we want to get on to a degree course, we've yet to see any real evidence that doing so will improve our chances over other methods of entry.

It'll come as no surprise to learn that, in addition to giving a welcome 'face-lift' to F.E. colleges previously left out in the 'non-academic' cold, Access has provided the opportunity for some colleges to claim they now do 'higher level' work (not 'Access', please – 'pre-degree, or pre BA' courses) and deserve more departmental Brownie points. These points, awarded to departments doing more advanced work that the usual business of F.E., carry extra cash to pay for more senior posts, and to help guarantee jobs for the boys (whose futures might otherwise be less secure).

For those of us not privy to all this information, Access can appear to be something which is to our advantage. In fact it just presents us with yet another set of hoops to crawl through. Not to put too fine a point on it, we think the whole thing stinks.

Most of the qualifying rounds take place in technical colleges or further education colleges, which frequently have their origins in the vocational training of male apprentices for industries wanting to control recruitment to skilled work in a more prosperous era than this. The legacy of their original purpose, despite opening their doors to different kinds of students, is often apparent in the pervasive stench of macho-culture and male achievement – albeit gritty working class male achievement – that pervades them. This ethos shows itself in pin-ups stuck around the walls of the teaching rooms much as they are in the workshops of Fords, the pool tables and the darts board, the groups of male students taking up space in the canteens, hanging over tables, spread-eagled across chairs, hands straying in the direction of any passing women spirited enough to invade this male territory. Pat Mahony has written about what she calls 'the training in social maleness' which takes place in schools, where boys learn their worth at the expense of girls by learning to take up space, monopolise teachers' attention and to systematically abuse and harass girls. Although similar studies of further education have yet to be done, as women students in these colleges we have no reason to believe that this miraculously changes when boys become men and occupy the lecture halls and labs of further education. Nor is this behaviour restricted to students. It applies equally to the women teachers who intrude upon the territory of men.

The violent atmosphere of that College was so threatening to me as a woman that there was no way I'd even think of being 'out' as a lesbian to the students. There, sexual harassment, whether from the uniformed security guards who staffed the entrance to the building, the students I walked past in moving around the college, to the sexual innuendoes present in almost every statement made in class by male students, was a way of life. And one very hard to cope with.

The first time I used the lift, for instance, made it very clear that lifts were no-go spaces for women. It was not only me as a woman staff member who experienced this, the young women students were routinely hassled, shoved about and jostled on their way to the classrooms. Not only did I witness this, but on several times met young women in tears in the loos. But this was all deemed trivial by the authorities. The security staff had long since given up attempting to stop fights between male students, and so a police presence was a regular part of life at this College.

Assaults on staff were frequent too (several men had been injured in the classrom) and while I was there, two women members of staff were seriously assaulted in the College, one having to spend a week in hospital and the other not coming back to work before I left. In this context I did not feel it possible to do more than teach my hours and keep my head down.

The only space I had to be supportive to the women in the College came after I'd done the part of the course on gender. Few of the boys bothered to stay, so at the end of the lesson I stayed on and chatted with the young women students. One of the things that came out of this was a women's self defence course and a few lunch time meetings on a very informal basis for which I booked a few videos and discussed 'women's' issues with any that were interested in turning up. But basically the atmosphere of hostility was such that I just went in and did my hours and was relieved to go home.

But in fact it was not that easy to leave it all behind. On more than one occasion I was followed to the tube station after the class I taught at the end of a Friday afternoon, by groups of male students and I felt safer riding round the tubes for an hour or so, rather than have them follow me to my door.

Even at home I was not completely free of the College. One week for example I had a series of obscene phone calls which, because the male caller called me 'Miss', I put down to male students from the College. They stopped after I gave up the job.

Not being paid for 'sick' days, I rarely took any, but there were days when I just did not feel able to go into College at all. I must have had about 5 days off sick in the term I taught there, more than I've ever taken before or since. A lot of the problems in that College could be put down to the general tensions of the inner city. The kids I was supposed to be teaching had chosen or been persuaded to take a further year in education, rather than join the dole queues at 17. They knew there was little future for them, the white kids as well as the black ones.

Race was another factor in the violence, but not in any clear or straightforward way. The NF [National Front] presence was small but visible, and this contributed to the tensions, but the alliances in the fights and attacks on women were not drawn around race line, but were much more difficult to unravel.

I did not seek for that contract to be renewed at the end of the term. I was aware that in walking away from the College, I was abandoning the women in the group, but at the time, I seriously thought my survival was more immediately at risk. I do still meet some of them, in the area I live. Only last week, now 2 years since I left, the check-out woman in Woolies says 'Oh it's you Miss' and as she was due for a tea break we were able to have time for a chat.

These Colleges are in a league of their own in our experience.

The big event

The analogy of the conveyor belt is often used to describe how young people are processed in the preparation for higher education. They are transported and deposited at the starting line in peak condition, ready for the big event. For working-class women running in the same race, a little later in life, nothing could be further from the mark. Rather, we've had to scramble over hurdles and around obstacles to arrive on the scene already somewhat punch-drunk.

University may represent 'the pinnacle of academic endeavour', the site of learning where 'the collected wisdom of the past' is transmitted and where 'creative thinking continually pushes back the frontiers of knowledge'. But for us it also holds conflicting messages. As working-class women we've seen it as the training ground of the establishment – the exclusive club of the white upper middle classes where membership is usually refused to the likes of us.

My feelings upon entering University as a full-time student were very mixed, ranging from mild panic to sheer terror. I was sure I was going to make a complete fool of myself – all of my pre-conceived ideas of Universities and the type of people who attended them came rushing back. No matter how times change, the idea of someone with my sort of upbringing actually becoming a student seemed totally unbelievable.

Yet on the other hand, those of us growing up during Macmillan's era of 'you've never had it so good' had been promised equality of opportunity if we showed ability and perseverance.

> On being accepted to do a Sociology degree course at Southampton University I believed, in my naivety, that my lack of formal academic qualifications and being a female, working class, mature student would make no difference to my capacity to join in and enjoy my course and to feel part of University life. I believed further education opportunities were open to all, regardless of class, providing you had the 'ability'.

In Harold Wilson's day the idea of expanding higher education to provide improved opportunities for those who previously had little chance of gaining entry started (and some would say ended). Different types of courses, in different types of institutions, seemed to mark the beginnings of a shift away from elitist notions of appropriate learning for those in training for power, to education linked more directly to social and industrial change. These developments, together with an improved and extended system of student grants, helped to make higher education seem like a real option for more working class people than ever before.

Even so, the gains were slight. The proportion of working-class students was still pitifully low and men still outnumbered women. What might have been the beginning of a new era turned out to be a brief chapter before returning back to the original story.

We have witnessed since the early 1970s the exchange of the catchphrase 'we are all middle class now' for the even older one of 'two nations'. The idea that increased affluence and opportunity would bite away at the sexual and social class fabric of Britain has, instead, bitten the dust. Any minor redistribution of income experienced in the 1960s has now been reversed. Massive unemployment, monetarist economics and social policy informed by Victorian ethics without philanthropy now prevail, bringing in their wake polarisation of the haves and have nots.

For those of us who still cling to the idea that ability is what counts, we're not left in any doubt about the truth of the matter.

> On starting the course I soon realised how wrong I was. The 'ability' I needed was the ability to take on the values and beliefs of the middle class and in fact to be middle class. The working class were something outside the University to be observed, studied and to make theories about.

If we are expected to leave our working-class identity in the changing rooms, and adopt the disinterested stance of the objective spectator observing the goings-on of the working class from a safe distance, it is even harder for us to abandon our gender. It's not just middle-class values that pervade the locker rooms of the academy. The warming-up exercises provided for the powers-to-be are designed with men in mind. We know that the Universities of this country were originally created by men for themselves and their sons, to promote and transmit knowledge collected by men and representing male views of the world. Women have been allowed in only grudgingly and never in significant numbers, especially as teachers and administrators.

These institutions are able to continue to promote male authority and perspectives, largely oblivious to the presence of women. Men are, of course, unlikely to loosen their grip on the resources which provide the coaching needed to operate the cogs of industry or those in the corridors of power. Women are intruders in men's clubs in which the original members have controlled the rules to their advantage for too long to want to change them now. Although the doors are increasingly being opened up to us as students, we still encounter rampant prejudice against us.

> After years of being referred to by the well known term 'just a housewife' and seeing adverts portraying us as getting emotional about a soap powder or not being able to cope with washing the floor, it is not surprising we doubt our ability when entering an establishment of higher education, especially when we find these places have the same attitudes as the people who adopt these advertising ploys.

In these institutions men have authority over us, as in every other area of our lives.

> I think the first thing any woman should do before embarking on higher education is to join an assertiveness training course. I wish I had. I thought I had come far enough in my independence to be able to cope with the authority of men but I think it took me a year into my degree course to realise that this was not the case.

The point at which class and gender combine together in a way which affects us as working-class women is in our lack of rights to economic independence. While most students are impoverished, for many it's a temporary stage, part and parcel of student life. For us it is the continuation of our struggle to survive. None of us can attend these institutions unless we have a grant, and persuading local authorities to recognise our rights to financial support, or the DHSS to cough up when grants are delayed or reduced, is a major obstacle for some women.

Money was always a problem. What pissed me off most of all was that every vacation while other students 'signed on', I couldn't get any money. Because I was a mature student with a child I was awarded a dependent's grant which was supposed to last for 52 weeks. Because I had a certain amount coming into the home I was not entitled to unemployment benefit or social security during the holidays. I was living in rented accommodation paying rent that I could barely afford. I literally had no extra money for things like shoes wearing out, school trips etc. The first year wasn't too bad as I got a rent rebate. Then all of a sudden that stopped – I received £1.98 a fortnight! My travel grant was reduced to £50 for the whole year – it cost me more than that a term. I tried applying for a hardship grant but no-one was interested. I kept being passed from one department to another and achieving nothing. Social security were obviously fed-up with me trying to get money and one day they phoned me at College to say they had contacted my daughter's father to get him to pay maintenance. I was horrified. We had not seen him for 12 years and he has never paid me any maintenance. I told them I did not want his money or anything to do with him. I was frightened he would find us and try to make some claim on my daughter. They told me it was not my choice, I could have no say in the matter! I was furious and shaken.

Some things felt like a nightmare, like finding out I wasn't entitled to Benefit in the summer holidays, simply because I wasn't considered to be an independent person. I was supposed to crawl to my long-gone husband for extra maintenance.

Although I am a single parent bringing up two small children, I am unmarried. Because my children are technically illegitimate I am not allowed to claim for them in my grant as my dependents.

Many of us are already familiar with the tactics of the DHSS, forcing women back into financial dependency on often violent men from whom we are struggling to extricate ourselves. We have experienced similar pressure from both DHSS and local authorities to claim financial support from ex-husbands – despite the potentially disastrous consequences. It can feel as though our lives are being played with, like a game of pass the parcel. Only in our case, no one wants to be left holding the package when the music stops. This reluctance on the part of funding authorities to acknowledge our right to independent financial support can have far-reaching consequences.

My grant was delayed for three months as the awarding body decided that, due to my marital separation, my husband should pay maintenance, and until he did so they could not assess my award. It didn't matter that he wasn't, and wouldn't contribute. This meant several visits to a solicitor during my first term – it also meant borrowing money from the student fund (£50 maximum) and instituting the help of a welfare officer. To live on £50 for three months was impossible so I carried on with my two jobs. The worry and concern for the future was distracting to say the least. To have come this far and be hindered by policies which bore no reflection of my true state of affairs was ludicrous. After December it was a case of leaving the course – a threat as well as letters from my tutor and solicitor eventually persuaded the grant office to pay me the full award. Hurrah, it was plain sailing now.

Not quite. Due to the still complex and antiquated laws in respect of women I had to continue in a state of financial repression. My grant was, by the third year, £3 000 – approximately £60 per week. My husband had left the house and was not paying towards its upkeep so now I was responsible for all the outgoings and incomings at home. The rent was £20 per week with a maximum of £4 off in rent allowance to students whatever their financial position. Gas, electric, food and clothes were also to be my responsibility solely. My husband was aware that to evade any financial responsibility was fairly easy – he would go unemployed or just disappear.

Due to moving my son also changed schools. This was a further expenditure of £250 in school uniform.

Gradually the bills and debts mounted as did my growing concern. Only one solution – to work and not declare it. The grant office had stopped payments during all the vacations to students with children (mainly women) as they included a child allowance in the £3 000. Single students without children could claim unemployment or dole, but not single parent families.

The only way to survive the onslaught of court orders and bailiffs was to work on a night shift and part-time in the day. Prior to my finals I was as near to a breakdown as I would like to get.

The pressures affected my relationship with my son. Home-life was extremely traumatic. We were constantly rowing and unable to meet each other's needs. I was not the normal mother. Unable to cope I arranged for my son to go into care for two months while I worked all out to clear the bills. This added an emotional strain in the sense that I felt guilty, cruel and a failure. My son felt I had rejected him and was confused. This was not how families behaved, not in story books anyway. The 'loving unit' should always be unblemished. After thirteen years what had I done wrong to allow the separation?

I worked at three factories in order to get straight as quickly as possible. As June neared I realised I could not sit my finals for my degree for two reasons. One, I was not able to revise and two, there wasn't the time.

The course chairman arranged that I could have a year off and sit them the next June. So for two months I worked like a robot until the time I had control of my financial situation. My son came home and I worked fewer hours and concentrated on repairing the damage and getting back to a healthy disposition.

During the following year I revised at home amid request after request to repay my grant. It seemed that as I had not sat my finals I would have to repay £500.

The course chairman was amazed and concerned – as this would affect later students. It had always been the policy to allow a student a year off under particular circumstances. My grant had been used for the purposes it was intended. I had attended the course right up until finals, all of the course work was completed and marked. So it seemed the educational authority, on orders from above, were changing their policies once again to suit Government cutbacks.

I was threatened with a court order – but I continued to refuse repayment due to lack of funds, plus I intended sitting the following June. The letters continued despite intervention from my MP, the course chairman and the student union.

I sat my finals in the following June and have not heard from the Grant Office since.

We don't need 'academic ability' to come through this kind of ordeal, we need grim determination to survive. It's not surprising that some of us give up. What is surprising is that most of us keep going, at least until the next hurdle.

I guess all three of us were experiencing doubts (about our capabilities) because we found it necessary to make a pact on that first morning. Right – we agreed – if one goes, we all go – for myself without that sense of responsibility towards the others I'd have cut and run for sure. Anyway we were there and we were staying – for the time being at least. It would be wonderful to be able to stay – so they stayed and yet another amazing success story emerges (as generally happens in the storybooks). But this was reality, and for my part nothing could have been further from the truth.

It's hard to explain to those who have no experience of feeling marginal – white, middle-class, heterosexual men – what it feels like to live in a system where we are continually at odds with dominant values, and where the experiences that structure the reality of our lives are rendered invisible. Even those who have some experience of feeling marginal, don't always recognise the condition in others, as black women quite rightly point out to white feminists. And we all know working-class or black men who are only too happy to confirm or exploit our marginality as women.

The experience of being culturally excluded and misrepresented in terms of race, within education, has been widely written about. In class terms it also makes us feel we don't belong.

> My first impression was that I had no right to be there at all. I was only a working class women. All the other students on the course were middle class, came from completely different backgrounds to me and all had academic qualifications of one sort or another. They spoke differently to me, used language I didn't understand and had different experiences to me. I couldn't join in conversations about lives, values or beliefs because they were so unrelated to my own, but within the university they seemed correct because they were the values everyone else had. Consequently, I not only felt that I couldn't talk but also that I shouldn't, because if I did I would be found out as a working class woman and ignorant, and as such shouldn't be there.

All of which contributes to the gradual but systematic erosion of our sense of identity, our right to make ourselves heard and to occupy space.

> I did a year's PGCEA (Post-Graduate Certificate of Education for Adults) at Surrey University in Guildford. All along I felt the odd one out in many ways; being poor, trying to support myself on just a standard student grant and being a feminist among other things. The other students on the course were overwhelmingly middle class, wanting to teach Art, English Literature, Management skills and one bloke was going on to teach officer cadets at Sandhurst. Not only did they clearly see me as a 'loony feminist' but I think they also considered me very 'common'. I once swore in a seminar and was treated very sniffily.

It can help if we have the support of a few like-minded friends but we know the problem goes deeper than this.

> Luckily I wasn't facing the ordeal alone as two friends who'd also been on the Second Chance for Women Course – the place where confidence is built and egos ever so slightly inflated – had also opted for the same degree course. We all met up outside in order to present a 'united front' when entering the building. Even with their support I was still really nervous. I think I half expected people to turn and point accusingly or for someone to turn and say 'who the hell let her in'.

We are left with the impression that it is our presence, women rather than men, which places us in the wrong. This impression is continually confirmed as we struggle to find ourselves amid the mass of accumulated knowledge about male experiences.

Although we may recognise our own experiences as different from the ones that men speak, write and teach about in these institutions it is their power to give greater significance to their own concerns, and to claim them as 'the norm', which makes us believe that we must be in the 'wrong' for feeling differently. If our experiences, when they diverge from men's, are wrong, then there is no need to take account of them. This, of course, all contributes to the consolidation of patriarchal control.

As working-class women, and more so if we are black or lesbian, we are likely to find ourselves at odds with the prevailing values of universities and colleges, which are those which contribute to the maintenance of patriarchal order and social inequality. Just how we experience the effects of all this deserves more detailed examination.

At one level it its the use of an alienating and mystifying language used to exclude us from sharing the store of accumulated knowledge. At another it is the nature of that knowledge itself. It is also evident in the power and authority of the teachers over the taught to assess us, grade us and to decide which of us will reach the finishing line. At yet another level it is the assertion of men's power to control us as women which presents the major obstacle to getting a degree, especially with our sense of identity and self-respect still intact.

The role of language in preserving elite power to define the world is now well understood. The effects of setting a standard of 'proper English' which ignores class, race and gender differences in access to this power is, as others have pointed out, tantamount to expecting many of us to communicate in a language which is not our own.

> Colloquial speech is lazy
> the English teacher said
> it shows a lack of vocabulary
> use the dictionary instead.
> Don't think in terms of dialect
> forget about your class

you are here to learn good English
and the accent is on pass.
Review your comprehension
rewrite what can't be said
They give high marks for dialogue
that's false and bland and dead.
Accept the written handouts
observe the hidden laws.
Shut your gob in other words
or they will shut the doors

Lecturers talked in a language and with words and sentence construction I'd never heard before, and how can you struggle to understand the concepts when you can't even understand the words they use to describe them? I couldn't take notes properly because putting things into my own words was impossible . . . it would have taken a week! The only way was to try to take it down word for word and then when you get home you haven't a bloody clue what it means.

This was the first time in my life I'd ever come across people talking in this way and no matter how much you tell yourself you're not thick it's very hard when you're faced with whole lecture rooms full of other students who seem to understand it. I knew intellectually that this was a middle class language and that it had nothing to do with intelligence, but the truth was that this was a middle class institution and if I was to get my degree I would have to learn this game and I just couldn't see how I could do it. So working class women are faced with not only learning men's ideas but also translating the middle class male language.

The ironic thing was that in the first year they taught us about Bernstein's theory of restricted and elaborated language codes – that working class people are disadvantaged in the education system because of the complex language of the middle class – but the joke was they taught us this in the elaborated code so I couldn't understand it!

The way in which language excludes us in class terms is perhaps the most obvious example of linguistic bias we encounter in academic institutions. Lecturers also use pretentious jargon as a way of highlighting the cultural gulf between working-class students and middle-class culture. At times it seems as if they deliberately set out to confuse and ridicule us, to put us firmly in our places right from the start. At others, their pompous affectation with language seems rather ridiculous in itself.

Obviously, having old ideas challenged and acquiring new terminology is part and parcel of learning, but there is a distinction between really useful knowledge and confusion for confusion's sake, for example: Do you know what analepsis is? Prolepsis? Anaphora? I don't. (If you care, don't go looking in your dictionary, because you sure as hell won't find them there.) Anyway, it wasn't until the finals 3 years later I found out that it didn't matter a damn – the only mention of the first two I ever heard again was a male lecturer snickering that the first years usually put them in their first essays, most often the wrong way round, tee-hee. What became of anaphora is not something I've lost any sleep over. It just seems a little cock-eyed to me to introduce new students to the most obscure terms at the beginning of a course.

Looking back over old notes I see that I've written 'interpolate' for 'interpellate', the meanings are quite different. I still have problems with the second, something about being hailed as a subject by ideology, but then it hadn't even been explained, and they do sound the same. How about pre-lapsarian? It means before the fall of Adam and Eve in the Garden of Eden. It might sound impressive, but it's actually quicker to say 'before the fall'. One lecturer was obsessed by 'rubric' - not an infuriating plastic cube but the title of one's essay – but to him, people did not get off a bus – they 'disgorged'.

Sometimes you'd know the words, but just think their use was affected. Take the lecturer (on another course) who said 'Is everyone clear on the organisational structure for next week?' when he meant 'Do you know what seminar groups you are in?' Fixing times for tutorials, I was told mine would be at 'seventeen hundred', that's five o'clock, if you are neither a sailor, nor an employee of British Rail.

But mostly, the message strikes home and we feel ourselves to be inadequate, especially if other students and lecturers see nothing wrong in using language to mystify and confuse us.

I sat through some lectures not understanding a word that was being said. One particular lecturer's motto seemed to be 'never use three short words that everyone will understand when you can use six long words that most students won't understand'. I talked to other students about this and although some admitted they didn't always understand the words used, they still didn't see this was wrong. I commented to one student that I felt the language used excluded a lot of people and was elitist and he told me: the English language is there to be used, certain (long) words explain things better than other (shorter) ones and if I was having problems I should try using a dictionary.

One particular tutor whose politics seminars I attended, talked in a very academic way and was completely incomprehensible to us all. But when we asked him to rephrase his questions because we didn't understand, we were told we hadn't done enough work and if we couldn't understand things we shouldn't be there.

The view of many who teach us seems to be that their language is the only one in which intellectual discussion can take place, so students had better acquire it – even if it requires a knowledge of those classics that never featured in our secondary modern school curriculum.

One lecturer always littered his speech with quotes from Latin or Greek. He argued that for him to speak any different from usual would be patronising to students. Refusing to acknowledge that it was equally patronising to use language which we were unlikely to understand, his reply revealed his arrogance and feelings of superiority: 'I never talk down to my students, I expect them to come up to my level.'

This is all to do with perceiving knowledge as power, where those who have the knowledge exercise power over the rest of us by conducting the debates in a language which excludes all those who have not been initiated.

It was useless, one long word which was used was unpronounceable where four or five shorter words in everyday language would have done. The term 'sociological jargon' was used to explain this and all the lecturers seemed to be afflicted by the same disease. It got to the point where if something was put across in a more simplistic way I began looking for the hidden meaning behind it.

It sounded vaguely English but the words which rarely contained less than eight syllables were words I'd never heard before let alone used. Even my hastily acquired dictionary of Sociology proved near useless as the spoken work and the spelling all too often had nothing in common. I felt I was drowning in a sea of 'isms'.

Whilst other students enjoyed the coffee breaks between lectures, either talking about the previous night's revelling or the previous lecture, I spent my time chain smoking in order to raise the nicotine level sufficiently for my brain to function at what appeared to me half the pace of everyone else's, and trying to borrow lecture notes in order to fill in the gaps I'd been forced to leave in mine.

The effects of this are often to question our confidence and our ability, so that we feel we should never have embarked on the course in the first place.

Towards the end of the first term I began to face up to the fact that I'd made a dreadful mistake. I felt totally out of my depth and realized that before much longer I would be discovered for the fraud I really was. Whatever confidence I had gained on Second Chance had long since disappeared. Deadlines for essays were looming ever larger and whilst everyone else appeared to be coping admirably I was having problems linking words together to form coherent sentences. I decided to give up. I tried to explain to my family and friends how I felt it really wasn't for me and how I thought I'd bitten off more than I could chew. But would they even come half way to understanding? THE HELL THEY WOULD! After all I was their shining example of what people like us could achieve, their 'intelligent friend' who went to University. The pressure from them was such that I felt I really couldn't let them down. So, with a touch of the Magnus Magnusson's (I've started so I'll finish) I continued.

The essays did get written, or should I say born, because each was ten times harder than giving birth to either of my kids, and surprisingly the marks weren't half bad – although this still did nothing to boost my confidence. Okay I'd tell myself, I've fooled them this time but surely next time I wouldn't be so lucky. I tried talking to tutors about the problems I was having, realising that if I was to continue I needed to talk to someone. What a waste of time that was. One told me 'Oh yes, I suffered the same thing, but don't worry it will all come together. For me it was in the exams'. My God! I thought, dare I wait until I'm sitting in an examination room to find out! I became renowned for challenging lecturers during seminars and out of them. 'Please, Please' I'd beg, 'could you bring it down to a level where it's likely to hit me centre forehead rather than sailing above my head!' 'You're coping okay' they'd say, 'I don't know what you're worrying about!'

The relationship between language, its construction and uses, and gender has been researched by, among others, Dale Spender in her book *Man Made Language*. She argues that men's language is a way of maintaining patriarchal control by constructing our marginality, if not our complete invisibility.

The process of removing women from language is a disappearing trick of mammoth proportions, cleverly executed by magician grammarians of centuries ago, who decreed that the male gender was more comprehensive than the female one, so that 'man', 'him', 'his' and 'he' should be taken to include 'women', 'her', 'hers' and 'she' – except of course when 'she's' cleaning the lavatory or feeding the baby. Put like this it seems patently obvious that the language which we regard as neutral and unbiased, and which we have no choice but to use, has been tinkered and tampered with to put us at a disadvantage. But until we actually think about it, it's not that obvious. We are so used to 'mankind', 'man's progress', 'manpower' and 'man-made' that we don't notice it at all. Like the hapless stooge in the stage pickpocket routine, we remain oblivious as our distinctive presence is systematically removed, under our very noses.

Nor does it end there. Women stand at every point in a different relationship to language than men. When we are spoken about, it is often in words taken from that rich vocabulary that men have developed to express their disdain, contempt and hatred for us. Pat Mahony, in her study of schools, refers to lists of more than 200 words used by boys to describe girls' sexuality. They represent, she says, the language of women-hating. Other words, once they have had any association with women, lose status themselves as a result. The worst insult you can pay a man is to call him feminine. The worst abuse he can imagine is to likened to a woman's genitals. If the way language has been constructed has secured our invisibility, the way it is used is to effect our silence. The problem is not 'what' we say, but the fact that we say it. We have all had experiences in seminars (and political meetings and social gatherings) where a contribution from a woman has gone ignored or been trivialised, only to re-emerge at a later stage out of a man's mouth and been taken seriously.

> Another lecturer made clear his feelings that women especially those of us who are married and/or have children – should not even be at College. In seminars he would often put us down or ignore or belittle our contributions, so creating the inevitable situation when we'd play into his hands and remain silent. When some of us tried to discuss these attitudes, his smug retort was 'Well, I'm a chauvinistic fart' (There wasn't a lot to say after that!)

When the norm for women is silence, any woman who talks at all is seen as garrulous. The popular image of the talkative woman and her counterpart, the hen-pecked husband who can't get a word in edgeways, couldn't be further from the truth. We don't need research to tell us what we know from our own experience – that men do most of the talking. They also control the topics of conversation and make decisions about how it is conducted. Whereas, we do the conversational shitwork. Working hard to find the right ploys, the right gambits, the right levers to trigger blast off, we follow without thinking the advice churned out in women's magazines and agony columns – 'find out what he's interested in', 'ask him about himself', 'be a good listener'. It becomes second nature to us. We stand on the side lines, like ballgirls at the game of life, lobbing the stray balls that come our way back into the conversational game to be taken up again by the real players.

> We frequently suffered situations when men took over seminars. (Rather astounding when there's sometimes only one or two male students and the lecturer in a group of ten or more.) Perhaps because we have all been taught about the 'natural precedence of men' we rarely interrupted them, nor were we expected to. This, combined with the unconscious (and in some lecturers not so unconscious) belief that academic discussion is more properly suited to men who can argue 'rationally' and 'objectively' often made it virtually impossible to stop some men dominating some seminars. This even happened when a woman tutor took a seminar.

If male students use their authority as men to take over seminars, male lecturers also use the authority of their position to do the same.

> The highlight of the day was the longest word he could come out with. He delivered lectures by rote. He knew it by heart. He talked and talked and if there'd been no one there he'd still have stood there and talked. We were just surplus to his requirements. No matter what, he would stand there and say his piece.

Considering the price we pay to get there in the first place, it's not surprising that we feel angry at our relegation to spectator status, while male lecturers ego-trip on authority to us, their captive audience.

> On a dismal January afternoon would your spirits be uplifted by listening to someone read Browning for two solid hours, without explanation? The spirits of the lecturer in question might have been, the sound of his own voice and good old Browning, most of us found them both very trying, and might have been able to read the verse for ourselves.
> It may seem that I'm giving a biased and waspish view of masculine affectation, we all have our foibles after all, but what would you have made of a lecturer who broke off from facing the class to address several of his remarks to the side wall of the room? Or another who persistently held his lapels when speaking à la Churchill? There was some excuse for the one who used to check that his flies were done up – he had once delivered a sermon in church when they were not. It was the arrogance that was enraging, what was the point of sitting the best part of an hour in

total silence in some seminars? All of us had other responsibilities and worries, and if some had not prepared, or were too intimidated to speak, there were ways of stimulating discussions, as the female lecturers invariably showed. They were also more amenable to lectures being stopped in mid-flow to answer questions, and their language was generally far less highfalutin.

One lecturer turned up with lecture notes so old and yellowing the British Museum would surely have been interested in them. He devoted at least half of every lecture to the latest rugby results, egged on by the male students. That was when he wasn't slagging off the 'boring old menopausal women' he had to deal with in his evening class teaching. Another lecturer had a fixation with soap and glazed oval sewer pipes. He was supposed to be teaching us about falling morality rates in the 19th century, but every lecture would inevitably lead him to his favourite topics, occasionally digressing to chat about wild flowers. The most important things going on at University were the discussions we had with each other over our pie, chips and gravy in the refectory if we had but known it.

If some of the lecturers had a sense that they ought to find more interesting and accessible ways of teaching, they frequently do it in a way which angers us. In the attempt to pitch their language at the level of their students, lecturers can be both patronising in class terms as well as grossly offensive to us as women.

If inadequate explanation or unnecessary use of long words widened the gulf between lecturer and student, the matey approach did not always help to narrow it. Speaking of one Marxist critic Althusser, one of them said: 'So what if he bumped off his old dear?' They weren't usually that horrendous, just patronising – 'I'm just an ordinary bloke' sort of thing.

As women, our means and style of communication represents a partial view of the world, one in which our invisibility and silence is encouraged. Men's language also serves to 'write us out' of those bodies of knowledge we've come to study. Without a mode of communication which takes us into account, we do not have the means to recognise or to record our achievements, our feelings or our understandings. We've been brought up to think of knowledge as something 'out there' waiting to be 'discovered', which once found will reveal the objective, neutral, proven truth about the world. In fact the knowledge we find in academic study only reflects the truths, the experiences and the values of powerful men who have been able to control the meanings and dominate the educational landscape for too long.

At the level of everyday life and common understanding this explains how, while labouring on the home front without pay or holidays or sickness benefit, we can turn to each other and say, 'I don't work, I'm just a housewife'. At the level of the abstract knowledge we come across in higher education, it explains the near invisibility of women and the proliferation of male experts in the subjects we've come to study.

Put like this it seems obvious. Yet many of us have been taken in by this partisan knowledge, feeling grateful to escape domestication and to be given the chance to learn important things. But in such disciplines the rod is self-denial and self-dislike. We sit next to the men, listening to the endless discussion about issues which are not our own, imagining we are part of the exciting interchange of ideas that takes place at university. It could make you weep for lost time, lost energy, lost selves – all of which could be put to better use. We could give endless examples of the exclusion and marginalisation of women in the context of what we're learning – an omission which seems to hold true whether it's literature or law, the sciences or sociology.

> These lecturers, all male except for a woman film tutor, were not replacements for my father, ex-husband, priest. Here they were teaching us things I had never heard of before, if they were teaching they had to be right . . . didn't they?

> It took me a while to question certain arguments, after all I was going back into education with only three O levels to my name. If the other students who had A levels were not disputing situations, who did I think I was? But eventually I made up my mind to speak out about things that worried me such as why there was only one woman writer (Virginia Woolf) on the whole of our literature syllabus. Why did the women students always have to play the stereotypical roles in our drama course? Why were the drama productions always produced and directed by male tutors etc?

> In Economic History I don't think women were mentioned once during the whole year. Presumably we weren't even being economically active. Same in Politics – women didn't feature in that course at all.

The lack of references to women in the course results not only in students considering women unimportant, but also in hostile reactions to those of us who try to broach the issue.

Apart from making me angry I'm also sad to hear an eighteen year old woman state 'Oh not Womens Lib – again, it's all old hat now'.

It's not unusual to hear such hostility or even official complaints of 'too much feminism' in seminars, even though the film seminars in question never once had a feminist analysis or approach. The fact was we were studying 'women's films' and this focused mainly on women. The male students, used to being the focus of attention, immediately labelled the proceedings as feminist and duly complained to the course Chairman. And of course they were listened to. The seminar tutor (a woman) was told to stop being so biased.

Occasionally women were studied but only as an after thought – a single one hour lecture tacked on at the end of a series after the important bits.

Many of us coming late to education as mature students have deliberately chosen subjects like Law or Sociology because we believe the subject matter would be of direct relevance to our own lives, and because we believed that studying them would give us understanding which would have practical application later on.

When studying Sociology we should have been suspicious during those early lectures about 'founding fathers' that something was amiss, but it took longer, despite our quips about 'founding mothers', to fully appreciate the sexist bias in the subject. One disturbing aspect of Sociology is its tendency to objectify certain groups, whether it's the working class, blacks or women, as 'not the norm'. It takes only a small shift in emphasis from being a minority group – ludicrous when applied to women and often insulting in its other applications – to be defined 'deviant', but this seems to be where we often end up.

For two years I had some influence in the deviancy option. This was a time of renewed interest in women's relation to the forces of law and order both in terms of what was happening down at Greenham and in terms of theory.

The effect of making us the object of study, as if we were specimens of a different exotic species, will be easily recognised by black students. Under the microscope our behaviour is observed, but our motivations, understandings and experiences are not understood or even solicited. Rather, we are expected to stand back and observe, invited to be voyeurs of our own lives, to see others be amused, fascinated or titillated by our antics.

One example of this was when I went to a lecture about 'Female leisure patterns' or, what working class women do in their spare time – when they have any, that is. It turned out the major leisure pursuit of working class women according to the research, is bingo. We were told how the lives of working class women are so 'awful' and bingo is the only available form of leisure that is acceptable as an escape from children and home. A visibly shocked lecturer told us the research had found that 'these' women's lives were so bad that some of them had said that they locked themselves in the bathroom to escape for five minutes from their children. Being a self-confessed working class woman who's not adverse to doing this myself, I must admit I didn't find this news too shocking, but on looking round the room at other students I saw that others did seem astounded by this 'revelation' into working class lives. The lecturer also told us that many working class women find it difficult to participate in courses and evening classes particularly when they have to go along to the first meeting on their own, and that all of 'us' middle class sociologists should be aware that it isn't as easy for 'them' as it is for 'us'. Considering my own lack of confidence at University this also was no news to me, but again looking round at the other students I realised how different I was from them. We were being taught about working class women by middle class men who thought they knew all about it. Although I, as a working class woman, knew and had experienced these things, I wasn't allowed to comment because the only valid information on the working class is that 'done' by middle class Sociologists and anyway, I couldn't be working class because I was at University!

Another incident during my first term demonstrated to me the judgemental attitude of many of the students to working class women. This was when we were studying poverty in Britain and we looked at a video showing the experience of women living on Supplementary Benefit or low wages. Following the video we had a discussion on poverty. The attitude of many students was to not take the subject seriously, it was just another part of the course to be studied and got over with. It was so completely unrelated to most students' experiences that it meant nothing to them to see people living in poverty with no hope of any improvement. Many of the students were not interested enough to make comments on the video but others made moral judgements such as 'Fancy having another baby when she's not married and can't afford to look after the one she's already got' or 'You can't say anyone's living in poverty when they've got a colour T.V.' Having experienced living on a limited income and knowing how difficult this is, I found these comments distasteful and felt judgements were being made on me personally. We were told that 'objectivity' was needed to define poverty and thus I presumed my 'subjective' experience was not valid. But how can anyone, and why should anyone, be objective about poverty?

And on a teacher training course, at the University of Surrey, came another lesson in class bias and sexist assumptions.

On one occasion we spent a morning 'role-playing'. We were all given different parts in a scenario supposedly about a slum tenement full of people with problems – elderly, unemployed, single mothers and so on. I was handed a card telling me to act out the part of a single mother living with her baby in one damp room, who is soon to be evicted for not paying her rent. I sat and looked at it for ages, not really understanding what was expected of me, then I saw the others charging around putting on what they took to be 'working class' accents and manners, ie. dropping aitches, wiping their noses on their sleeves etc. I started to feel quite ill, and departed to the nearest toilet where I sat for about an hour chainsmoking and crying, trying to get myself together. I must be slow – it took me ages to cotton on that they could take the piss like that because they all lived in big houses in Woking and Farnham, and all thought they would never be in this situation. What had never occurred to any of them was that amongst them might be a single mother, desperately hard-up, living in a bedsit, in terror of being homeless and losing her kid. When I came back no-one even noticed or asked me what was wrong. If someone had, I don't think I could have told them that they were asking me to act out the realities of my life for them to poke fun at.

This might well be the hurdle that finally does for us. It's hard to survive such experiences on top of everything else. It takes more than a quick pit-stop for a rub down and a massage to get us back on course.

All of us went through a cracking up period. One after another we went down with crying fits, mostly due to exhaustion, feelings of not belonging, not knowing what was expected, trying to read too many unreadable books in a week and listening to incomprehensible, obscure or plain old boring lectures hour after hour, that had no relevance to our lives and simply made us feel put down or knackered from having to rush home at 3.00 to sort out children, cook dinners, clean houses and trying to write essays at midnight, mostly wondering why the hell we ever wanted to be there in the first place.

If we are forced to retire due to injury, the chances are we'll feel that it's because of our own inadequacy and this view of often used to reinforce the idea that, as working-class women, we're not 'up to it'.

For those who stick it out for a few more laps, there are more obstacles around the next corner. If we imagine that the liberal ethic in higher education might protect us from the worst abuses of sexism we are wrong. Matters of sexuality are never far from the agenda of any exchange with men – whether we are studying at university or working on the shop floor. In the past it has been extremely difficult for women to tackle sexual harassment for the same reason that rape survivors think twice before taking legal action. We know from experience that it is women who stand accused, certainly of taking 'a bit of fun' all too seriously, but also of 'provoking' the attention in the first place by 'flaunting ourslves'. by our choice of clothes, by how we walk or sit and by a myriad other messages we are said to communicate to men to exhibit our availability. Not that our 'availability' is something that matters all that much when men decide to pounce. Our presence as women is enough. The buzzer sounds and the men in question move into auto-pilot, their 'natural urges' uncontrollable and requiring immediate satisfaction.

It has been through the Women's Liberation Movement that we have found the courage to name sexual harassment as an offence against us and have come together to support each other in campaigns against it. But we have also learned a lot from feminist research. In challenging some of the myths about male sexuality, we can now see the wood for the trees. Now we know that there is no biological imperative for men's sexual behaviour, no uncontrollable urge and certainly nothing natural about a male sexuality that requires that we are seen only as sexual objects robbed of other aspects of our human identity. We don't, as the 'founding fathers' of sexology proclaim, enjoy subjection, or the infliction of pain. We now know that men have a vested interest in maintaining these myths, which they do just as forcibly in the law courts of the land as in the pages of the daily tabloids. We have come to understand that the construction of maleness seems to rely heavily on our degradation and humiliation and we observe that many men continue to believe that all women – young, old, married and lesbian – are fair game.

Just as the plastic bullet and the baton charge are tangible proof of state control when all else fails, when the iron fist is brought out of the velvet glove, so sexual harassment and sexual abuse represent the blunt instrument of patriarchy, brought out to keep us in our place.

We have shown earlier how male lecturers are well placed to use the power which attaches to their position in the hierarchy. We have already given examples of their exhibitionist behaviour, of academic machismo launched upon a captive audience of students with better things to do than bear witness to it. But we also know of lecturers taking an almost sadistic pleasure in exercising their power over women students particularly.

I always got the impression he was sneering at us. He liked to make out it was all informal – you know, put the chairs in a ring, sat with his feet up – then he'd spend the whole session setting some woman up to be his stool pigeon, to look very foolish and I've got to admit, I rarely opened my mouth. If anyone said anything he'd shoot them down.

We have other examples of them using their patriarchal power over us. At one level it is directed in the form of those 'jokes' we are meant not to take 'too seriously'. Like the politics lecturer taking the opportunity to discredit the GLC (Greater London Council) by referring to 'grants to A.I.D. lesbians to have babies' and the economic history lecturer describing the living conditions on the slave ships during Britain's involvement in the slave trade as being 'worth stopping to think about – all those lusty wanton black women chained together in a confined space'. Or the lecturer showing medical students a slide of a woman being prepared for an operation with the comment 'Now here's a big fat lump that needs sorting out'.

> One of the worst things at College was the constant 'jokes' or comments made at women's expense. One example of this was in a seminar when we were analysing a film scene which showed a man fondling an unconscious woman's breasts. Quite neglectful of the implications this has for women, the tutor remarked 'Well, that was quite pleasant'. The angry reply 'Who for?' made him 'realise' how offensive his remark was, yet he still tried making a few 'wisecracks' to laugh it off. But we often had to listen to similar 'jokes' and remarks – from lecturers and students – that were obviously intended to denigrate women generally and offend and embarrass those women present, such as the lecturer who 'explained' everything in terms of the 'problems of menopausal women'.

The insistence that these are 'only jokes' is not as harmless as it might appear. It provides the cover for men to make sexist, insulting remarks which they would probably think twice about making as serious statements, and it removes from us the right to show justifiable anger at this kind of hypocrisy. If we do, we are told 'we can't take a joke' and that 'we've no sense of humour'.

Like domestic violence and incest, it's hard to give an accurate estimate of the full extent of sexual harassment though we know from our own experience, in one way or another, that it happens all the time.

> Sexual harassment and sexist comments are quite common. Some lecturers move the chairs around so they can sit next to someone they fancy. The new intake of students each year is an opportunity for male

lecturers to take advantage of women students. Certain lecturers have reputations that other lecturers must know about yet their conduct remains unchallenged. It is certain that many women are afraid to report them for fear of the repercussions.

As women we know only too well what to expect.

One particular lecturer was always sexually harassing women students. All the signs were there: the excessive attention to some women's appearance of 'looks'; the way he stood talking to women in corridors – pinning them down by facing them and placing his hand against the wall; his 'mentally-undressing' looks; the ruses to speak to women in private, etc. etc. – even the warning from women students in other years.

In a survey about sexual harassment at Southampton University, the anonymity of the questionnaires enabled women to give examples of behaviour that is more often suppressed.

Sexual harassment happened to me and I did nothing about it because I did not want to jeopardise my chances of a degree. At least now I will become part of the statistics. I just want people to know it happened. All women students are vulnerable because the way the system exists now we're in a weak position regarding the lecturers. Although now I know it was not – at the time, I thought it was my fault.

The survey found that examples of sexual harassment were most common in the faculties of law and medicine – two faculties which have claimed great credit in recent years for increasing the numbers of women accepted as students.

If we refuse to go along with the sexual advances of male lecturers we may find that they use their authority to mask their pique and down grade our work.

One of the lecturers was a sex obsessed drunk and the other was a complete Howard Kirk (History Man) look-alike. He tried his slimy seducing charm on a variety of women students, me included, and if he was rebuffed, which he mostly always was, he would then ignore us, cut us dead in corridors, and down grade us.

After his abortive attempt to get me to visit him, (while his wife was at work) he had to mark a piece of my work which I was rather pleased with. I felt he marked it too low, but did not do anything about it.

Two weeks later in a seminar, we had to read our work out to other students. I read mine and it was received very well. It was then that I told him I thought I deserved a higher mark and he agreed but told me it was too late as the marks had already gone forward for processing.

Sexual harassment can also affect the quality of the work we're able to do.

> Two women in my year suffered sexual harassment from a lecturer not only in College but also outside, in their private social life. Their academic work suffered, as well as having feelings of not wanting to continue with the course. Although no doubt men who behave in such ways are unable to see their actions as wrong and offensive, and would deny that intimidation was their intention, it is clear that this is precisely the effect their behaviour has. Confidence is sapped, women feel helpless to deal with the situation and invariably begin to feel it is somehow their fault, that they 'asked for it'.

It also circumscribes our freedom of speech and movement and our participation in college live, in much the same ways as girls are affected by sexual harassment from boys in schools.

> Whenever I had to do work for him I chose to write about women's issues, as that was what interested me most, eg. women in trade unions, violence against women, women and alchohol, child abuse . . . I was then labelled a hard, aggressive feminist. There were other instances of lecturers offering extra tutorials in their rooms when the rest of the staff had gone home. At first I did not know quite how to cope but eventually I had as little to do with these particular men as possible. It sometimes limited what I did at College but at least I avoided their hassle. I wish I had been able to look up and say what I felt without feeling I was going to be reprimanded in some way. Stupid isn't it?

The idea that favourable treatment in the exam will be the pay-off for sexual favours is repugnant to us, as is the fear that if we speak out about sexual harassment tutors will use their authority to mask their anger and downgrade our final degree. It is the fear that we will pay the cost for their behaviour that often prevents us from speaking out on our own account.

> A close friend of mine was accosted by a drunken tutor who several times asked her to sleep with him. She gave him no encouragement. If she did what he wanted he'd give her a 2.1. She was too embarrassed to complain to higher authorities and she left last year with a 2.2.

When as women we support each other to try to challenge sexual abuse through the official channels, we do not always fare much better. In one polytechnic department some liberal lecturers set up a staff/student monitoring group to discuss student experiences on the course, but they behaved in a remarkably illiberal manner when faced with women students using this opportunity to bring up complaints about harassment.

> During our second year, the department organised a 'Monitoring and Support Group: Student Survey' with the intention of probing student's feelings about the course and making changes where necessary. Although it was not the only reason for attending, two women decided to bring the whole issue into the open. Not only did they raise the matter at the meeting, but they got so frustrated and angry at the belittling of it all by most of the men present, that they gave more examples, particularly from their own experience, than they intended, as well as 'naming names'. Yet the only reference to this in the published report was dealt with in two sentences: 'Some lecturers were felt to inhibit the participation of women in seminars. Notably these staff however were popular with most of the men at the discussion.' It wasn't even specific that the complaint was about sexism and sexual harassment by some lecturers; merely a few convenient and bland words in a tone and style which suggests that it was only a minor concern and one that could be rectified quite easily. (If it was felt to be necessary of course, considering that 'these staff were popular with most of the men . . . ') There was no further comment at all, not even in the conclusion which re-emphasised certain points: 'However, students were forceful about . . . ' That's one way that women's experiences and perceptions are marginalised and trivialised. Another was when a couple of us discussed the problem with the chairman of the course and were alternatively disbelieved, practically accused of being 'trouble-making feminists', told nothing could be done unless the women concerned themselves made an official complaint (which, of course, was to him) and generally fobbed off. Some students reactions – male and female – were equally awful. At one time I was told I was only making a fuss because I was jealous!

Being 'out' as a lesbian takes its own courage, but it is no protection against sexual harassment from male lecturers.

> I went to see the course chairman to ask for an extension – my mother had been ill and I hadn't done the essay in time. Suddenly he came and sat next to me and he said 'There's a tension in this room'. And I said 'I feel quite nervous'. And he said 'There's a tension in this room because I'm attracted to you'. I was amazed. I said 'But I'm a lesbian . . . ' so he said 'Oh yes, but you've got two children – you must have been into men once'. It was very embarrassing – I couldn't get out of the room quickly enough. I said about it to a woman lecturer and she complained. But then she got reported for ignoring the men in her seminars and he just kept looking daggers at me for shopping him. I thought 'Well that's it, I've buggered my chances now' – given who he was and everything.

If we have concentrated so far on the abuse by men who are in positions of authority over women, it is not because we believe that male abuse stops there. Women who are 'in authority over men' get the same treatment.

> When I went to work at a teachers' training College in the seventies I don't think the term sexual harassment had been invented – although the practice was alive and well. I was shocked by the extent to which my male colleagues – especially the young and trendy ones – regarded young women students as part of the perks of the trade. I found out later that my 'sexual conquest' was the subject of a wager between two or three of my colleagues, and that a number of their cronies among the men students were also involved in the speculation about who would win.

When it comes to class, race and politics there seems very little to choose between the men who feel free to harass women.

> I have no more illusions left that working class, black and socialist men are any more enlightened than any other men about women's oppression as a result of being oppressed themselves. In my experience they despise women on the whole – they may have policies and rhetoric to disguise their antipathy, and it may surface more swiftly in bar room banter and misplaced chivalry than in direct aggression – but the deep rooted disregard for women and speedy recourse to sexist and sexual attacks makes nonsense of the view that authority is attached to the position of tutor or comrade when the tutor or comrade is a woman.
>
> Middle class students are no better – though their performance may be marginally more subtle. Most of them don't enjoy the feeling that a woman might know more than them – it goes against the grain – though some are happy to resort to flattery and flirtation to disguise their ignorance or failure to produce any work. I have found men students on In Service Diploma and Masters Degree Courses in discussions about inequality and gender – to be living examples of the arrogance, aggression and attention-seeking which they so adamantly contest is an exaggeration and distortion of male behaviour. In the heat and anger of these kinds of 'discussions' it is clear who has power – and it isn't women teachers.
>
> It seemed pointless to discuss the matter with my male colleagues who used the same tactics to bully, interrupt, misrepresent and silence me in staff meetings as their fellow men used in the classroom. And I have yet to attend a residential conference, with eminent and respectable authorities on whatever the conference happens to be about, who don't talk excessively about their own eminence and authority, whilst at the same time trying to manoeuvre the minority of women present into bed.

The base line then, is not just men abusing their authority in institutions, but men abusing women. It is men wielding the power which attaches to their maleness in a society in which women, whatever our position in the heirarchy, stand in an unequal power relationship with men.

When we enter the obstacle race we don't usually anticipate this. We may know that the going will be tough, a long haul marathon in which our stamina will be tested to the limits of our endurance. We may have had a taster during the qualifying rounds of GCSE' and 'A' levels or on Access courses which are meant to prepare us for the big race. What most of us don't know, when we sign up for the competition, is that is is also an obstacle race, in which the hurdles are not only our own lack of training, our lack of confidence or intellectual prowess, or our home commitments, but anti-woman values which consciously or unconsciously permeate the entire game. The hurdles are devised to weed out all but the fittest, leaving only the most determined among us who are not prepared to be knocked off course by the unfair tactics of the spectators, the other competitors or the judges of the game.

It's bound to be hard in these circumstances to run the course straight, holding on to our sense of ourselves and our principles. It has been tempting for some to cut the corners which allow a more comfortable route through to the finishing line. To keep our heads down and our mouths shut. To produce the right kind of essays and dissertations which prioritise men's issues. To allow men their heads in the seminar rooms and elsewhere. We understand why some women take the line of least resistance – it is enormously draining to struggle perpetually against the odds of male control wherever we are. But we can find ourselves down a blind alley. If we take on the values of white, male, middle-class institutions we find ourselves in the no-woman's land between the world we left outside where we are already marked out as different, and the new, in which we'll never be fully accepted. But worse than this, we take into ourselves a male view of the world, reflected in the knowledge we have learned at the feet of the masters, and when we hold this knowledge up to light we can find no corresponding reflection of ourselves – only men's views of reality.

We have the choice either to make it our own, to give up our identity and offer ourselves over to colonisation by theirs, colluding in our own denial. Or to live in a state of schizophrenia – a ritual mouthing of someone else's words while desperately clinging to another consciousness inside our heads.

To toe the line also leaves the game unchanged for any woman that follows us, and cuts us off from the powerful source of support that as women 'coming together' we have experienced elsewhere. The message is not that we should not enter these institutions – we have little choice. In a patriarchal society we cannot avoid them. But we should never leave them unchallenged. We know that it takes courage to be the one that never lets anything pass, and that we run the risk of feeling even more isolated and marginalised.

But speaking out also has its own rewards. We might be voicing the silent thoughts of other women, and in doing so we can provide a focus for women to come together to survive the course and challenge the system that makes us feel marginalised in the first place. Certainly there's safety in numbers, and women organising together can achieve more than on our own. We also have the satisfaction of knowing that we are resisting the pressures experienced by generations of women to take on male values if we wish to 'succeed'. We are making our own contribution to shaking the complacency of those who have had it their own way for too long by demanding that there are alternative bodies of knowledge and ways of learning from those presented to us when we go back to study.

We shouldn't expect that we can change the system single-handedly. It's not surprising, when men monopolise 99 per cent of the world's resources and the power that goes with them, that we can't change it overnight. But at least we'll escape with our integrity intact knowing that we have made our own contribution to the struggle for genuinely liberating education.

4

Deals and Dilemmas

The pursuit of qualifications in the male educational empires of
further and higher education is not the only alternative open to
women. There is another educational provision that's worth
considering. Adult education is often aimed particularly at women
and frequently staffed by women. However, it's rarely controlled by
women, and in our experience is not always in our best interests. We
need to be clear about the dilemmas in store for us once we begin to
sample the different varieties of adult education on offer to us.

Trivial pursuits

Adult education – run by the Local Authorities (LEAs), the
Workers Educational Association (WEA) and Extra Mural
departments in universities – is one of the few kinds of educational
provision in which women students outnumber men (probably
because adult education is about the least well resourced, least
powerful and least serious form of educational opportunity there
is). Students tend to be middle class, although most providers,
depending on their politics, make some commitment to unemployed and working-class students in ways that are far from
satisfactory. In general, adult education is associated with 'learning
for pleasure', recreation and leisure activities and is not greatly
concerned with the business of changing lives – let alone changing
the world. In recent years, like many other services to the
community, adult education has been a victim of government
spending cuts, with the result that provision has declined and fees

110

have increased. As a 'leisure pursuit' it is now even more restricted to those who can pay.

In university adult education, classes to do with ancient history, medieval culture and contemporary religion are legion. Most of them deal in obscurity and irrelevance with the fervent dedication of those obsessed by Trivial Pursuits. But while academic excellence is the rhetoric it is not always the reality.

> If they had any commitment to educational standards the course would be closed down tomorrow. The same old ladies troop in every year. It's always oversubscribed. Usually you can only get a place if someone dies. The tutor switches off the light and shows them slides of country houses and gardens. Half way through, those who have fallen asleep wake up when the coffee is wheeled in. Then there's another three quarters of an hour's illustrated lecture before they all go home. It's dreadful but it makes an awful lot of money.

And the making of money is an increasingly important organising principle.

> The university, it is claimed, represents the best in enlightened, civilised and cultivated thought. Increasingly, though, because of cuts in government spending and the concern to save academic jobs – university adult education has tried to popularise its approach and attract a wider audience. Now you can do a course on Roman cookery – using authentic Roman recipes and 'enjoy a Roman meal served on neo-Roman tableware'. You can make a study of 'the extravagant and often absurd ceremonial dishes at medieval aristocratic feasts' and compare how 'the less well off survived' by enjoying a 'medieval ploughmans' at lunchtime for the payment of an extra £2.50. The season of 'Masterpieces of the Indian Cinema' includes a free curry 'thrown in' for all participants, and if you want to sing madrigals and early church music, 'what better place than in residence for the week end at a National Trust country house' – full board and lodgings included. All of this could be said to reflect adult education moving with the times and responding to commercial competition in the leisure business and yet 'the study of the best that has been thought and said and done' is still claimed to be the purpose of it all.
>
> At a time when millions of people are out of work, and when the lives of blacks and working class people and women are getting harder all the time, what is the point in learning about Roman cookery? Or singing madrigals in English country houses? Is this what the early pioneers of adult education had in mind when they campaigned for political education and 'really useful knowledge?'

Local Authority day and evening classes provide more of what some might call 'women's education' than anything else – various kinds of cookery, craftwork, beauty culture, childcare and aerobics, for example. Most of the students are women and a high percentage of the part-time tutors are women. Men dominate the career structure however – nine out of ten of the people with responsibility for planning programmes are men – and this they do with the assumption that they are providing the kinds of things that 'women want to learn' and which they think will be appropriate for us.

Very often those of us who attend flower arranging, machine knitting and keep fit classes do so out of a sense of loneliness and isolation rather than anything else. The number of social meeting places that are safe territory in which we can gather together are few and far between. An adult education class can be the place to meet people and make friends – the content of the course is often much less important than the opportunity to get out of the house – and to do something legitimate, for a while. But this can lead to a very patronising assessment of our needs.

> You have to remember women want to talk to each other – but not have to read or think too much. They certainly don't want to do any study at home. It is an 'interest' – not a full time course. Usually they feel happiest if there's a social element and they can meet new people – the coffee breaks are very important.

The fee for a ten week course – even allowing for concessions if you're on supplementary benefit – can prove an expensive way to enjoy a coffee break! In fact, most of us are looking for something a little more substantial.

> Yoga, badminton, car maintenance – you name it I've tried it. I figured there had to be more to life than Friday night at Sainsburys. Evening class seemed to be the place to look for stimulation, interest, company – all the things you don't get as a full time housewife. Problem is what to do if you're not into cookery in all its various forms? That wipes out nine tenths of the options right away. I was willing to try almost anything – but not cookery, please. As it was I struggled to turn out something edible every day – the prospect of getting out of the house to do it even more didn't excite me in the least. As promised I was certainly soothed and relaxed by the yoga – although the atmosphere was so serene and low key I never got to speak to another soul on the course – we were too busy concentrating on our asanas and breathing exercises. And as for any of those courses changing my life – they didn't. All I learned at car maintenance was how to watch men tinkering with car engines –

something which I already knew quite a lot about, having done it for years without having to pay for the privilege. Only the badminton proved worthwhile mainly due to the creche. At least it gave me an hour and a half a week when I didn't have total responsibility for my two year old. However, I was looking for a more radical solution to my depression and stagnation than hitting a shuttlecock around – something I never did find out about at evening classes.

Of course the pressure caused by government cuts, the need to protect jobs and to justify what is happening has encouraged some local authority centres to get into the business of 'Access'. As we have already seen, Access can seem an important development and very often women are the focus of concern – courses to help those of us who have been 'out of work' or 'out of education' for a while get 'back into the swim of things'. Access courses might well be regarded as positive discrimination in favour of women – and are certainly claimed to 'meet the need' for training and equality of opportunity. They should, however, be approached with caution.

At our place, we're in year two of the development and at the moment the major initiatives are in the department of Fashion, Food Studies and Child Related Studies. Not surprising, since 68% of our students are women and the Fashion and Food Studies Department was, until recently, the largest in the institute. As a department, they've taken a lot of stick from feminists who've criticised the traditional subject bias of adult education. They've been working hard to get in tune with major trends in education today.

So we have a course called Return to Learning in Fashion, the first of its kind in London, so much admired that other institutes are beginning to copy it. It's supposed to lead on to the City and Guilds Course available in further education colleges, and it involves pattern cutting, learning to draw designs, using a machine and garment construction. The idea is that the students spend a year rehearsing the syllabus in order to have a better chance of success doing the real thing the following year!

And what do the students think of the course? Half of them have done the time-honoured adult education disappearing trick. They've voted with their feet and gone to a course for the unemployed at the London College of Fashion, which is a direct route to trade, i.e. assembly work in a factory. The City and Guilds course is an outdated syllabus, geared to quality work and not mass production which is where the jobs are. So, in effect, we've delayed those students by six months from going on a course precisely tailored to their needs. We've constructed an extra hoop where good educational and training advice would have put those students in touch immediately with all the local opportunities.

Far from helping women to break out of the traditional employment ghettos, we seem in fact to be directing them towards the very industries and training which will ensure their continued subordination and oppression. We're just a mirror in adult education of what's happening in the big wide world.

To me, it all begins to look like a game of snakes and ladders. With women in the majority of the student body, it's women and women's traditional courses which are becoming littered with hoops and hurdles. Those of us teaching and organising seem to be involved in manufacturing the currency to pass through one g..teway and onto the next obstacle.

Perhaps, instead of us all politely opening and shutting all these gates, we should be doing a comprehensive course in breaking and entering. Time is precious to women returning to education and work, and what we're being offered now is a cynical diversion. That exciting awareness of the potential of adult education for the growth and redevelopment of women has been used to entrench us even deeper into the traditional mould in the classroom, at home and at work.

It's an old product in new packaging. What used to be needlework is now 'fashion studies' and what used to be cookery is now 'food studies'. You can get a certificate in cake decorating if you pick the right centre and do some kind of secretarial course almost anywhere.

We learned shorthand, typing, the basics of commerce and secretarial duties (which was basically how to fill in forms for your boss) and most revolting of all (or so I think now) Domestic Arts. Wednesday afternoons we would all sit aroung trying to look like secretaries, you know 'efficient', and be shown the accomplishments of how to walk with a cup of tea in your hand! Apparently the secret of not spilling the tea in the saucer is to sing, or hum, in your mind, 'Here Comes the Bride'. Of course we were instructed in the art of making a good cuppa prior to this. Perhaps I should mention here that the making, or carrying of the tea, is not for your own pleasure – but for the new man in your life – your soon to be Boss.

Other Domestic Arts classes involved 'laying the table'. I seem to remember that there are no such thing as serviettes, only napkins – but it might be the other way around. 'Floral art' was included in this class too. After learning how to 'make him feel comfy' we then progressed to learning 'how to look nice for him'. We had a lesson on 'how to brush your hair', which involved fascinating facts on the best hair brush to use and even how to shampoo and condition your hair. We didn't have a class on painting your fingernails because we all know that's tarty anyway, and men don't like it, but we were shown how to trim nails and push the cuticle down, and of course 'there is nothing The Boss hates more' than bitten fingernails.

Looking back, it all seems incredible that none of us thought these classes strange. I'm sure we all thought it useful info to help us please The Boss, if we were lucky enough to ever get one. That was all part of being a secretary – pleasing The Boss.

What they forgot to teach us were the basics like 'What to do when your boss grabs your tits' and 'was it your own fault for not brushing your hair properly and having bitten fingernails'. 'Did he think he had the right because he thought you looked like a "tart"?'

Most LEA programmes, and the mainstay of WEA and Extra Mural provision, however, remains locked into the restrictive notion of women as homemakers or as consumers of male culture and ideas. As ever-vigilant meeters of needs and greedy salesmen in the search for customers, extravagant claims made about specialist programme planning turns out, in practice, to be much the same wherever you go. You can do hostess cookery, old tyme dancing and upholstery anywhere.

It is not unusual to find that adult education centres, in the middle of provincial inner cities for example, in which most of what goes on is a reflection of white, lower middle-class aspirations and hobbies, are full of students who travel into classes by car from outside the immediate neighbourhood. Those who operate according to total ignorance about feminism also pay scant attention to social class and race as critical concerns in the content, teaching and provision of what passes for adult education. Except that there is now money to be made and jobs to be protected by the cultivation of a conscience and the recognition that 'disadvantage' is a legitimate liberal cause for concern.

Managing the poor

> I am I am I am
> the deserving poor.
> Bring your cast off clothing
> to my door.
> Thank you thank you thank you
> You're so pure
> You help to keep us going
> Like Manure.
> Old dressing tables, bed spreads,
> Carpets on the fade.
> Record players on the blink
> We've really got it made.

They don't know how I manage
They don't know who I am
They just know that I'm grateful
So they don't give a damn.
We don't refuse a single thing
Who knows what might turn up
Some rubies in the rubbish
Some tea leaves in a cup.
And we should be so lucky
And sorting is such fun
And its bound to come in handy
Ammunition for my gun.
I am I am I am
the deserving poor.
God help the ones that aren't
thats for sure.
Thank you thank you thank you
You're my friend
We'll get it sorted out
in the end.

One of the most transparent government strategies used to disguise the impact of unemployment, and to deflect criticism away from the accelerating hardship and poverty caused by their economic policies in recent years, is to encourage, and make limited funds available for, educational initiatives with those of us who are the victims of those policies – especially women, blacks and the unemployed.

Adult education, with its historic concern for the 'individual', is an ideal instrument of government intervention. It can mobilise an extensive language of consideration, caring and salvation, reiterating with ease familiar claims about 'meeting needs', 'personal fulfilment', 'rebuilding confidence' and 'self development' – while at the same time making it appear that social problems lie in individual deficiencies.

There's nothing very new in all of this. The British ruling class has always succeeded in sugaring the worst aspects of its self-interested policies with a simpering concern for the 'deserving poor'.

But when there is no intention to bring about radical social change, the number of available options to protect the status quo are limited. If working people are not to have decent jobs or enough money to live on, we need to be distracted from a proper sense of grievance, outrage and anger by the promise of new skills, retraining, educational qualifications and the constructive use of 'leisure'.

If we are always going to be locked into the poverty trap, in inner city ghettos, with support services cut to the bone, we need to be encouraged to 'help ourselves' and 'build up community spirit' in ways which imply that our poverty is the result of apathy.

If, as women, we can expect nothing more than economic dependency on a man or the state and a future constrained by domesticity and making ends meet, we need to be encouraged 'to cope' with unsatisfactory circumstances and develop the 'social skills' necessary to endure 'everyday life'.

Adult education has been quick to respond to government pressure – to take the money – and to agree to manage many of the schemes that will keep us in our place. Courses for the unemployed, discussion groups for women based in community centres, porta-cabins attached to infant schools and neighbourhood clinics. Basic literacy and numeracy courses. Jumble sales and tea parties with a spot of fund raising and some advice on child care. Drop in centres and toy libraries. All of these are attempts by professional community and education workers to make contact with the disadvantaged and 'do them some good'.

One project, receiving government funding and the assistance of adult education, was set up to find 'useful voluntary employment for several adults in ways which would be beneficial to their community'. It involved 'cleaning up civic statues, clearing waste ground for recreational purposes and visiting and helping the housebound'. There are some of us who remember when paid local authority workers and a welfare state took care of such things – but there's progress for you!

When women are identified as being 'in need' of this kind of treatment, it is our competence in childcare, domestic skills and coping with unsatisfactory circumstances which is seen as the problem. It seems we 'lack social skills' and, even more disturbing, 'life skills'. But never fear:

> The major aim of our modular teaching system is to provide unskilled, unqualified, unconfident [and ungrateful?] women with a facility that will enable them to grow.

How? You may well ask! 'Using the telephone', 'developing the confidence to deal with every day life', 'coming to terms with beginning to help yourself.' Makes you wonder how we ever managed to survive at all before all of this education arrived on the scene. And just in case you forget that the inspiration for such ideas is heavily influenced by the concerns of capitalism and images of a production line or a ferry terminal: 'We expect in the region of 16 students on a roll on roll off basis, for one day per week, for six hours duration.'

This is what one scheme for unemployed women in Hackney, Lewisham and Hammersmith – when the Greater London Council was at the height of its radical influence – decided would be appropriate.

> The programme will depend upon the needs of the women concerned – but we envisage demonstrations and involvement in crafts and culinary arts, speakers from the local community and local voluntary sector as well as outings to the local places of interest.

It was expected that

> this education in itself will provide the women concerned with a great deal of confidence as well as knowledge.

The complexity of racism, poverty and powerlessness was dealt with in a single sentence.

> we hope to bring together women of all ethnic origins to foster an understanding of each others cultures – so inculcating a feeling of community.

Another scheme in Kent comments on the fact that

> unemployment by its very nature leads to stress in many areas of life – particularly money, marital and social problems. There is a high incidence of wife battering, child assault, violent crime, single parent families and other related examples of social deprivation in this area.

No suggestion here that male violence is the root cause of all these 'examples of social deprivation'. But neither is unemployment seen as the problem either. Women are the target for educational attention: 'to help alleviate some of the pressures and restore some self esteem'. Does this mean organising collectively against male violence? Poverty? Government policies? Of course not! The role of adult education is

> to show women how to cope – not only with being unemployed themselves – but how to support and reassure an unemployed partner.

So he doesn't beat you up presumably, or if he does, help you to understand why it was necessary. In practice this means a curriculum focusing on

> How to become more interesting; finding out how to make the most of individual potential; self analysis, creating the right impression, the art of conversation, how to be a good listener; how to make friends and influence people; planning a social event and seeing it through . . . '

Not surprisingly, the concern of community outreach workers employed on such schemes are not always appreciated by those of us identified as being in need of their attention.

> She would stand in the school playground throughout all that awful winter – rain, sleet and snow – and try to persuade the Mums in for a cup of tea. They'd got a portacabin on the same site as the school – she'd have the tea on the go and then she would try to get us into conversation about what else we'd like to do in the portacabin. 'Nothing too heavy at first, you know, jumble sales, Mother and toddlers, sewing, that kind of thing.' But we all just sort of smiled and said 'Oh yes', gulped the tea down, and left.

The philosophy underpinning such schemes is simplistic and patronising, concentrating on women's alleged deficiencies rather than our strengths, our inadequacies rather than our capacities and our limitations rather than our potential. Education is rarely named by the intruders for fear of alienation. The job of the teacher/ outreach worker is to guide, to facilitate and to contain. Sometimes even to act as a 'role model'. But not to engage in critical social analysis or action. And certainly never to make recognition of the fact that as women we're all in the same boat. 'Keeping a professional distance' makes it possible to talk about 'these women' as if we are the members of another species.

Although frequently the recipients of special grants, such schemes are understaffed and poorly funded, given the enormity of the resources which would be needed if relieving poverty was really the intention and we were to be genuinely compensated for our massive economic disadvantage and political powerlessness. So often in these circumstances the organisers assume there is virtue in thrift and self help. The view is that 'we can't wait for the revolution, or decent funding, or proper building or a creche – so let's get on and make do'. And while the energy that this implies is all very commendable – the consequences can be counter-productive.

> So far as men are concerned – if women want to tackle the gross injustices of poverty and inequality on the funds raised from jumble sales and coffee mornings – they're only too pleased to let us get on with it. There's no chance of us getting anywhere and it keeps us busy in between doing the housework and seeing to the kids. Some of them even like to pose as anti-sexist sympathisers on the sidelines smiling their support as we struggle on against the odds.

And if men are not to be trusted in this respect, neither are some women. To be 'well meaning' is not in itself enough.

> To the freedom-seeking women
> or at least to those I've met
> I write these words of bitterness
> but not without regret
>
> With your flair for starting jumble sales
> and meets of every kind
> sifting yourselves the decent stuff
> and leaving the shit behind.
> And when you say that's twenty pence
> from the other side of the table
> you just collect, as you've always done,
> from those who are less able.
> We think we can remember you
> from school in '53
> with your homework nearly always right
> and your special friends to tea.
> We knew you'd pass the eleven plus
> though we didn't know then why
> just had a sort of feeling
> that it was all a great big lie.
> Sure you want the revolution
> you've had your problems too
> left outside the circle
> with your stockings almost blue.
> Our hands that sort like lightning

through the jumble that you sell
have served their time in menial work
and most of it was hell.
While you wrote clever pieces
or danced in student rags
we wrote for jobs as mother's helps –
an excuse to pack our bags.

They worked us for low wages
we called them middle class hags
and the only perks in those jobs
was insight plus king size fags.
While you knew poems and read books
that made you feel alright
we were in the factories
our dream was Friday night.
There was something about the lot of you
that we didn't understand
you seemed relaxed in coffee bars
and you often had a tan.
We were in stilettos
it was difficult to run
our faces thick with Outdoor Girl
melting in the sun.
Some of our men fancy your kind
you are different to us they say
we hear you are not above adultery
just like in a play.
The wives, they nearly die of course
and the children suffer too
but still you're right in theory
so what's all this to you?
We never could vote Tory
or Liberal or just daft
and we know the way it is with men
but still our men do graft.
If this writing's just a jumble
and reading is a strain
we won't hold it against you
a bit like rain in Spain.

It's not that we lack vision
or we think there is no hope
it's just that we got tied up
in a different kind of rope.
We know that your intentions
are probably quite good
but somehow we don't trust you
did you really think we would?

Such schemes are also short term – six months, a year, two years at the most. But then the intention is not to solve social problems overnight – only to be seen to be acknowledging them.

The best thing that can be said of them is that their contact with us is slight as those of us who participate regularly are few. While this reinforces the 'commonsense' definition of our poverty as being the result of apathy, it provides some protection for those of us who escape from the prescriptions and management of yet more misguided missionaries.

'Ah! You're a single parent aren't you?' Everything is put down to depression from then on. From this attitude I must suppose that if I married tomorrow my daughter would turn into an angel, I'd be content to play mother and housewife all day – perhaps do a cleaning job in the evening – and console myself with the idea that it's all for the love of my husband. Somehow, this doesn't appeal to me and I'll take their dreaded depression anyday.

I have joined many groups – mothers and toddlers, Mainly for Women, and Scope – great places to moan about the kids and lack of funds – but would always be told 'you ought to go out more – meet a nice young man'. I didn't realise there was such a thing!'

Adult education and the class struggle

There is another tradition in adult education besides the liberal concern to civilise the masses. It dates back in our history to times when the working class received little or no education and when it was believed that 'really useful knowledge' could help us in the struggle to improve the circumstances of our lives.

Some of the earliest discussions about adult education in the early years of this century were concerned with who could be trusted to provide adult education for us the working class, and who should control it. Women's education was less frequently a part of the agenda. It was as if the experiences and issues which affect our lives as women were of no concern or could be subsumed neatly within the general assumptions made about the working class as a whole.

We all know about early Separatist organisations like the Women's Co-operative Guilds, the Suffrage Movement and the early women's trade unions where women's own definitions were allowed to surface. In these organisations women became skilled in political organising and devised educational programmes for themselves which did justice to the realities of their lives. But none of this was achieved without opposition from working-class men who did not respond at all well to women taking political action on their own or, more importantly, stepping outside their familiar and allotted roles. So it continues today. Increasingly, men have elected themselves the spokesmen of the Labour movement. They have preferred women to stay at home, or to make the tea and address envelopes at Labour Party gatherings.

These men have gone along with the bosses' system of bosses, which exploits our free domestic labour and cheap unskilled labour, in the pursuit of profit. The Labour movement has never allowed issues to do with women's wages; our right to paid employment, shared responsibility for childcare and domestic labour; sexual harassment at work or the reform of men's behaviour towards us, to become matters of social priority. They may have been encouraged to learn a little more of the language of women's liberation in recent years, under considerable pressure from some of us active in the Labour movement, but if policies and practice are anything to go by, most of it remains rhetorical.

Some of us know from personal experience that those who are most eloquent in the defence of the rights of workers are likely to be as oppressive as the next man when it comes to women's rights and the politics of family life. More often than not they have been content to define us as conservative, passive, or apathetic when it comes to politics.

Making deals with the male Left creates a number of dilemmas for women, not least of which is the chauvinism of the Labour movement in its view of women, class priorities and loyalties. In our experience working-class adult education for community activists, trade unionists and the unemployed, for example, invariably means men's education.

I'll give you an example. I've been on a few trade union courses for shop stewards on day release from work, about law at the workplace, health and safety at work and bargaining skills. The courses were sponsored by the T.U.C. and taught by the W.E.A. As often as not, women stewards were completely outnumbered by men and taught by men. Most of us kept going – out of concern for our members and to maintain our right as trade unionists to paid educational leave. But the combination of sexual harassment and being talked at and down by the men was enough to reduce all but the most outspoken of us to silence. Each new course brought in its familiar contingent of cocky romeos, old lads who'd been to more union meetings than 'You've had hot dinners', and those intent on a skive.

As often as not the discussions about sex discrimination and equal pay were timetabled for the last session, after everyone had been to the pub – a reflection of the priorities of the men in charge of the course as much as the interests of the participants. I quickly came to understand that 'drinking with the lads' and 'plotting the revolution' at the bar was a feature of course activities which belonged only to those in the men's movement.

The sexual harassment of women stewards and women tutors on trade union courses and residential courses is notorious. No one likes to spill the beans about the less heroic exploits of working class heroes on 'flying picket duty' or away from home 'on a conference' – especially when they've had a few drinks – but if the rumours are to be believed about coarse jokes at women's expense, sexual assaults and even the breaking down of doors to study bedrooms to get at the women known to be sleeping inside, the prospect of the revolution doesn't seem to promise much that's very different as far as women are concerned.

One of the current pre-occupations of the so-called 'radicals' in adult education is work with the unemployed. The problem yet again is that of ignoring the extent to which unemployment is also a woman's issue. For much the same reason as women don't turn up to trade union meetings and trade union courses, we are unlikely to turn up in vast numbers to courses for the unemployed which are about the jobs that men have lost, or which don't have a crêche, or which are based in premises and meeting places associated with trade unions – working men's clubs, snooker tables and darts boards. It's not that we don't care about being unemployed, or that we don't identify as being unemployed. It's just that we can read the signs and we know that women aren't expected.

Generally the course was about the politics of unemployment but 'the politics' were imposed by the university lecturers onto a group of mostly angry men who were angry, hostile and aggressive about their situation. We split into the same groups each week. I was the only woman in my group. Once I mentioned I was pregnant. Well that's all. There's no more to that story. It got about as much attention as it has just taken me to write the word. Over the weeks we were given handouts of statistics, graphs and information sheets looking at Ford International – the profit and loss game; the multinational; Ford operations in Europe; the UK economy – profitability and spending; main developments in the British educational system; industrial distribution of employees in GB in 1973 (ten years out of date); the cost of dying (about Pinto cars being a fire hazard); death rates of babies by occupational class (i.e. of their fathers); unemployment in Southampton Docks. We also looked at videos of men who had industrial diseases.

I had to conclude that the organisers had (a) a fixation about cars (b) the idea that unemployment is a male issue (c) no idea that politics comes out of your own experience – not theirs. One week a woman was brought in to do a session on the role of men and women. Arguments were heated and at the end of the session she looked angry and flustered. I don't believe anyone's lives were dramatically changed by this slice of feminism inserted into the course – not that the word feminist was ever used. There wasn't a creche – 'no demand' the organisers said – 'didn't seem worth throwing one together'.

Although adult education influenced by a political commitment to the working class has got to be better from our point of view than the usual round of trivial pursuits, the sexist assumptions of the Labour movement about women and politics that feature in this kind of education are unlikely to make many of us want to get involved.

5

Worming into women's studies

Faced with men's domination of the education system as teachers, students, organisers and creators of that which counts as academic knowledge – women influenced by the Women's Liberation Movement have not been slow to demand some changes. Knowing how men's education in colleges and universities makes us seem invisible, and how adult education is often used to preserve the status quo – when we see women's studies courses advertised our first reaction is to feel both pleased and grateful. Grateful that someone's making women a priority. Pleased that our cultural, practical and political concerns are being taken seriously.

The growth in women's studies courses over the last twenty years or so has been quite significant in both adult and further education as well as higher education. University extra mural departments and the WEA particularly have been a popular breeding ground for Women's Studies. Workshops, day schools, short and more intensive courses about women's literature and history and psychology and health, for example, have become a feature of every self-respecting liberal studies programme; whilst courses in self defence, assertiveness training, women's sexuality, welfare rights, peace studies and feminist politics have helped to remake what usually gets defined as relevant curriculum for women. In the FE and LEA sector we have been able to learn non-traditional skills like building, carpentry, motor mechanics and electrics. Some courses, especially those sponsored by the Manpower Services Commission (MSC) like Wider Opportunities for Women have been concerned with women re-entering the labour market. Others like New Opportunities for Women have provided the re-entry

126

points into higher and continuing education for those of us whose choices have been restricted by marriage and childcare and lack of opportunity. The growth and development of new technologies and scientific knowledge have inspired programmes providing positive discrimination for women in areas concerned with science and computing. Some, encouraged by the Equal Opportunities Commission (EOC), have offered 'Women into Accounting', 'Women into Management' and 'Women into Public Life' courses, aimed at women trying to break into areas of employment and influence usually monopolised by men. The variety is as enormous as is the nature of the response to feminism which they reflect.

If we take the view that 'anything is better than nothing', then courses influenced by an understanding of feminism and intended to make women the focus of study, have to be applauded. We know that very often a lot of fierce debate has gone into getting them funded and properly recognised. We don't underestimate the persistence and commitment of many of those who have worked from within the corridors of power to see them established. But if we take the view that 'anything' is not actually good enough, we can see that Women's Studies still has a long way to go in providing the proper kind of political challenge to men's education that would begin to make real changes for women.

It's perfectly possible to turn up to a Women's Studies class only to find – men.

> I couldn't believe it. There were three blokes doing our course on the Changing Experience of Women. One of them was a 'right on' social worker – well used to taking women's kids into care and 'getting families back together again' after fathers had abused children. I didn't trust him an inch. Another kept going on about his wife's feelings of isolation and frustration. Claimed he'd come on the course to 'understand her point of view a bit better' – whilst she was stuck at home feeling isolated and frustrated no doubt. The third one was a pervert I'd say, and kept wanting to 'get onto the bit in the course about sex and violence'.

Neither is it unheard of for men to be doing the teaching. A group of us worked hard to get a 'Feminist Perspectives' unit included in the course we were doing, only to find the tutor in charge was a man: 'He put it on between 2 and 4 – knowing that most of us women had kids and would have to leave half way through.' In this case the tutor's experience and behaviour was clearly quite relevant to what

was being studied – male power. It was not quite the vantage point
we'd expect in a Women's Studies course.

> In 'Feminist Perspectives' we were doing something on wife battering.
> Annie walked into the office and heard ——— tell ——— that he'd
> beaten his wife up – and he was taking the seminar! And everyone thinks
> he's so 'right on'. He plays the part quite well – but you can see through
> him. I mean he walked around with that baby strapped to his chest. But it
> soon wore off. When the baby started crying or demanding bits and
> pieces – he'd hand it over to one of us. And of course he abused his
> position. I'd say he was more interested in procuring female students
> than actually teaching them.

It is by no means uncommon in higher education to find men
teaching options about women. We are supposed to be impressed
by this. We are supposed to conclude that 'men care too' or (a more
pernicious view) that men's commitment to women's studies helps
lend credibility to something which could otherwise be dismissed as
partisan.

The prospect of men teaching us about women is not entirely
revolutionary however, although historically men have been most
preoccupied with their own ideas and experiences of the world.
They have also made themselves the authorities on women.
Historically, much of women's writing has been ignored, suppressed or discounted in favour of men's analysis of our intelligence,
psychology, sexuality and physiology – the legacies of which
continue to restrict and disempower us to this day. So there's
nothing very new in men teaching about women. But we should
learn from this experience. Their teaching has been to our
detriment in the past and there is no evidence to suggest that now it
would be otherwise.

In adult education, most of the part-time tutors and most of the
students are women – although they are not all feminists. Because
little attention is paid to assessment and qualifications, there are
plenty of ways in which the curriculum and teaching methods can be
influenced by feminist practice and feminist concerns. But the
career structure in adult education is still dominated by men and it is
much more common to see cultural and literary versions of
feminism finding their way into centre programmes rather than
radical feminism. In organisations like the WEA, because of its

grass roots and more democratic base, as women we have been able to take more control of our own learning, become teachers and organise in ways which are less constrained by patriarchal infiltration.

But despite its historic concern with working-class education, the WEA over the years has proved increasingly popular with middle-class students. One consequence of this for the Women's Studies programme is the preoccupation with counselling and therapeutic feminism – a middle-class tendency in the discussion of women's education. It's a view reflected, for example, in the WEA pamphlet, *'From a Different Perspective: Change in Women's Education'*, which lays great stress on 'women's dependency needs' and the search for 'harmony of inner and outer worlds'. It's a view that we are not only held back by 'structural barriers of inequality' (whatever happened to patriarchy?), but also by 'the negative bonding between women which is resigned, quiescent, passive' and by an 'internalised sense of worthlessness and inadequacy'. (This sounds like another version of the 'blaming the victim' theory.)

Accordingly, it is argued, 'we need to move away from the dislocated sense of self which women develop in response to the cultural distortions of psychic reality with which we live' (whatever that means) to a 'recognition and fulfilment of our dependency needs' – which could be said to be precisely what patriarchal arguments in favour of marriage have always been about. Except that it is to other adult women – friends, neighbours, colleagues – that women turn and it is the 'encouragement, support and the love of other women offered at a depth of involvement' which is being recommended. If all of this is a coded argument in favour of lesbianism, why not say so?

Except that those of us who are lesbians are looking for loving but independent relationships – not other women to lean on. And those of us who are feminists are looking for an end to male power, not personal therapy. Based on Kleinian (neo-Freudian?) and object relations theory and the work of Carl Rogers (haven't we had enough of all this?), this psychoanalytical approach to women's studies has very little to say about patriarchy or women-hating, and even less to say to the majority of working-class and black women for whom therapy and counselling (behaviour modification?) is not quite the radical solution to our poverty and oppression that we are looking for. Neither is it something we'd wish upon our middle-class sisters just because they think it's fashionable or because finding problems within ourselves is somehow an easier option than confronting men.

In arguing for Women's Studies courses, compromise is very often the name of the game. Some of the compromise has to do with money. Because we are defined as a 'minority group' with 'special needs', women's courses can attract – in adult education terms – quite large grants of money and special funding, principally from the European Social Fund and the Manpower Services Commission. European funding can be lavish, but it is tied to co-operation with public bodies. Grants are not given into the control of the women participating in the projects which are being funded. A more common relationship is that between further education colleges and MSC, whose declared commitment to training of various kinds and social education in preparation for responsible citizenship is well known. The philosophy underlying MSC is also well known. It is rooted in conservative values of limited self-help, virtuous thrift and individualism.

Students, tutors and the curriculum are supervised by representatives of MSC and unnecessary luxuries like crêches attached to women's courses are conspicuous by their absence ('in case women become dependent upon support services that will not be provided in the wider society'). MSC are opposed to schemes which can be defined by them as political or critical of prevailing government policy – in practice this leaves courses for women which concentrate on traditional job skills and traditional job expectations – even though those skills are not valued in the present economic climate and the opportunities for women in the labour market are negligible.

Dependency on short term grants and external funding is an excellent way of keeping women – as well as other disadvantaged groups – in competition with each other for scarce resources. So long as the energies of project workers and project participants can be distracted by the relentless search for short term funding, the chances of any significant changes being achieved are minimal. Also this form of poverty control and management is most susceptible to applications intended to pacify potentially disorderly groups. Projects directed at cooling the anger of the male unemployed or black people in inner city areas are more likely to be successful than schemes seeking to increase women's access to employment or educational opportunities.

Apart from those who want 'to get in on the act' – especially when 'jobs for the boys' and European funding is involved – the majority of men are not pleased to see the growth in Women's Studies courses, and the everyday sexism of man-made institutions is frequently the backdrop against which they operate. In adult education the opposition is not particularly subtle either.

> The bloke who thought he owned the workshop was reluctant to leave it when we had our women-only class. He used to give out the tools really grudgingly and was always interfering and passing comment on what we were doing. We had the feeling that we were second best and not taken seriously by the regular staff. We had to be careful not to step on anyone's toes for fear of our courses being stopped.

Various forms of sabotage are not uncommon.

> Three or fours years ago we ran a New Opportunities for Women course. In the draft of the prospectus this appeared as 'New Opportunities for Women in the Twilight' and 'New Opportunities for Women in the Dark'. This was explained by the person who compiled the prospectus as a joke. I didn't think it was a joke and neither did the tutor, the students or others when in the final prospectus 'the twilight' had gone but the 'dark' remained. We never got the written apology from the person (male) responsible, the Principal (woman) protected him by saying as Principal it was her responsibility. For several years there were also 'printing errors' in the prospectus. Courses for women were either omitted completely or the vital words 'for women' did not appear. Consequently this lead to men wanting to join, for example, self defence or computing classes intended for women only. This left the staff in the branches, usually women, powerless to prevent men joining. Classes being omitted from the prospectus meant that women didn't come, so those who wanted it had the evidence that women didn't want these types of classes.

Custom, practice and ignorance often make a nonsense of our attempts at innovation.

> We have the crazy situation where, for example, plumbing, bricklaying and electrics for women come under the head of liberal studies yet woodwork comes under the head of art. Equally a women's art history class comes under the former and a women's art studio under the latter. This is illogical, stupid and confusing and suggests to me that women's education is not understood and not taken seriously. It also means that the existing structures are not adequate to deal with new developments. This situation can only be resolved with the appointment of a woman with knowledge and commitment to the education of women. At the

moment you have the situation where a man can be responsible for the assessment of women only classes. Difficulties arise over the qualifications and experience of women tutors of non-traditional subjects because these have often been gained in non-traditional or in non-male ways. This causes all kinds of problems.

In higher education everyday sexism of universities, polytechnics and colleges may be more subtle, but feminism inserted into the curriculum rarely goes unmodified.

Only a minority of the men could cope with feminism without resorting to extreme defensiveness. Feminism, we were told, was an offshoot of the Bloomsbury Group (whilst studying the Suffragettes in another part of the course). It was little use citing Mary Wollstonecraft – she was an offshoot of Jacobinism, whatever that means.

Constant study of male ideas and achievements often makes us too grateful when we're offered anything else.

I was once told by a woman who calls herself a feminist not to criticise a history lecturer for his neglect of women because 'We've got a course on women next term'. The long awaited course turned out to be 4 one hour seminars and they were almost all about women in relation to the family and domesticity – about women and women's roles seen through men's eyes. I suppose there could be scope for discussion about the revolutionary way women are trying to control our own lives on our own terms, but from past experience I know it's unlikely to happen when the seminars are set up in this manner.

Much of the controversy revolves around content, assessment and evaluation. Feminism is accused of being subjective, tendentious and not sufficiently rigorous in an academic sense. Clearly this presents problems for feminist teachers.

The power to award good grades to sound pieces of women's writings feels good. I suppose at some level it is validating for me. Struggling with male tutors or external examiners over whether feminism is a 'personal view point', 'bias', 'simply polemics' (whatever that might mean), 'not sufficiently objective' (another strange word which is intended to describe their ideas and put down anything that challenges them), 'insufficiently critical' (i.e. if men's ideas are disregarded) is necessary political work, which at times can be empowering.
    But the real problem is in evaluating work which is in academic terms 'weak'. What is being said to a woman when a third or fail grade is being awarded to her work, particularly when she's writing in the area of women's studies?

Good and bad grades are of course the lifeblood of competitive individualism and the basis on which judgements in men's education are made about winners and losers. In seeking men's approval Women's Studies is in danger of forgetting feminist practice when it comes to making distinctions between 'good' and 'bad' students. There are also dangers involved in trying to appease men's definitions of objective knowledge and scientific method.

Central to most understandings of feminism is the belief that our own experiences as women are valid sources of knowledge. In contrast, central to academic work is the belief that knowledge lies in published books. On the one hand then we believe our experience counts, and the books we refer to say the same, but the practice of social science, for example, tells us that personal experience is not a valid source of knowledge and every statement we want to make has to be supported with reference to published works. Since feminism and women's studies took off in academia, a generation of women theorists and writers have emerged as 'the experts'. No student essay or project will now be acceptable without some reference to these experts. The 'founding fathers' of male social science have now been joined by the 'foremothers' of Women's Studies. So in my work with students on essays and projects around women's issues I am caught in these contradictions and end up more or less saying 'yes, your experience counts but you will have to find a book that said it first'. This also brings out contradictions in terms of hierarchies between women. The women's liberation movement has always rejected the idea of 'stars' or allowing one woman to speak for other women. All our voices count, all experiences count, was what feminism was about, but I was told Women's Studies is not women's liberation!

And of course when we are black or lesbian or working class – or all three – there are additional problems.

The voices of black, lesbian and working class women are excluded from the books on the shelf called 'Women's Studies'. For all these women, Women's Studies, as taught in malestream colleges, is just another academic subject. Here I mean 'academic' in the sense of being irrelevant to our lives.

As a lesbian I teach lesbian students, but there are few lesbian voices in the books. Actually it's worse than this. Many of the writers are lesbian, but they are not writing as lesbians. The message then I'm offering students in referring them to the books is not a strengthening one. It's more, if you want to be accepted hide your lesbianism.

As a white woman working in London, I'm teaching black women, African women, Afro-Caribbean, Caribbean women and Asian women from many different communities. Their voices are missing from the bookshelf too. I can refer students to the writings of white academics who have stolen black women's lives. I can agree with them that 'Women's studies' is the study of white women. In this way their lives are split in two. As black women they are invisible in Women's Studies. As blacks (which in practice means men) they are invisible in the Race Relations option.

But where's the space for their lives, their culture and history, as black women? These absences are reflected in the teaching staff and inevitably in the content and style of what is taught. Although the department is mixed – men and women – the very few black tutors, with one exception, are temporary and/or part time. What happened a couple of years ago shows the ways in which racism, sexism and heterosexism of the established academic world compound each other. One of my tutees outlined a well thought out project in which she wanted to compare black lesbian writings from Britain with those from the States. In discussing this, we realised that she could either be supervised by a white lesbian, who knew next to nothing about the 'sociology of literature' and clearly had not lived a black existence, or by a white, male, heterosexual specialist in sociology of literature. Hardly surprisingly she dropped the project altogether.

In Local Authority controlled adult education classes Lesbian Studies courses have never been common. Since the passing of Section 28 of the Local Authority Act, which prohibits local authorities from doing anything which could be said to promote the acceptance of homosexuality and lesbianism as a valid and chosen preference, attempts to challenge heterosexism and homophobia in higher education, although not controlled by Local Authorities, are also made more difficult by such legislation. And of course Lesbian Awareness courses in schools, further education and Local Authority controlled adult education are now illegal. In higher education any official encouragement to pursue Lesbian Studies or recognise lesbian perspectives are extremely rare. In those which claim to be liberal institutions, while 'tolerance' is claimed as a quality of academic freedom, heterosexism knows no restraint.

If feminism was threatening, lesbianism was completely off-limits. It would be untrue to say I ever underwent any direct discrimination at the Poly as a result of being an 'out' lesbian, mostly staff and other students were accepting, but there was a very subtle undermining of one's credibility with some members of both communities. One seminar we had to discuss Murnau's film *The Last Laugh* in which there is a shot of two bellboys asleep on each other's shoulders. I mildly pointed out that the repetition of and lingering over this shot was homoerotic and that this was not surprising since Murnau was a homosexual – it was patently obvious, in most silent films it would be a boy and his girl shown snuggling up – so I was unprepared for the shock–horror that ensued. I was told that there was no evidence to support my remark, so I quoted chapter and verse from a set book which stated Murnau was homosexual. Not only was this dismissed, but a male student said 'Oh, you're just biased', the lecturer laughed – oh yes, very amusing on a course which is deeply concerned with exposing ideological roots of much that is considered 'natural' in our society – clearly the supposition that everyone is heterosexual could not fall into this category.

I came unstuck speculating on the effect repressed lesbianism may have had on the life and work of Virginia Woolf. I was told off for pursuing my own interests. One lecturer did go as far as admitting there was 'some species of homosexuality' underlying the work of D. H. Lawrence. Can you imagine the reverse, some species of heterosexuality? It was as if they did not want to besmirch the memory of the dead with the taint of homosexuality. We were told Buckingham was James I's favourite. I later discovered (not from set reading) their relationship was homosexual, which made much more sense of court intrigue. To be fair, it was a male lecturer who pointed out the seeds of gay liberation in the work of Oscar Wilde, and a female one who tried the matey approach with the Harry's Game video, 'Come on women, who do you fancy Harry or Billy?' – I didn't like to answer 'Josie'.

Of course some lesbian teachers do try to raise the issues about heterosexism and homophobia.

Without the support of another lesbian feminist on the staff and the friendship of some of the students, life at the College would be very hard. A lot of time is spent thinking and discussing how we should cope with things. Included in these discussions is how as lesbian feminists we can offer support to women and lesbian students. Until about a year ago, I thought I was sufficiently 'out' to be known through the networks. After all I had been allocated projects based on lesbian themes to supervise. But at an exam board I learned that a lesbian student was in danger of failing her degree because of what was described as 'her personal difficulties' and the difficulties 'she had in relating to her male tutor'. This forced me to have a rethink. I realised that the lesbians I knew were 'out', those I'd seen around the lesbian community, or just happened to be amongst the few students I teach. This was clearly not enough.

From our discussions around this, the idea of a heterosexism awareness day emerged. Plans were already in hand for a racism awareness session as part of staff development. Working with the two gay men in the department, we set this up and it was included in the staff development programme. This was all we thought we could attempt at first. We hoped maybe with the support of the staff in the department, it could be opened out to include students later. In the days leading up to the event, several staff sent apologies but some of them came. Being nervous, as it was the first time any of us had done anything like this, we'd invited speakers who had done this work before. We pitched it at what we thought was a non-threatening level. Certain things were achieved. First we had all named ourselves clearly as lesbian and gays. Second, we had made it clear that we were willing to offer support to any lesbian or gay student in the department. Third, we had made direct links with the student lesbian and gay society. We had provided lists of contact groups for all staff, with a request they were put on their walls where students could see them. We also pointed out that there were no courses in the department where sexuality was not relevant – from economics to psychology – and suggested that staff might consider how they could both introduce relevant material in their course and encourage students to identify and challenge homophobia (a nasty word meaning fear and hatred of lesbians and gay men) in the books and in their contributions to discussions. This session was an opener. It was planned as the first of an ongoing programme. For several reasons we did not immediately take responsibility for further meetings. As part-timers our input to and presence at the session was in our own time and not part of our paid jobs, unlike the full-time staff. Secondly, we did not feel that responsibility for confronting heterosexism should lie only with lesbians and gay men.

In the majority of colleges and universities the prospect of staff engaging in homophobia awareness training seems about as likely as Margaret Thatcher joining the Women's Peace Movement. Lesbian and gay academics who are outspoken about lesbian and gay rights, and who are perceived as having any influence whatsoever over students, are likely to be viewed as dangerously corrupting – sexually rather than politically.

It's not surprising that many lesbian teachers and students chose not to come out – except that their silence makes life much more difficult for those of us who do. Equally, many feminist students and teachers find ways of quenching their anger or modifying their views in an effort to stay put. But strategies which involve modification and good behaviour can quickly become the unacceptable face of compromise. The danger is, of course, that in clinging on to what has been achieved – however modest and insignificant it may be – you forget what's been relinquished. To those who are concerned that Women's Studies should bear rather more than a fleeting relationship to women's liberation we don't advocate the following recipe for success in academia – although we suspect that the caricature presented here may jolt the consciences of at least some of our readers who have made academic feminism their career.

You have to be respectable – which means you should look as 'normal' as possible. Long hair, tatty jeans and baggy jumpers are alright for the ageing male hippies on the staff – but if you want to have any credibility as 'a serious academic feminist' you should try to avoid looking anything like a feminist at all and especially not like a dyke. Forget the spikey hair and dungarees. Never go to important meetings wearing trousers – and remember 'the smattering of lipstick' to fend off any suggestion that you're queer.

You also have to be academically respectable. It helps if your higher degree(s) and published works include considerable attention to non-tendentious knowledge i.e. are nothing to do with women. Your interest in women has to be supported by easily recognisable (to male academics) credentials – like male theories and ideas applied to the study of women; a language rooted in male scholarship; copious references to other published works – at least a half of which should have been written by men – as supporting evidence. It is legitimate to be critical of male scholarship and male ideas about women – but only in a way which is indistinguishable from male scholarship and ideas. You need to believe in the business of 'beating them at their own game'.

If you want to get Women's Studies options included in the curriculum you need to plan your manoeuvres like a military campaign. First of all you have to be 'nice' to your male colleagues. Don't threaten them with your greater intellect, pay attention to their boring pre-occupations, have lunch with them occasionally and accept their invitations to parties and to dinner. So long as your behaviour gives no indication that you believe what you want to teach, or that you practise what you preach, it'll be alright.

You'll need to make strategic allegiances with likely allies – in the event this will mean gay, black and socialist men – non of whom can be guaranteed to care very much about women – especially 'petit bourgeois feminist deviationists' from the gay/black/class struggle, but they might enjoy helping you to put one over on the old guard.

There'll be others too – anti-sexist men looking for a home – teaching *your* subject to *your* students now that there is 'work' in women.

Most of the 'allies' will also want to believe that your interest in women is purely academic – so be prepared for the usual cut and thrust of sexual intercourse and harassment that is the life blood of academic exchange. So far as bad. Now you have to persuade the reactionaries and moneybags. Make sure you can count on attracting foreign students, research grants and international staff exchanges. Universities and Polytechnics are not charities and are no longer concerned with public service.

Learn to couch what you have to say in language which doesn't give the wrong impression. Never use the terms 'patriarchy', 'woman-hating', 'lesbianism' or 'oppression' when you could use 'inequality' of opportunity', 'prejudice', 'sexuality' or 'discrimination'. Always refer to men as well as women, and don't lose the day by insisting on women-only courses or women-only tutors. Hopefully not too many men will be interested – but if they are – use this as further evidence of the significance of what you're doing.

When decisions about funding and course proposals are being made – remember to brief your 'allies' well in advance. Turn a deaf ear to their sexist comments about female students. Go out of your way to take an interest in your other colleague's concerns about 'everyday latin' or 'flying model aeroplanes'. Don't object to terms like chairman, gentlemen and chaps being used in your presence at meetings – even though it makes you feel invisible. The reward for moderation and reasonable behaviour on your part may be a foot in the door. The price, of course, is that the costs of achieving so little are so immense, that you cannot now afford for it to be all in vain. The toe hold must become a foothold and the foothold a permanent place in the academy. This means more manoeuvring in the corridors of power – more modifying of demands – more evidence of credibility (publications, academic honours, consultancies, television appearances, research grants).

Whatever the content of your course might be, its credibility will be judged by its academic respectability – in male terms – which means marking, grading, examining and classifying students in the usual way: D – for Women's Experience. A Lower Second for sexual identity. A 'Masters' in Women's Studies. In times of plenty the academy can afford to be generous but in times of stringency – like now– 'fringe subject areas', 'deviants' and 'trouble makers' are the most vulnerable. You'll find yourself in competition for scarce resources with your old 'allies' on the left – who will increasingly see you, rather than the old guard, as the immediate threat.

By now, whatever connection you might once have had with the first principles of the Women's Movement – about valuing women's experience, recognising that the personal is political, rejecting elitism and linking women-centred learning to political campaigns for change – will have completely evaporated. Your knowledge and your assumptions will bear precious little relevance to how the majority of women live our lives, and your language will be one we recognise no more readily than the language of oppression which men have always used to keep us in our place.

The dilemma facing feminists in Women's Studies varies depending on which part of the education system you are studying in, although the basic problem is the same everywhere – men remain in control. Further education has a long history of vocational chauvinism and any deals struck with the MSC to fund women's training and access courses will never be free from anti-feminist scrutiny and government control.

In adult education the prevailing view of women as either feckless incompetents in need of role training, or culture vultures in search of interesting diversions to satisfy our leisure needs remains pervasive. Attempts to infiltrate Women's Studies have been successful insofar as they remain unthreatening – which leads to a preponderance of Women's Writing courses, co-counselling and therapy. Courses and initiatives more explicitly concerned with women's liberation have little chance of success unless – as we describe in the next chapter – we do it for ourselves.

In higher education the main dilemma is to do with academic respectability – a deal which frequently involves teaching Women's Studies in partriarchal ways. In the attempt to be 'academically respectable' the first principle of the Women's Movement, which is that our personal experience as women is the source of our knowledge and the point of our action, so often gets jettisoned in the grab for grades and the concentration on objective evidence and male academic approval.

In all of these respects, the missing link which leads to the de-radicalisation and incorporation of feminism in malestream education, is women not being completely in control of the work that we are doing. As long as we involve men directly, or we modify our behaviour and demands to meet with their approval, or we borrow their ideas to find ourselves in need of therapy, the possibilities of radical social change are considerably reduced.

For feminists who believe in coalition with other progressive groups and in the power of eloquence to change men's attitudes, then men's education systems like other institutions can become the site of struggle in which concerted action might bring about changes in personnel and policies. It may be, in these circumstances, that moderation rather than liberation is more likely to achieve results, but it is a matter of interpretation whether the results achieved by good behaviour are worth the energy required. When feminism becomes respectable – and if the world hasn't been turned upside down as a consequence – the significance of our achievements needs to be examined very carefully.

6

Doing it for ourselves

A 'friend' told me the other day that I should have been born a man. She was wrong of course. I don't want to be a man. I just want to be a plumber!

In comparison to what we learned at school, and what some of us have learned from traditional adult education or from entering higher education as 'mature students', our experiences of women's education are altogether something else. Coming, for the most part, from white, working-class backgrounds, it is unusual to find 'education' a relevant or empowering experience. We know from the words of black women included here, and from lengthy discussions with black sisters, that the chances of black, working-class women receiving anything of value from white, middle-class mens' education are even more remote.

With the education system so obviously geared to the self interest and concerns of white, middle-class men we have found no better alternative than to take matters into our own hands and 'do it ourselves'.

Learning with other women with feminist intent implies a number of important principles. They may seem obvious to those of you reading this book, but they are by no means the common experience of most women returning to education. Together they form the basis on which women's education concerned with women's liberation should be based. Principles like women-only classes, a curriculum which is based on women-centred knowledge; teaching-learning approaches which break down hierarchies between 'experts' and 'others'; an atmosphere which discourages the divisiveness of class privilege, racism and lesbophobia; the validation of personal experience; knowledge which is politically useful in the battle against patriarchy; good childcare; flexible timing; minimal fees and freedom from male interference and control.

Our starting point is obvious. Courses need to be arranged at times that fit in with our domestic commitments.

> What is great about the course is that it is geared to the needs of women. The hours are perfect for us with children at school – you've got enough time to take them to school in the morning, and pick them up again in the afternoon. And you don't have to worry about half-terms and holidays and who you can get to look after them – we're off at the same time as the schools.

But as we've seen such considerations are the exception rather than the rule in most adult, further and higher education.

It's also important that good crêches are provided for women with pre-school age children. Not a box of broken toys and three schoolgirl volunteers in a makeshift space, but a well-run crêche, with experienced workers who also have a political understanding of their educational responsibilities.

> At the moment I am working in the Centre crêche. We ensure that women with small children can enjoy courses knowing that their children are safe and having a good time.
>
> The crêche exists not just as a place to leave the kids, but as a very important part of the Centre and its commitment to working in anti-sexist, anti-racist and anti-classist ways. Children are encouraged to explore and learn new tasks and experiences, and learn to play together in a sharing and co-operative way.

At the Women's Education Centre we have always placed a lot of emphasis on good crêche provision and tried to make sure that workers are well paid and properly recognised for the important work they do.

> The WEC is rightly proud of its crêche. Few other educational institutions can provide one of such a high standard or so regularly. This is due to the efforts of women at the Centre who have given time and energy to its creation and operation – and still do so.
>
> Society deems crêches to be an unnecessary luxury; not surprising since it values women only insofar as they reduce society's costs. But our

crêche is no luxury. It is a vital necessity for women to begin learning in a small space of their own, often preparing for a working life as a single parent in the future. Absence of a crêche effectively relegates low-income mothers to the breadline for the future.

It is also important in women's education that any fees charged for courses are kept to a minimum and easily waived. We know from our own experience that the majority of us could not have joined courses like Second Chance if we'd had to pay high fees.

I was only able to attend Second Chance because my fees were waived – Supplementary Benefit (now Income Support) does not recognise the 'luxury' of education for women. Education, however, should never be a luxury or a privilege, dependant on financial status. It must be a right. Any insistence that fees must be paid by women such as myself means that right is then withdrawn.

The course helped me more than I can say, and it must remain open to all women regardless of their financial status. I am now doing a degree course. I owe that to some remarkable women who believed in me and not my cheque book.

Even now we are prevented from doing courses because we can't afford the fees.

We have always lived on a low income, so I could not afford the daytime courses offered in Adult Education and certainly could not find money for nurseries or childminders as well. I have never been able to get to evening classes because of the unsocial hours my husband works. I thoroughly resent the fact that working class women like myself have such a hard time taking advantage of the further education we are supposedly entitled to – those who are able to obviously already have several advantages over me!

I applaud moves to run free courses for unemployed men, but I cannot understand why the same principle should not be applied to women who are single parents, or unwaged mothers or who are living on a low income.

For women with little money to call our own, arbitrary demands for cash as evidence of our commitment to learning is grossly insulting.

A low income family, no way could I have afforded fees to go on a Second Chance. Besides, my self importance rated me barely visible – to spend money on such a luxury as education for me was unthinkable, especially when food, clothes and children's shoes was a pressing reality.

In the present economic climate the struggle to preserve good childcare and cheap and free courses is enormous. Like many other women's groups we've seen these resources cut back to the bone in recent years by those who provide our funds. But the issue is not just to do with money and the derisory amounts of financial support given to women – it is also concerned with political priorities. In a society which pays lip service to equal opportunities and women's rights, we find our rights and opportunities continually under attack. The backlash against women in the present political climate, and the ways in which this affects our education, is something we'll return to in the next chapter. First we need to remind ourselves of what is at stake.

For many 'adult education' may be viewed as a 'pastime', a 'non-essential', a 'frill'. Something to fill in the time during winter evenings or when 'too much leisure' becomes a problem. In some circles – as we've seen – education for women has become the latest of many professional bandwagons. This is not our view. For most of us – with few resources to call our own and little enough power in the world – we think of education as a tool. Something to help us change our lives and help re-create the world in a different way. Not just by getting qualifications or even a well-paid job – although both of these are useful assets which most of us don't already have – but as a way to challenge the present order of things. The sort of women's education we have in mind is an education controlled by women for women. It means taking resources usually monopolised by men away from men and concentrating them in the hands of women. It means learning together effective ways in which we can challenge patriarchy in our everyday lives for the benefit of ourselves and for women generally. Women's education, as we define it, is political education linked to women's liberation.

Considerable numbers of education courses aimed at women aren't of course based on this assumption, especially when their organisers have patronising ideas about the limitations of our expectations, or thinly disguised male views of scholarship and excellence. But courses that are set up by women, with feminist intent, and which place commitment to women's lives and struggles before any other consideration, are likely, by the very nature of their women-positive, pro-women character, to be concerned with social change and liberation. Sometimes, even when they're not, the experience of being with other women, and in the company of feminist ideas, can trigger lift off.

I'm not sure what attracted me to the Changing Experience of Women course. I'd been studying with the Open University for years, and this was the last ½ credit to get an Honours degree. During my studies I'd become a Marxist. I was active in CND (Campaign for Nuclear Disarmament), a steward at work for Nalgo (National Association of Local Government Officers), working with unemployed kids on YTS (Youth Training Scheme) etc. I was divorced, living contentedly alone. Feminism was something I'd heard of vaguely, and seemed trivial and dull. The course wasn't much different from any other OU course that I'd done. So I thought. But then came THE SUMMER SCHOOL. This included analysis of ordinary cinema film, a workshop to design a sex education course for school children, and a workshop of role-playing a Trade Union dispute with male managers and male union officials (role-played by women) representing the aggrieved women's workforce. And much more.

In particular, the summer school was almost completely women only. No group had to have one of the 2 or 3 male oddities in with them if they didn't want. I opted for women only groups throughout. And there was a women only disco one evening – the first disco I ever enjoyed in my life! The freedom to *dance*. I know this was a 'turning point'. The *experience* of the Women's Studies one week school was such that 'nothing would ever be the same again!' I noticed, when revising for the exam at the end of the year, that my pre-summer school essays with their Marxist line seemed, well, dull and trivial.

Within a year of finishing Changing Experience of Women I had left my 'straight job' (no more straight high income), sold my house, got a job in a worker's co-op and changed my surname. I cannot seem to find the commitment I used to have to working-for-change within the organisations (patriarchal) that I used to care about. Changing Experience of Women was the only bit of my whole education that *I lived*, rather than just read-up.

When courses are more explicitly committed to black and working-class women, to our increasing independence, our economic advancement and our growing self-esteem, we know that we're into something pretty remarkable.

I knew as soon as I had those pipes in my hand that I wanted to be a plumber. I don't know why, I just knew that I couldn't get enough of this. I wanted to learn all I could. I was amazed at how easy it was. I was always led to believe that the tools were dangerous, but here I was using them. Things that I had been told I would never be able to understand, I could.

The Women's Training Scheme has given me a lot more than just skills in Auto Engineering. It has given me confidence, staying power, opportunities, support and friendship. And the will to support other women who want to go into male dominated skill areas. And pride when

I realise there are things I *can* do. Things are not as difficult or alien for us as men would have us believe.

I can't begin to explain how much it meant to me, but I do know that because of the course my life has been enriched beyond measure; it has virtually meant a new life for me.

Some of us got involved in women's education at critical times in our lives when we were in danger of going under.

It was the best thing that happened to me at one of the worst times of my life, and without it I feel I could have gone to pieces. Sharing experiences with other women has been very supportive. It's helped me regain a perspective and the hope that life still has a lot to offer.

I felt I had wasted so many years. Where had I been, what had I been doing all this time? It seemed really urgent to regain myself before it was too late, to do something worthwhile and interesting. After being silenced for so long it was difficult to feel confidence in my own voice. But I was freed from silent life where my thoughts and needs could never be fully expressed because no-one had really listened or cared. I had become a slave of my own oppression: always giving in, compromising my true beliefs to gain nothing, always trying to please everyone else but never myself. Thinking I could not survive on my own, dependent on those who gave me very little in return. What was I? What had I been? Someone's daughter, girlfriend, lover, wife, mother. My needs and ambitions never really being fulfilled, an identity that belonged to others. I had been servile, hidden, put down. Always conforming to please others to gain affection and love that was in reality empty of loyalty and depth.

I was at a crossroads in my life after having been married for 22 years and having brought up my children. All this seemed to end when my marriage was ended by my husband walking out of my life for good. He had left me. I didn't know any other life. I was left empty, nothing in my life to do and no proper qualifications. I am broken-hearted about my marriage ending, but I knew I had to start a new life somehow. That's when I started Second Chance.

It's not unusual for women to feel insignificant and marginal. Its very clear where the power lies in our society and what little importance is attached to the quality of women's lives. Poverty, racism and women-hating are effective controls on any sense of pride, confidence or ambition.

My life seems to have been mapped out for me in this dependent role. I wish it had been different – that I had been given alternatives to learn from, to aim for, having a choice that would make me financially secure, so that I could have then decided on equal terms if I wanted a man to share my life.

Of course quite a lot more has to change before patriarchy takes a topple – but the more we pick away at its foundations, and reclaim some control over our own affairs, the less dutiful and the more independent we become.

I have benefited by having a chance to discuss my ideas with other women and to realise how much we have in common – so many of us have doubts about ourselves, about why we have certain things or why we feel certain ways. This gives you confidence and support. You no longer feel isolated and this leads you to start looking for answers, not just for yourself but for women in general.

Before this course I felt like I was in a cocoon, unable to break out. Since starting I have broken out and am just spreading my wings. My colours are starting to show through. I know that by the end of it I will have learnt to fly.
This course should be the right of all women, not only for the skills but also for the confidence and self-esteem. It's an awakening.

Being on Second Chance has made me revalue myself. A school failure perhaps – but why should I take all the blame? I didn't fail the system, it failed me. Second Chance has given me confidence, and like a candle I burn brighter when I'm with other women who are the same. It's much harder and exhausting now – the same flame is flickering when placed in the everyday hassle of life, but I still burn. I'm not putting myself down. I don't want to lose the truth I've found or the confidence of my own worth.

I began to liken myself to the last onion in the vegetable rack, the one we get so familiar with we don't notice until it gets beyond use; the one that when we finally start to peel off layers of skin, emerges as a bright and firm and very usable onion after all.

Whatever images we use to describe our 'emergence' as bright and useful onions, 'flickering flames' or 'spectacular butterflies', increasing self-esteem, a new sense of purpose and rekindled courage are common responses to feminist education.

All my life I've always taken second best, but I know now what I want to do and be and no-one is going to stop me. Let them try and I might go down, but I will go down fighting. Then I might just surprise them and get up again. Just because I'm a woman, they can't say no.

And it's not only because we feel inspired by the promise of new skills or a job, but also because we are relieved to have our significance confirmed.

> Qualifications nil – straight into a factory, that's ME. It took Second Chance to assure me that what was pressed between my two ears *was* a person, and that what I had to say *was* important.

One of the major achievements of patriarchy is to fill us full of doubts about our own worth. Anti-woman propoganda and misogynist information on a massive scale can, as we have seen in earlier chapters, make us feel useless and even responsible for our own predicaments. Those of us who feel angry, restless or rebellious about the extremely little lot usually reserved for women get maligned as 'difficult' or 'embittered'. Those of us who get smashed by poverty, violence of hatred get defined as 'mad'.

It is highly empowering to discover in discussion with other women that as individuals we are far from unique in our reactions to poverty, powerless and isolation. To want more out of life is not a personal deficiency or a minor insanity. The appropriate response is not to feel guilty. We are not victims of our own inadequacy. Quite the reverse. When we start looking outside ourselves for explanations that make sense of our lives, male power and women's oppression are quite clearly related.

> When I started Second Chance I was feeling resentful and bitter about my inability to change my relationship with my husband and improve things for my family. But now I feel less dependent on him for approval or decision making, and am learning to feel better about myself as an independent woman with my own needs. I like to think that I no longer care what my husband thinks about me.
>
> I have been using him as a measuring stick for my success or failure for too long – now I shall start using my own standards. I think it is possible for me to be myself, as well as a wife and mother. I feel more optimistic about my own future now and more determined than ever to do some of those things I have always wanted to do.

> Until I became involved in feminist education there were whole areas of my life that I never spoke about to anyone: experiences from way back that I never been able to discuss, and least of all with the people I was supposed to be close to, like my husband, my family.

> Some women on the course said that it took them a long time to feel safe to talk about certain things, but to be honest I was so amazed that

anyone wanted to know about the skeletons in my cupboard I didn't stop to think – I just couldn't believe that the deep, dark secrets I'd been hiding for so long had happened to other women too. Like feeling angry and resentful towards my son, feeling trapped and out of control of my life. The panic attacks, feeling strange about going out sometimes. having been beaten up by a boyfriend, and feeling ashamed, thinking it was my fault, actually allowing myself to be persuaded that the beatings were proof that he cared about me.

It's hard to describe the relief in discovering that you really aren't mad, that if the world feels strange it's because it is strange and distorted, not your fault at all, and that there are actually words to describe all of that which makes perfect sense to a whole lot of other women.

We also know that feelings of personal failure aren't confined to black and working-class women.

Before undertaking the course I thought I knew exactly where I was in society and what the future held for me. I had been brought up to believe that a 'good wife' kept the home clean, did the washing and ironing, shopped for, prepared and cooked the food and, most importantly, was always smartly dressed for her husband. The cardinal sin for my generation (born 1939) was the wife who had 'let herself go'. Where she had gone no-one was sure, but in ceasing to care for her appearance, she had ceased to be of value. She was an abject failure. In my professional life (upon whose scene I was a very late arrival) I have doubted my own capabilities (despite obtaining a good degree) and, if I am honest, I have always deferred to the opinion of men.

Now, seventeen months into this course, I feel that I have been the subject of massive brainwashing for the past 47 years, and have been coerced into a role which I no longer feel can accommodate my needs. I feel a growing sense of awareness and my confidence and competence are developing daily.

'Developing awareness', 'competence' and 'confidence' are all experiences that we can relate to. Whereas our other experiences of 'education' contributed to putting us down and keeping us in our place, learning together with other women in the spirit of feminist education produces a quite different effect.

There was a sense of belonging with other women – women who felt the same commitment to a cause that cares about women, our rights to equality and independence and the struggle for power. Usually my mind was spinning with emotions when I got home: anger and sadness because of women's oppression and the violence we suffer; enthusiasm and hope for the future projects and campaigns; affections and togetherness for the women who care and those who had become my friends. Emotions which had lain dormant except as a servant of others were now *my* emotions, sharing needs, hopes, dreams. I felt on a sort of 'high' a lot of the time. I felt elated, happy, inspired, useful – felt I could take on anything and win. It set me on the path to regaining my identity.

Before I went on Second Chance my life was one big boring existence. Tuesdays used to be one of the days I went to a centre for the disabled, where I was expected to make baskets or stools or do knitting. My life was going too quickly, and yet too slowly. I had to do something else. Second Chance is doing for me exactly what the title says. It's certainly given me the chance to learn that I am not a freak or abnormal. I'm just another woman, as normal in the head as the next. It sounds crazy, but if I wasn't sitting in this wheelchair I think I'd have quite forgotten, now that I am different. I've always hated asking for help but sometimes I have to, but most women on Second Chance know I need help with the toilet, so I'm no longer embarrassed to ask. I now don't feel anywhere near as chair-conscious as I used to, thanks to the support I've gained here.

I felt very nervous to begin with, it felt like going into the unknown, I've never done anything like this before. When I was married I was at home all day doing housework, then a cleaning job, in the evenings, but my job came to an end when my husband left so all I had was the housework. By going on Second Chance it was a challenge to me, to save my self respect and confidence and, most of all, to learn more so I could in future be able to get a job.

At first I found it very difficult to concentrate, but I began to feel more at home when we began to share our own personal experiences. Then I was able to settle down to do the work because I had support and understanding from the rest of the women and also the tutors. They all became my friends, which I've never had before. They are helping me get through a very bad time of my life. So I coped with the work involved on the course. I haven't before done any sort of writing, only Christmas and birthday cards, so I never even wrote letters. But I felt so relaxed on Second Chance and look forward to every Thursday when I could go again and see my new made friends. I was now able to study and I began to see things differently, and I had no problems about coming here, no matter how bad I felt inside. I was beginning to think for myself, not feeling just a machine. I am feeling better about myself because I'm using my brain. Second Chance has given me an education which I want, to go into life with hope of a better job – one which I can call a career as well – and also to go on with life, coping with my problems, with the support of all my new friends. It has given me the will to get on with my own life instead of thinking to end it, which I thought many times before coming here.

There is a moment in the experience of women's education at its best – which in different ways, at different times, for different women – allows 'the blinkers to come off', 'the penny to drop' and 'the light to dawn'. It's an experience which we often hear women refer to. From the point at which we realise that our dissatisfactions are not unreasonable our anger is justified and our problems are political. We have the makings of a whole new perspective on the world. And whatever the discussion, emotion or personal association is that brings us to that point of recognition – of ceasing to blame ourselves and beginning to recognise the power of patriarchy for what it is – we know that, inside our heads at least, nothing will ever be quite the same again. From that moment – to use a well-known feminist cliché – there's no turning back. And these are moments which come not from the 'influence of extremists' but from the piecing together the truth about our lives in serious debate with other women. It can be a passionate and emotional experience. Its the kind of passion which leads to making monumental changes and to questioning old loyalties.

> I like being in a women-only group that's feeling emotional or passionate or angry about something. The careful, engrossed attention from those listening, with contributions bursting out of an exacting concern to reveal the complexity of truth and emotion and meaning – testimonies of women – anecdotes to validate insights and experiences across different barriers of age and race and background. Spontaneous irreverence and jokes, and bodies registering courage, resistance, strength. The woman who makes us laugh or cry or bleed, or who gets up 'to do the actions' she is describing. The woman who says 'Yes, that's right, that's how I feel too'. In those women's groups I have felt love for women and pride and delight in women. I've hugged women I'd never met before and I've felt close to women in ways that men could never make me feel. When I listen to what men do to women I find it hard to like them anymore.

Which is not to suggest that 'old loyalties' don't die hard. As working-class women we'd be naive to forget the ways in which the middle class organise society for their own benefit, and that middle-class men don't need to worry as long as middle-class women like Margaret Thatcher are taking care of their interests.

> God knows we can understand
> your thrifty little ways
> brought up to slice the bacon thin
> and save for better days.
> But some of us are wondering now
> what else you've got in mind
> you want the fat, you want the lean,
> you even want the rind.
> And god knows we can understand

the business of the scales
brought up to weigh the basic needs
and she that loses fails.
But some of us are thinking now
about those weights you use
we think you've hung them round our necks
and that is why we lose.
And god knows we can understand
why you're still selling things
brought up to mind the counter
and not to pull the strings.
But some of us are tired now
so when you say your prayers
could you tell the big inspector
that we're after even shares.

As lesbians we know that ignorance and prejudice still comes from women who have chosen to believe men's lies about us. Or women who are so used to thinking in heterosexist ways that we remain invisible.

I spent 2 years doing a diploma in Women's Studies – the only lesbian in the group so far as I know – although some women dropped out and talking about your personal experience wasn't encouraged. Only two sessions in two years focussed on lesbian issues. I felt completely invisible in that group and was reduced to silence – even during the two sessions they decided to discuss me.

Ignoring lesbian existence and making heterosexuality 'the norm' is a common occurrence. But while ignorance is bad enough, prejudice and hatred are even worse.

I remember co-leading a discussion about 'loving women' to which enormous numbers of ostensibly 'straight' women turned up. It always amazes me how popular such discussions turn out to be among women who 'are not lesbian but . . . ' and who often look more like dykes than dykes. However . . . we were talking about the ways in which lesbians are stigmatised in ways that, as well as being personally damaging, are also used against us in custody battles and in de-barring us from jobs. In the event we didn't need to 'import' illustrations of what we meant into the group. One woman said she'd never allow lesbians or gays to babysit for her children just in case . . . Another – waxing to her theme of insatiable promiscuity – said she knew about lesbians, 'they did it like dogs on the carpet'.

A commitment to feminism doesn't automatically eradicate racism, as many black feminists have discovered to their cost.

I went to the meeting to talk about 'feminism'. By the time I got there – 14
miles on public transport – I was late. I was the only one who in their eyes
didn't 'measure up' to the group. I understand perfectly what they were
on about but what's different about me is that I don't look like them, or
dress like them, or live like them, and by making the effort to go to the
meeting, I have spent money that I can ill afford. I think they like to think
of themselves as 'liberal feminists' – they're all white, they've got good
jobs, comfortable homes, husbands. If this was to happen to me a year
ago it would put me off feminism for good. They would have depressed
me down to the ground. Women like this used to be able to do this to me
the same as men.

With old loyalties still intact and old contradictions still in evidence,
we have considerable work still to do in resolving the conflicts we
have inherited from men.

Not all women's groups feel so good. There are differences between us
which we didn't create, but which we've inherited from men, and which
still conspire to divide us. I think we should be angry with each other and
certainly we should be critical of each other. But when we can't talk to
each other anymore, then we're doing men's work for them. We can say
the differences don't matter – in a weedy liberal kind of way – or retreat
into therapy or meditation as an easier option. We can say that its all too
painful and turn our anger inwards, or our feelings of betrayal onto each
other. But then nothing will change. Patriarchy will win so long as we
help to keep alive the hatred men have created and the systems of
oppression that go with it. Women's groups don't feel so good to me
when we can't see the wood for trees and when its men who get in our
way.

Preventing men from 'getting in the way' is, of course, much easier
said than done. Two thousand years plus of patriarchal power won't
shrivel up and go away because some of us have decided to give
priority to ourselves and other women rather than to men. But
reclaiming our self-esteem and taking more control over our lives is
not a bad place to start.

At the Women's Education Centre in Southampton the struggle
to establish, and hold on to, a small, under-funded and borrowed
space for women has been enormous. Funding bodies have been
critical of our feminist politics and women-only provision.
Traditionally-minded sponsors of some of our courses – the
university extra-mural department, and the Local Authority – have
exercised continuing interference in our work which has been at
best unhelpful and at worst utterly destructive. It is some tribute to

the persistence and courage of women over the years that, despite an increasingly hostile backlash to feminism generally in society and a specifically localised attack on our existence, we continue to survive. But more of this in the next chapter.

The hostility to women-centred education from anti-feminist groups of one kind or another does not detract from the benefits we know we have gained from what we have achieved together. No doubt 'the powers that be' would have given us an easier time if we had agreed to compromise, let men take part in what we do and exert their influence over our decisions. But then, we'd have been back into the usual business of learning altogether different lessons about the world – lessons which wouldn't have been concerned with women's liberation. Arguments for women-only classes are sometimes presented as remedial provision, as though we need to 'cling together' and 'build up our self-confidence' in a 'sheltered environment' away from the 'rough and tumble of everyday life'. As those well used to the rough and tumble of the real world knew its not self-confidence we need, but power.

We don't exclude men from what we do because we're 'practising' so that we can 'cope better' when it comes to the 'real thing', or men's education, later on. We're involved in making our own separate and different education tradition. We don't include men because we have our own history and culture to reclaim, our own knowledge to create, our own skills to identify and use and our own political priorities to attend to. We're not concerned about 'copying men' or 'seeking their approval', we're concerned with making our own freedom. And this means refusing to be diverted by the usual submissions which are made on their behalf.

As far as I'm concerned, words are cheap. Men can and do say all sorts of things but never mean them. If a man wants me to believe he's trying to be non-sexist then he's got to show it – he's got to *live* it – not just keep telling me. I may want to believe him – but I won't trust him.

The fact is, although a partcular man may not personally harass or intimidate or abuse women, that is a *choice* – he has chosen not to act in the approved male way. But he could change his mind at any time, and he knows it. And, according to the sanctioned power over women he has by virtue of being male, he will get away with it.

Others, we are told, will improve with education.

I get really pissed off hearing the same old thing – 'Why don't you let men in, they need education as well?'

Well, I'm sick of being expected to do everything for men. If they want to know why we're so angry, if they *really* care about the way things are in this sick world of theirs, then that's fine, I'm all for that. But they've got to go and sort it out themselves – get together with other men and tackle their own sexism and behaviour – not expect us to tell them yet again. Women have spent hundreds of years telling men what the problem is – them – and what could be done about it, but they don't really want to know. They pretend, they pay lip service to women's rights, but at heart they don't want to, and won't give up their power. The quicker we realise that they're all dead keen on keeping the differences and inequalities between us, the less time we'll have to spend wasting our breath explaining and negotiating with them.

Often, it is claimed, men's support will give us more credibility.

We don't want men to be present to give it bogus 'status' or respectability. We don't need it. Women's Education is the most important activity that we have engaged in in our lives; it already has the highest possible status in our eyes, and we don't care what men think of it.

Although not all of us agree that men are 'the enemy', we do agree that they don't contribute very much to making things any better.

After a lifetime of listening to them droning on about football, sex, real ale and politics in that order, I just know what it could be like having men in our group. Reducing our urgent and desperate questioning to why don't we want doors opened for us anymore! Most of us don't give a shit about doors being opened for us, unless when we pass through there is financial independence and freedom of choices in the way we live our lives waiting on the other side. Most doors have 'Keep Out' stamped on them, and its only men who *can* open them.

Doing it all ourselves is of course very threatening to men. Who knows where such behaviour will lead? Keep fit classes and jumble sales are one thing, but becoming a plumber or going to Greenham suggests defiance, moving in and taking over – an altogether different challenge to men's authority.

Men do not concern themselves with the separate worlds we live in – we can spend most of our time with other women just so long as we never forget that our role is really all about looking after and servicing men. We can join cookery classes or slimming clubs, or go to Tupperware parties or Mother and Toddler groups because they are 'safe' activities – safe for men. They make no challenge to our role of wife and mother and housekeeper. But most of all, they present no threat to male power.

Involvement in Women's Education, however, *is* a threat to male power – and they know it. Witness their panicked and desperate tactics to try and stop us: the image of the fat, ugly, loony feminist, the guilt they load on us about 'neglecting' our children, 'experts' (men) telling us how we will 'lose' our femininity, and their distortion of women loving and caring about each other revealed in their hate-filled and offensive insults about lesbians.

Seen from our point of view, of course, the absence of men is the very ingredient that makes the experience of women's education empowering.

I'm no longer invisible. Now I can challenge what people say, I can speak my mind and feel confident.

I was never specifically taught these skills – we didn't sit down and actually learn how to be confident, or how to question things or express our opinions. This process came about through doing courses with women where we worked collectively, learning from each other, and where there was an atmosphere that gave us freedom of voice. Ideas were created, old memories were reborn. We were on the same wavelength – irreverent jokes sparked off spontaneous laughter, important insights received validation. We listened to each other and we all cared if someone was going through a problem, or we all rejoiced when someone took another step towards her liberation. The only place where this can be achieved is in feminist, women-only courses, because then the knowledge we need and want is *ours* and is relevant to our lives as women. We need to be on our own because, as one of our sisters frequently reminds us, 'you don't plan the jailbreak with the screws in the room'.

After years of self-denial, losing confidence and any sense of self worth, I'm at last feeling I am important. My reasons for not looking out for myself, for not thinking about what I wanted or needed, fitted neatly into the mould expected in a patriarchal family. I was aware that I might be at odds with all that and feel guilty – now I *know* I'm at odds with it and I'm *enjoying* it.

Two ingredients are important in the curriculum of women's education. One is that the content should be women-centred – about womens lives, about the world seen through women's eyes, about issues, skills and information likely to increase women's independence and choice. Knowledge, attitudes and assumptions about women which are intended to restrict our independence, misconstrue our past and mislead our futures are not in our best interest and have no place in the curriculum of women's studies.

The other ingredient is relevance. Relevance not to the limitations and restrictions which are currently imposed upon us by domesticity and powerlessness, but relevance to what we need to know and what we need to do to transform our lives.

While many different women would make all kinds of claims for including different information, ideas and skills in women's education, the test of their relevance is as much to do with intention as content. The purpose in feminist education is concerned with our liberation and independence and with learning politically and socially useful knowledge in a positive and encouraging atmosphere.

Too often, as we've already seen, courses aimed at women are deliberately arranged to avoid contention. Those who want to educate us think that, as working-class women, we'll be afraid or put off by any suggestion of feminism. So we get offered things like keep fit and machine knitting. Although many of us writing this book wouldn't have called ourselves feminists when we got involved in women's education, we knew there was plenty that was wrong with our lives and that we wanted dramatic changes. Now, being feminist means we're actively involved in making them. It's much less contentious, of course, to keep looking for problems within yourself than start making the connections between male power and women's oppression. And some varieties of women's education are in danger of preserving such delusions. Assertiveness training, for example.

I think for many of us assertiveness training seems to be a logical step in trying to find ways of dealing with the world that don't leave us feeling more powerless and frustrated. I suppose that we all, at some time in our struggles, cling on to the naive belief that if only we ask in the proper way, express our needs and wants clearly enough, be assertive enough, we might get our fair share of the world.

Naive it certainly is. You only have to look at some of the mass of current literature aimed at helping women to be more assertive, for example, like *A Woman In Your Own Right* by Anne Dickson.

I would have to say that the central struggles of my existence, and of the women I see around me, do not consist of getting waiters to serve me in a restaurant, returning a steak that is not cooked properly or holding out for the best apples in the greengrocer's pile. I suspect that I could role play these situations until I got an Oscar, but I would, like most women, still be denied the right to a decent job, a decent standard of living for me and my kid, and would still be unable to walk out alone unmolested. And if I ever got closer to a steak than gazing at it in a butcher's window, on my way to buy the sausages, I wouldn't give a bugger how it was cooked. I take issue with Ms. Dickson when she suggests I argue my way out of sexual harassment with the cool logic of her assertive techniques. Suggesting that women can talk themselves out of being raped is as bad as men telling us we provoke them. The logic of both arguments is that sexual harassment and rape are our own fault – the new twist in the tale presumably being that these won't happen to us if we are only assertive enough.

A great many women could testify that men will persist a great deal more strongly than this – they will threaten and use fists or knives or bottles, and will claim afterwards that 'No', no matter how assertively said, really meant 'Yes'.

Are our problems as women really caused by not being assertive enough? Certainly we are conditioned to put our own needs last, but we also have to acknowledge that men have the power to make sure women's needs continue to be ignored. Seeing ourselves as deficient in 'Social Skills' isn't really going to change that.

Neither is the concentration on the kind of games and exercises which seem increasingly popular in some Women's Studies courses.

I feel as if in my search for answers to serious questions about my life, I've wasted an awful lot of time playing silly-bugger games. After half a lifetime of being put down, trivialised, mocked and treated with contempt by men, I can't believe the games I've been willing to put myself through thinking I might learn something. Trust games where you lean on each other, games where you close your eyes and wander around, where you draw pictures of yourself (particularly humilating as I never could get any further than stick people). Games where you hop around the room or wear a drawing around your neck. I'm not saying some of it wasn't fun, but what did it achieve? If fun is the object I'd rather spend my money in the pub. Doing unthreatening things like trust games in the company of lots of nice women can feel safe, make me feel good, but I think I've achieved more when I've been angry and upset at what men do to us.

The lurch towards counselling and therapy models in women's education, apart from being thoroughly middle class in inspiration, it also politically dangerous for women.

The problem with all of these approaches is that they all sidestep the real issues of male power and control. They don't attack the structures of dominance that are used by men to keep us in our defined place. They don't confront male power and attempt radical social change, which is what we need to improve our lives as women.

We also need our anger. It can be creative. We must not allow it to be dissipated. We don't need it to be 'smoothed away' by meditation, or to be transferred on to a white-coated 'expert', or to be shown how to 'manage our anger' through therapy; we need our anger to galvanise us to work and fight together.

Like psychotherapy – from which all of these developments in women's education have their origins – they also encourage their own brand of 'white-coated expert'.

In a world of 'caring and sharing' and 'working on' your problems, the reverence given to co-counselling adds to the deception of equality. Just as those who are being paid as 'counsellors' to listen and cuddle and question do not reveal their own vulnerabilities and anxieties to those they regard as 'clients', neither do women's studies tutors 'experienced in group work' forget the importance of their own detachment. It may be explained as 'protecting students from becoming too dependent' or 'enabling students to arrive at their own solutions' or preventing tutors from being questioned in ways that stop students from 'facing up to their own problems'. But all of these are ways of rationalising a distance which is based on the assumption that tutors and students are somehow different. Although the atmosphere is often caring and the language is kindly, the underlying assumptions are nontheless those of 'experts' and 'others' of 'us' and 'them'.

One of the criticisms we have made of men's education is its hierarchical and competitive approach to learning – the reflection of male power structures in the wider society. We've also seen how academic feminism is in danger of repeating the same patterns because of the concern to establish some kind of respectability for feminism. 'Therapeutic' approaches to women's education may appear to be more democratic, but are actually dependent on tutors not getting 'too emotionally involved' with their students, rather like conscientious social workers. This is not the kind of relationship on which women's equality and liberaton will be based.

In the Women's Liberation Movement here has always been a suspicion of experts, hierarchies and leaders because all of them prevent us speaking for ourselves, taking control of our lives and finding better, less divisive and oppressive ways of organising ourselves and living together. We think that in women's education the emphasis should be on learning from each other, on making sense of our own and other women's personal experience, and making theories together which do justice to the complexity and difference of our lives. Tutors might have skills that we can learn from – like electrical engineering or computer programming – but they have no business to set themselves apart as some kind of role model. Neither should we forget that we also have skills that are just as valuable.

In this sense we are all teachers and we are all learners. If we have been persuaded to believe in our own ignorance by the oppressive messages of our early education and our everyday lives, we have to begin revaluing ourselves and reclaiming our lives in the company of others we do regard as our equals.

We also have to expect that such a transformation of what is usually regarded as education may take a little while to get used to! At its best it will be a mixture of emotional and political intensity, so that nothing will ever seem quite the same.

I am *not* enjoying the course. I go along every Tuesday, quite happy in my mindless, self-denial world, only to be slowly woken during the hours of the day. Suddenly I find that somehow the sincerity of the women around me makes me feel safe – that it's alright to talk of those inner-most pains and fears and no-one will say those dreaded words 'Oh stop being a martyr. Pull yourself together.'

The women there listen with intensity of genuine concern, companionship, empathy. That's it, we have empathy for each other. Because of that we really talk to one another. It is *wonderful*. Real people talking about real happenings, important issues and maybe affecting each other's lives, not only by removing communicative barriers, but also within ourselves.

I, for one, have dared to confess to myself some of the thoughts that I would not listen to. Those thoughts that hurt right into the depths of my soul. Not only did I stop and listen, but I spoke of them as well! Everyone listened, no-one told me off for dramatics. I showed my real self and I was accepted. Oh, the elation. I feel supported, cared about, and glad that people know I need to be hugged. Sometimes a hug can hold a person together. In a friend's arms I feel safe and if someone cares about *me* enough to hold me whilst I crawl out of my head, then what a *great* friend I have.

But no, despite this, I can't say I enjoy the course. It makes me think so hard and so deeply, I have to start facing up to the fact that if I'm not to blame, someone or something out there has got it in for women. Its no longer possible to keep believing the usual old lies. When I go home I am drained, emotionally washed out, exhausted – almost glad it's over. I will tell you this though. Through the tiredness I do feel that was a day well spent. I have learned more about society, more about my friends and more about me. It *is* challenging but satisfying, frightening and enlightening, intrusive but awakening, frustrating but hopeful, annoying but calming. And a great many more mixed emotions.

So all in all it's probably one of the best things that I have ever done with my life.

At its best it will help make a 'reclaimed identity' into a whole new identity.

At 28 years old, I thought that the best job I could get if I was lucky would be in a shop or a factory. Then I got a chance to go to college via the Nottingham Women's Training Scheme, and I have never looked back. I chose to do Electrical Engineering, something I never would have seen myself doing – until I got the chance.

Naturally, I've had some snide remarks about me wanting to do a 'man's job', but I don't see why I, or any other woman, should only be thought suitable to be cleaners, dinner ladies or typists. Even if a man has the same job as a woman, the title is different. A man is a chef, whereas a woman is a cook. The word chef stands out to be important – a cook doesn't. Who is to say that electricians, plumbers, mechanics and lorry drivers have to be men only? – I cannot see why women should be thought incapable of doing them.

Going back to learning is the best thing I've done for a long time and I'd recommend it to any woman – no matter what subject she is interested in.

At its best it will provide inspiration and the courage to make difficult political choices.

When I listened to the Latin American women – who are political refugees in Britain – talking about revolution and machismo, I felt utterly inspired by their strength and their conviction. The Women's Liberation Movement feels extremely timid here at times, and whilst we can explain all this as an exhaustion born of fighting anti-feminism and the massive social and political backlash against women, nothing could be more crippling than the conditions of women in El Salvador, Chile and Guatemala.

Talking with the Latin American women made me feel even more impatient with the complacency and liberalism of some British feminism – the naivety with which we put faith in attitudinal solutions rather than face up to the implications of gross inequalities of wealth and power and resources, the reluctance to hear what working class and black women are saying about class and racism and the attempt to keep lesbian women quiet in case we give the Movement a bad name.

The Latin American women were quite unequivocal. Social change for women needs to be both a political and economic revolution as well as a cultural revolution. Men may not be the enemy but they have to stop acting as the oppressors. When I think of the tangles some British feminists get into to avoid the truth about all of this and the continual 'benefit of the doubt' we somehow managed to sustain in the face of gross male violence, enormous poverty and widespread racism, it makes me very angry at our prevarication and retreat.

What makes feminist education special is that we're making women-centred knowledge in collective ways. We're linking together personal experience, powerful ideas, strong emotions and political action on our own behalf, in a way that makes education not just about being clever and getting qualifications but about changing the world for women.

It's not only *what* we learn, it's *how* we learn that's important, and in both of these respects we have to be in control of what we do. The over riding power and potential for interference from men will never be far away. We have no illusions about the patriarchal world in which we're trying to build some space, but we also know that, in the end, 'doing it for ourselves' is the only way in which we'll ever change that world.

It's not role models we require – successful women doing men's jobs and beating the boys at their own games – but a vision that includes greater freedom for us all. At a time when popular pundits are already proclaiming the Women's Movement dead and feminism defeated, it feels more important than ever to hold on to the truth of what we know, what we need and what we want for the future.

7

Beware the backlash

> Frigid, prude, dog, bag,
> Bitches, cranes, slut, slag.
> Names to pin on flesh and bones.
> Frump, tramp, whore, nag.
> Gold-digger, virgin, strumpet,
> Painted hussey, piece of crumpet.
> Tart, doll, gangster's moll.
> Good figure. Like it, lump it.
> Minimise, tranquillise –
> Prescribe until we're ill.
> Hospitalise, sterilise
> We will pay the bill
> Drag us through the system
> Use us till we're scrap
> Call the undertaker
> Another nude to wrap

As the twenty-first century gets nearer, women at the sharp end of poverty, abuse and right wing government policies, wherever we are, know only too well that our liberation is still a long way off. In the present political and economic climate it is harder to maintain the early excitement and optimism many women felt in the 1960s and 1970s coming together in the new Women's Liberation Movement when, 20 years on, the real bastions of male power remain unbreached. We don't intend to perform a lengthy post–mortem on the WLM. We think it's still alive. Nor do we intend to lay the blame for failing to end two thousand or so years of patriarchal power at a stroke, at the feet of an already maligned movement.

Blaming ourselves is something most women are good at. It is one of those things we're encouraged to excel in. For most of us, the right to stop blaming ourselves, which feminism has given us, is a liberation in itself. although some of us are too young to have had this experience and most of us the wrong class or colour, those women who were part of the Women's Liberation Movement in the early days found that much of what we experienced as personal failings were shared with other women who felt the same. Women like us who felt perpetually poised on the brink of failure, whatever our situations – mothers of young children, workers trying to cope on our own with what we later came to name as sexual harassment, lesbians, trying to find some reflection of ourselves in the media images of women in the 'swinging sixties'. With its emphasis on the personal as political, and the importance of personal experience as the starting point for political analysis, in the WLM we learned to be honest with each other.

We stopped believing in the messages directed at young women, devoted mothers, successful career 'girls', sex kittens – all rolled into superwomen – and began, in the language of the day, to 'tell it like it was'. It points to the power of ideology that for many of us, it was a revelation to learn that other women felt the same way. Together we were able to discover how this con had happened, and to learn that what we had in common was being on the receiving end of a system in which men made the rules to their own advantage and we kept quiet about it.

Once the light dawned, it spread quickly. But our growing understanding of the problem hasn't in itself been enough to bring the walls of patriarchy tumbling down. Which is not to underestimate the significance of what has been achieved.

The idea, if not the realisation, of Women's Liberation has forced its way into the public consciousness as an issue everywhere, whether in local government committees or the pages of women's magazines. Women have worked alongside men in every institution – political parties, education, trade unions, the legal profession – to represent our views of the world and to confront theirs. We have set up alternative networks for battered and raped women, to cater for our health needs, to rescue our history, to publish our ideas and to control our own education. These networks set up by and for women have been personally and politically important for many of us. Indeed, for some of us (and we'll have more to say about this later) they represent the best way forward as a real source of strength and hope in an increasingly hostile world.

Nevertheless we have to explain why, after the most energetic and sustained period of feminist activity since the end of the last century, we'd be hard pressed to show significant ways in which, for instance, Parliament, the City or the Judiciary, have changed to our advantage.

Childcare is still seen primarily as our sphere and our responsibility – except for lesbian mothers who continue to have our children taken away. Most trade unions still function largely with the male workers in mind and have done little to encourage equal pay. Many more women than men face poverty at some point in our lives and low pay and punitive DHSS regulations keep many more financially dependent on men. Maternity grants have been abolished. Only 41 women sit in the House of Commons after the 1987 election. Our right to control our own fertility is increasingly under attack, though the methods used vary, depending on whether we are black or white. Marital rape is still not recognised as an offence in the eyes of the law. Male violence towards women and children has reached horrific proportions. Pornography is a multi-billion dollar industry and goes increasingly unchecked. Some schools do their best to fight inequality, despite government opposition, while many more don't even try. Judges, schoolboys, employers and men in pubs continue to manifest rampant sexism, differing only in the means at their disposal, and too often individual men continue to hold sway over individual women in the privacy of personal relationships.

Now some would say that this is an unduly pessimistic view, and many more would attempt to deny these facts as evidence of a massive reluctance on the part of men to relinquish personal and institutional power. Some would say that 'Women's Lib' was never popular with 'ordinary women', that it never really 'caught on'. And of these, all would probably agree that Women's Liberation is no longer needed now, it's a thing of the past along with student protest and flower power, part of the debris of the 1960s.

One way of trying to camouflage or minimise the extent of an oppression whether its apartheid, poverty or patriarchy is to cite superficial or peripheral improvements. So we hear quite a lot about individual women who have 'done well' in spheres previously associated with men as if this is somehow the measure of equality for all. But the 'successful woman' is all too often the token woman who manages to 'make it' in career terms, in what is still a man's world, usually without making any real changes that will alter the system one iota for women in general

The General Secretary of the Union, the successful business woman, indeed the Prime Minister, all get used as examples that old prejudices are dying out and new opportunites are there for women with the energy, determination and personal qualities to succeed. The implications for the rest of us are that we are lacking in some respect and that our far from perfect situations are the result of own deficiencies and lack of 'get up and go'. The myth that 'things are getting better for women', as exemplified in 'the successful woman' syndrome, becomes yet another rod with which to beat the rest of us. If learning not to blame ourselves is part of our history, as feminists, it's a lesson which we still need to take to heart, at a time when poverty and social problems are seen more than ever before, since the nineteenth century, as the product of personal failure.

Moving right

It is impossible, of course, to discuss the state of the women's movement without placing it in the context of an overall shift to the right. Three terms of Thatcherism to date in Britain, and almost as a long period of Reaganomics in the States, have made mighty changes in the political composition of both these countries. Tory politicians in Britain see a reduction in the power of trade unions as one of their greatest achievements. The Left has been discredited. The Labour Movement is now several more stages to the right than it was ten years ago. Coupled with the effects of long-term economic recession, for many women it seems that rather than experiencing 'new opportunities' our room to manoeuvre is being reduced. Rather than getting 'a piece of the action', we feel increasingly ground down by the struggle to survive the effects of Thatcherism. It's more to do with clinging on by our fingernails than scaling the peaks of success. Thatcher's policies may offer a bigger slice of the cake for some, but for most of us we see ourselves swept out to the margins by the tide of other people's prosperity.

But its not just that economic recession makes it harder to keep our heads above water. To many of us, it seems there's a more deliberate attempt to re-submerge us. It's not our lack of energy or persistence which has prevented our liberation. It's more to do with the reaction to our demands, which we think amounts to a deliberate backlash against women aimed at stripping us of the meagre gains we've made over the last 20 years and preventing any further improvements.

Like all oppressed groups we feel constrained, our lives are controlled and restricted and we are all too often denied the freedoms which are taken for granted by men. So it seems appropriate – if tongue-in-cheek – to explain this backlash against us using the metaphors of captivity and containment. Our attempts to seek freedom and escape from a system in which our lives are not our own, in which we are denied equality of power with the other half of humanity, have met with reprisals. It seems to us that these consist of four main strategies.

Firstly, there are sniper attacks made against those of us who've managed to escape, or avoid, the front line of direct control by individual men, and who lead reasonably independent lives – unmarried women, divorcees, single parents, feminists and lesbians. The object of this time-honoured strategy – of crushing extremists, discrediting deviants and labelling outsiders – is to divide and rule , to scare and silence us, to drive us underground and, of course, to deter other women from emulation. The propaganda used against us is meant to ensure that any woman in her right mind will avoid identification with undesirables and dissidents at all costs.

The second strategy is to concentrate on the rest of us, those detainees who as yet have not sprung the trap. Here the weaponry of ideology is used, in a cultural blockade to convince us where our 'true duty' and 'proper responsibility' lies – with the family, the children, the country, the community, the microwave. Anywhere, that is, except with ourselves.

The third manoeuvre is to close down any avenues of escape by cutting off routes to economic independence, restricting our opportunites for decent employment or useful education and by ensuring that divorce will cost us in more ways than one. All of which makes it more difficult for us to survive on our own or to have any real measure of independence or power within our rela-tionships. The point of this strategy, of course, is to convince us that we have a little option but to stay put and stop complaining.

The final assault, if all else fails, is the threat of violence. At a time when violence against women is an ever-present factor in constraining our lives and keeping us in the compound, we can also expect that if we make demands or step out of line we'll be judged guilty of provocation and inviting 'justifiable' use of force. Our right to demand redress, if we live to tell the tale, is questionable because, after all, we did 'ask for it'. Now it's not the first time in history that women's demands for fair play have met with this sort of reaction, but this time we intend to spill the beans by recording the tactics used against us as they happen. If we don't make clear what's going on no-one else will. But more than this, we need to understand what's happening ourselves if we are to resist the backlash and survive with our principles intact until the present climate of oppression changes.

FAMILY FORTUNES

Tory Government policy is decidedly frosty towards anything that smacks of feminism – in fact towards any suggestion that women might put any of our energies into ourselves. Of course it isn't unusual for radicals and socialists to be critical of the current social and economic climate characterised as Thatcherism. There is considerable anger from the Left ranged against Conservative government policies on unemployment, reductions in public spending, the destruction of the welfare state, the attack on trade unions and local authorities and the privatisation of publicly owned utilities and corporations.

We wouldn't wish to deny the significance of any of these issues, which together have changed the political, economic and social face of Britain. For sure, they are attempts to wipe out the hallmarks of a caring and civilised society and replace them with an ethos in which selfishness, greed and sharpening social divisions flourish. But why, we might ask, is much less attention paid by the Left to the escalating oppression of women which also lies at the heart of much of Conservative policy?

Tory family policy is a fundamental part of the current backlash against women. It serves to identify and punish those defectors and dissidents who live our lives outside the grasp of the patriarchal nuclear order, while at the same time reminding the rest of us of our commitments to the family and closing off our escape routes. And yet, the ideas and arguments about 'the importance of the family' which have been expressed in Tory government policies on health, law and order, social security and public spending have not often been the focus of criticism by the Left. Perhaps that's a reflection of the extent to which family policy sits uneasily, straddling the divide between public and private life.

Mainstream political parties of all persuasions rarely include in their political agendas any critique of personal relationships. Most often these are seen to lie beyond the proper sphere of politics. Even those left-wing groups which are concerned with the unequal distribution and exercise of power draw back from analyses which identify the inequality of power in intimate personal relationships between men and women. When they do admit that inequality exists, they choose to interpret this as evidence that both women and men are equal victims locked against their will in the stranglehold of capitalism. They fail to point out that men, unlike women, benefit personally, in a whole range of ways, from this relationship, It could well be that Tory Family Policy doesn't make the centre pitch with opposition groups because, after all, they don't see too much that's wrong with it. And if they want to talk about women, it's easier to concentrate on the public aspects of discrimination and about arguments for and against legislation, than on a reappraisal of men's personal relationship to power.

The Labour party has not been slow to adopt the current rhetoric of the Tory Party and about self-reliance, independence, choice and ownership of property because it carries with it the smell of election success. If ever such ideas were meant to be extended to women as distinct from men – if women were to be encouraged to aim for self-reliance, independence, freedom of choice and property ownership – the present state of marriage and the family would be turned upside down. Women encouraged to rely on ourselves rather than on men might stop deferring to men. Women encouraged to be independent might seek our own means of financial support. Women presented with freedom of choice might choose not to have children, or to have them in our own time, or on our own terms. Independent, property-owning women might not choose to enter permanent relationships with men.

As we have already seen, it's often lack of financial independence and real alternatives which keep women in unsatisfactory marriages once the veneer of romantic love has worn thin. But if we did, the balance of power within those marriages would be very different. Clearly this is not what any political party intends. We have mistaken the messages. These catch-phrases are for catching the imaginations of men as head of families, not women. The emphasis upon self reliance and independence refers not to individuals as much as family units, and women as ever are subsumed within the family rather than regarded as individuals in our own right.

The importance of the family lies at the heart of Tory policy and serves it well. For a party with an overwhelming commitment to the accumulation of private property 'the savings of families', according to Geoffrey Dicken MP form 'the very basis of capitalism. Strong families pay the tax bills which allows the government to govern . . .' Capitalism also relies heavily on the continuing unpaid labour of women in families, which is seen as our real sphere of work – feeding, clothing, nursing and nurturing family members.

Equally, the Tory government has set itself against the state, pledging to reduce its power, and thereby much of its responsibility for the care, protection and policing of those who need it. Again, the family comes up trumps as the ideal institution to perform these functions for free.

Of course, all of this emphasis upon 'the family' has nothing to do with a willingness to examine the personal relationships within families that we mentioned earlier. What actually happens within the family – the dynamics of relationships, how the work allocated to the family by the government and the state gets distributed between members – none of these are considered to be the province of politics nor the concern of government. It is the family as an institution that the Tory government is concerned with. Unconstrained by any consideration of what real, lived in, family life is like, the Tory collective imagination has been free to make it into an institution which serves all its requirements. The family is viewed not as a method of social organisation as much as a natural and even biological necessity made up of men and women in monogamous permanent relationships and their dependent children. Together, as tightly knit units, families provide for all the basic needs of their members without undue reliance on the state or undue concern for anyone else.

If it's a biological necessity that we live only with those with whom we have a reproductive/sexual or blood relationship in a permanent unit, it helps to create the impression that families are natural and therefore unchanging. The family becomes a monolith and is placed on a pedestal, out of the reach of historical changes, unaffected by war, unemployment, bad housing and poverty or domestic violence. It assumes that all families are the same, regardless of class, race or location, and that relationships within the family present no problem.

The differentiation that does exist within families is seen to be a difference in roles, not power or status. Men are seen as the heads of families, providing financial support and excercising discipline. Women are the guardians of the home, providing emotional support and domestic servicing. These roles are seen as interdependent – an equal partnership. Men are to operate in the world of paid work and public affairs for the good of the family, women and the privacy of the family are indivisible.

Now clearly this is all something of an 'ideal', that any party, let alone one with a woman as its leader, would have some difficulty in translating into acceptable policies. Margaret Thatcher cannot be seen to head a government which prevents women with children from working outside the home, but Graham Webster-Gardiner, Chairman of the Conservative Family Campaign, in a speech entitled 'Putting Father Back at the Head of the Table', can ask, 'Who can doubt that men's employment would be higher or men's unemployment lower if married women with school age children did not go out to work?' What Margaret Thatcher's government has done, in fact is to reduce the number of nursery school places and make it extremely difficult for women with children to register as unemployed. This removes from many of us the feeling that we are entitled to paid work, and contributes to the backlash against us.

Tory family ideology, of course, rests its case on the idealising of a particular brand of family which represents only 11 per cent of all households in Britain. The nuclear family, consisting of a male breadwinner with dependent wife and children, is no longer the norm (if indeed it ever was). Many couples have no children, or no dependent ones, many of us live with people to whom we are neither married nor related, and many of us choose to live on our own. Not all women have children, and many who do live with them without a man. Collectively what are 'anomalies' according to Tory doctrine amount to the living patterns of approximately 89 per cent of all households.

These facts haven't prompted the Tories to abandon a view of the family which reflects the reality for only a minority, nor to acknowledge that people live in a variety of ways which shift and change over time. Nor have they chosen to take stock of the possible reasons for this. Despite some concern about 'the instability of the modern family' the Tory line, at the end of the day, has been to play down the instability and doctor the evidence. Using all the ideological means at their disposal, the Tory magic circle has transformed a mere 11 per cent into a moral majority. Documents issuing from the Centre for Policy Studies tell us that the decent normal family soldiers silently on, albeit under attack from a small but vociferous group of misfits.

Deviants, dissidents and defectors

Women living without men, as heads of our own households pose problems for a society which relies so heavily on the family as the first line of defence in preserving male power. Together with homeless men and single young people, women living without men are escapees from the gulag of family life characterised by a male breadwinner, a dependent wife and children. Irresponsible mavericks evading family responsibilities, homeless men dependent on the state and without families to head are as Bea Campbell points out in *Wigan Pier Revisited*, the antithesis of a masculinity which is derived from having power and authority over others. That's why former Social Security Secretary Patrick Jenkin cut their benefit. Similar treatment has been given to unattached young people who've moved out of the parental home. In the 'ideal' family, children remain under the care and discipline of their parents until they are financially independent, by which time they ought to be considering marriage, forming an independent household of their own and setting the whole process in motion again.

However, for many youngsters today there is very little real work available to provide the economic passport to independence. They face prolonged dependency on parents since the government has cut benefit rights to young people who leave home. Middle-class kids might be eased out of childhood by going to university, or helped to find a decent job or to be set up in a flat funded by their parents.

Some working-class girls do it by becoming mothers themselves. Motherhood surely sorts out the women from the girls, and eventually might improve their chances of getting out from under and into a council flat of their own. This is not the kind of initiative and enterprise that gets Tory approval, however, for it all adds to the growing numbers of undesirable, single parent families.

Homeless men and wayward children – there's an unwritten assumption that women are to blame for this 'breakdown' in family life. Our demand for 'a life outside the home' is often given as the main reason for the high divorce rate. Certainly we know that it's generally women, rather than men, who are unsatisfied with the realities of married life. In fact 75 per cent of divorces are initiated by women these days. If we're looking for explanations, a good starting place might be men's behaviour and privileged position within the family. More often the fault is laid at our door. We are told that we have 'unreasonable expectations' or 'unfulfilled aspirations' that make us perpetually disappointed with marriage and 'never satisfied'. Or else we are accused of having 'an eye to the main chance', of using divorce as a way of separating men from their money by excessive demands for maintenance, of forcing divorced men on to the streets.

Whatever the explanations, the outcome is not approved. The Tories like men to remain in charge. Geoffrey Howe in 1980 emphasised the importance of 'the idea of the state dealing with the family unit headed by the father' when he tried to transfer child benefit payments from mothers to fathers. Other politicians evoke images of wayward woman and children engaged in a conspiracy to swamp the nation and defraud the state. Rhodes Boyson, for example, has claimed that 'single parents have made their case so well that they have expanded their subsidies from the public purse from £15 millon in 1960 to £1 billion in 1983'. And what is worse, some of us do it on purpose: 'Low paid members of normal families are taxed at the standard rates to subsidise not only those forced to be one parent families by misfortune, but also to subsidise those who have specifically chosen to be one parent families.' Geoffrey Dicken MP claims that 'broken families drain the national coffers in welfare' and that 'in practice, the rising numbers of people dependent on welfare is fast replacing trade union power as a weapon of socialism'. Now if you're a single parent, this caricature of yourself as a politically motivated urban guerilla might come as something of a surprise, particulary if the only conspiracy or struggle you're engaged in is to make ends meet and to survive the scrutiny of DHSS investigators.

This is a real experience, you've got to be on it and then you know all about it; although it was not my choosing. I've been put into this awful situation without any fault of my own. It is an ordeal, filling in a book of forms, all about your personal business, down to every detail, and you must not have any money coming in to qualify, as they call it. Then they only allow you the smallest amount to live on for instance, for food, clothes, bills and as for luxuries, they call having a telephone, a television, a bar of soap luxuries, and if you have a pet, like I have a cat, it is a luxury, an extra mouth to feed – they tell you to get rid of it, and trying to get any extras out of them is like trying to get blood out of stone. You have to have no sheets, be sleeping on a bare mattress, then they say they have to decide whether you are entitled to it. They say you can't claim if the sheets are repairable as I've already experienced. So its sewn up sheets and second hand clothes as the money does not run to new ones. It makes you feel like a pauper, you've got to write down every penny you spend and where it went to. Some weeks you go without a lot for a little pride, to afford make-up, make do with a wash instead of a bath daily. You have one meal a day if you are lucky enough not to have to pay a bill that week. Soaking wet washing on a wet day because you can't afford to run a tumble drier, the tumble drier I already had before going on DHSS. As for things like household items, washing machine, iron, etc. you have to pay for out of your allowance, which is a pittance. If you do not have a washing machine, its washing by hand, and like the old-fashioned days, scrubbing board and red hands. As for heat in the winter, you can't afford a lot of heat, so you are squashed up in the warmest place, with about 3 jumpers on if you are lucky enough to have these. And in winter you need more clothes and food but the DHSS say it's got to come out of your personal allowance, which is impossible.

But that's the way they work. This DHSS authority is wicked. I'd like to see some of them try to live, eat, buy clothes and keep warm and pay bills on what they allow you. They treat you like dirt, people like me, genuine in my circumstances, are treated like a thing out of the gutter. I only wish I didn't have to live like this, but I have no option. God knows when this nightmare will end, you've got all this worry day and night, how to try and budget, but it is impossible when you are on DHSS. I could write a book on this, but until you've got to rely on this I don't think people would believe you – its like a living nightmare, I could go on about this but it's a never ending story; being on DHSS and under their authority.

For many woman becoming a single parent isn't something we've actually chosen to do, and certainly not as a conspiracy to defraud

DHSS or change anything except our own lives. Usually it's been the lesser of two evils or something we've had no option about. Most of us have been too busy coping to notice the accusations mounting against us. But it stands to reason that if women's dependency on men for survival, a home and a position in the world is the cornerstone of patriarchy and sizeable numbers of us have escaped that dependency, then fears about its continuation might be justified. For instance, Tory politicians have been in no doubt about where to lay the blame. Webster-Gardiner is convinced that 'years of militant feminism and harmful legislation like the Equal Opportunities Act have undermined the clear biblical concept of the father'. Rhodes Boyson fervently believes that the family is under attack from 'extreme feminists, youth cults and homosexual lobbies'.

Single parents might be a drain on the national coffers and dislodge fathers from their rightful place at the head of the household, but feminists and lesbians are accused of wanting to destroy the family altogether. As feminists we are well used to being lampooned and stereotyped, but now the level of abuse has gone beyond a joke. The attacks on feminists have become more vicious as our voices have become angrier. In the early days of the WLM we were more optimistic about the justice of our arguments being acknowledged. We concentrated our demands on equal rights issues, on legislation and education. We wanted state support for childcare, equal pay, encouragement for girls at school and positive attempts to break down prejudice and stereotypes. This approach became most notoriously associated with the policies and practices of the Greater London Council in the early 1980s. Under pressure from feminists, machinery was set up to begin a process of positive action to change attitudes, to acquire skills and to create a climate in which inequality of all kinds could be genuinely and effectively challenged. For almost the first time projects which had previously been run on a shoestring, relying on the work of dedicated volunteers, acquired adequate funding. In 4 years £30 million was given in grants to nearly 1000 different women's projects providing children, refuges and resource centres, advice and education services, health projects and employment opportunities. Womens issues weren't just 'hived off' and contained within one sector of the council's work, but were fully accounted for in all other areas of council activity. Wherever the GLC came into contact with outside agencies the principles of anti-sexism and anti-racism were to be upheld. Many other Labour local authorities followed suit and, by 1986, women's committees or working parties were operating in 33 of them. It gave us a taste of what can be done when the political will is present, but it was a rather brief affair and we all know what happened.

Subsequent vilification of GLC-funded projects as a 'ludicrous' and 'criminal' waste of resources, and the 'squandering of ratepayers' money' culminated in the abolition of the GLC and the metropolitan counties and in rate capping of other recalcitrant authorities by a Conservative government determined to have no effective challenge to its policies. The attack on feminists and lesbians became much more acute when it looked as though we were being taken seriously. Publications such as 'Tackling Heterosexism', produced by the GLC Women's Committees, were lambasted by Rhodes Boyson as 'the flaunting and propagation of homosexuality and lesbianism'.

For those of us living in less enlightened areas there was never the same recognition or political support for our cause. We were forced to realise just how firmly entrenched our inequality was. It wasn't just a question of changing attitudes and educating men. As more of us spoke out we saw that our original concerns were the symptoms rather than the causes of our oppression. The language of our analysis changed from that of 'equal rights', 'discrimination' and 'sexism' to 'oppression', 'domination' and 'power', as we began to fathom the full depths of patriarchal control.

Rape, domestic violence, child abuse and pornography came to represent frightening examples of the extent of woman-hating that is tolerated in our society. Inevitably, many of us concentrated our energies here. We set up rape crisis lines and refuges. We pieced together an analysis of our oppression to remind us that the attitudes and values involved in that oppression are rarely left behind at the kitchen or the bedroom door. It has not been easy for some of us to accept that the most intimate of all personal relationships are shot through with ideas about male dominance and female submission. The response to us now is less to do with the patronising and infuriating jibes at 'Womens' lib' as with accusations that we are extremists. As Thatcherism lurches further to the right, those of us who stand our ground and refuse to tone down our protests are accordingly left out on a limb. The Tory Party speak of us as 'pariahs' and the Labour Party accepts our designation as 'the loony left'.

The strategy of divide and rule is used again to mark out feminists as extremists who are against the interests of 'ordinary', 'normal' women. More so if some of us are also lesbians, in which case our sexuality is presented as threatening and predatory. Our interests are assumed to be different from and alienating to, more moderate, manageable women. Everything from plays to political campaigns get put down for having a feminist theme or as being 'only concerned with women' as if a comment on the lives of half the population is not enough.

MPs in Westminster can raise a laugh, even from the opposition, by referring to the absurdities of projects aimed at 'disabled black lesbians' or 'AIDING lesbians to have babies'. At a personal level this kind of abuse increases the feelings of isolation and fear many lesbians already experience – especially when we're working class and living in the middle of large housing estates where graffiti gets sprayed on our walls, our windows get smashed and our children get beaten up.

> Sometimes I feel scared to death. I'm scared for my children, myself and my lover. There are days I walk down the road and hold my head low – stare at the pavement – does it show in my eyes? Can you tell by my smile? Do I look different, sound different? The most awful thing I can imagine is my children suffering because I've chosen to live as a lesbian. My life shouldn't infringe on their freedom so I try to keep it secret from the outside world as best I can. People stare sometimes. They ask questions. They weigh up the possibilities. But as long as they don't find out I feel safer. Safe – that's a laugh. I'll never be safe, I sometimes feel I'm on a tightrope. My ex-husband holds one end. The children are at the other. I balance in between trying to stop myself falling . . . because there's no safety net for me to fall into. I know at any time he can push me off – he has all the power. I have none. The children are 'the prize' – if I can ever get to the end of the rope.
>
> And the rest of the world? Well, they'll be cheering him on. I'm on my own except for a handful of close faithful friends. The rest don't want to know once they find out the truth – suddenly I'm condemned as sinful, evil, perverted – people I've known all my life turn their backs on me.

At a political level the intention here is to deter other women from behaviour that might prove contagious.

Detainees

Given this kind of treatment its not suprising that other women back off from identifying with those of us who have been marked out as deviants, dissidents and defectors. Faced with this scapegoating, the message for the rest of us is to conform, knuckle under and not rock the boat, if we want to avoid the tide of hostility turning against us too. But those of us serving our time in conventional family situations don't escape the backlash altogether. As long as there's the possibility that we too might feel like a change, see an opening and 'go for it', we need to be kept fully occupied.

The doctrine of community care ensures, that even when our children no longer need us there's others who will. The demands made upon women in the family and the community to meet other peoples' needs are now greater than ever before. Its no longer just a matter of physical or emotional care – now we also have the responsibility for the psychological and intellectual development of our charges. Politicians and pundits are quick to lay the blame for all manner of problems – from soccer violence to child abuse by men – on our lack of proper care. And in the late 1980s we've been given another task to do. In the wake of the spread of the AIDS virus we have been appointed the guardians of the nation's health and morals.

The AIDS scare has presented moral re-armers with a heaven sent opportunity to revive a flagging cause. In fact, some have gone as far as to claim that the virus is 'the Wrath of God' visited on a sinful world like the biblical plagues of Egypt. For those who take a more down to earth approach it does, however, provide a twofold opportunity – to pinpoint and isolate deviants and dissidents on the one hand, while on the other endorsing women's vital role in preserving the heterosexual and monogamous nuclear family from attack.

This has lent fuel to the fire of gay-bashing. There are calls to isolate all victims and introduce compulsory testing of all homosexuals and other high risk groups. There are demands to sack homosexuals from the clergy, teaching and medical professions and to repeal the Sexual Offences Act. Individuals have been beaten up and harassed by hate letters. It has stirred up rows about the content of sex education in schools, and in the church, about different interpretations of the Christian doctrine on homosexuality. It has been used as a justification for the inclusion of Section 28 in the Local Government Act. Anyone who lives beyond the pale of the mythologised nuclear family gets included in the list of those likely to spread the disease to the rest of us.

In the context of the family, the moral panic around AIDS is presented as a 'new morality' endorsing monogamous sex and the sanctity of family life, set against the so-called permissiveness of the two previous decades. In reality, it is the old morality taken out of mothballs with messages for women that are aeons old.

We don't welcome back an era of sexual repression. Nor do those of us who live with men want to be charged with the responsibility of their sexuality and lose sight of our own in demands for safe sex, chastity, monogamy, condoms or celibacy. Of course, some us would like to say that we already know that there is a form of sex that's free from AIDS, cervical cancer, pregnancy and which also gives us more pleasure – but no-one seems to be listening. The penal code, as we know only too well, demands intercourse.

The so-called new morality of the 1980s, flourishing in the wake of AIDS, is also a very partial and selective one and its implications for women are confusing to say the least. Many of us find ourselves in something of a dilemma in the sexual morality debate. Although we have little patience with the Mary Whitehouse brand of morality, many of us would agree that we need a serious reassessment of prevailing ideas about male and female sexuality. While we dislike censorship for its association with political repression, we do believe in the criminalisation of pornography on a much wider scale than at present. We also find offensive the violent and degrading images of women on television, pop videos and films, in magazines, newspapers and advertising, which we consider to be pornographic. We take the view that pornography is an incitement to woman-hating and violence and ought to be outlawed just as material inciting racial hatred has been.

We need a sexual morality in which expressions of women's sexuality are not bound up in notions of submission, availability, passivity, sexual abuse and woman hatred – nor in terms of male aggression, domination and power.

Moral issues presented for popular discussion, and the emphasis placed upon them in the public debate, are usually rather different than our feminist analysis, however. Few commentators make any distinction between the roles of men and women in all of this. Declining moral standards are blamed on promiscuous 'people', women and men are presented as equal perpetrators of sexual violence, child abuse and pornography. Even lesbians, the group which must surely be the safest and least affected when it comes to AIDS, are found guilty-by-association and suffer in turn from the anti-gay flack generated by a disease which afflicts gay men.

In this moral context, the flip side of the backlash against women who live without men is to increase the surveillance on the rest of us, and leave us in no doubt about what we should be doing. We should be keeping out of the labour market as much as possible, unless it is to do those jobs which are too badly paid or menial to attract men. If we must work at a paid job, we should still concentrate our main energies upon family life and community care. Women should ease the pain of redundancy and unemployment for men, continue to service older children who are unlikely to find work and keep them off the streets, and take care of the ill, elderly and disabled members of society jettisoned by public spending cuts. In other words we have important work to do implementing government policies.

The Tory dictum of 'freedom of choice' for us is to give us the freedom to choose to stay at home and not to feel any pressure to seek work outside the home. As Margaret Thatcher repeatedly points out, most of us are not like her. Being a career woman isn't everyone's cup of tea. But while a change of government might feel like a relief, we shouldn't expect that its views on women would be any more enlightened. The last Labour Prime Minister, James Callaghan, stated in 1978, 'We have to pay more attention than we have done in the past to how industry organises women's role at work so that her influence in the centre of the family is not weakened. But equally, and here I want to make a very important point – one which I think is not made often enough – those women who choose their families as their life work, devote their energies to their homes, their husbands and their children are equally valuable members of society and fulfil themselves.' Of course he's absolutely right – we are extremely valuable. Who else would do all that work for free.

We are not arguing against women who stay at home. We know the value of the work we do at home only too well to put it down. Nor are we arguing that we should selfishly ignore the needs of others. But these pious sermons from male and male-identified politicians and experts stick in the throat. They sound extremely familiar to us. We've heard it all before from husbands who tell us 'what a good job' we're doing, then in the next breath complain about 'what a hard life it is at work' compared to the 'cushy social round' we're supposed to enjoy at home. The denial that paid work might give us some kudos, a sense of independence and, more important, our own money, insults our intelligence. The elevation of the status of motherhood as compensation has been tried before, in many places, but women, for the most part, remained unconvinced.

Blocking off the exits

In a country like Britain it isn't acceptable to resort to force. Much better to use 'gentle persuasion' and to rely on ideology. Neither is it possible to lock up and shut up those who disagree. But when enough of us stop believing the messages and start to look for escape routes a contingency plan is needed.

Avenues to independence are turned into blind alleys as we find our exits blocked off before our eyes. The inroads that some women have made since the 1960s into education or the labour market now look like cul-de-sacs, and in the current economic and political climate our chances of 'changing the system' to the advantage of women seem slim. Many of us feel that the first step is to change our own lives. Greater freedom, independence and financial resources of our own might also give us greater power to tackle the institutions that preserve male power. But of course its not that simple. Good jobs, useful education, improved legal rights all provide routes towards independence – but increasingly they are hard to come by. The backlash against the women's movement has set in motion the measures which are designed to reduce women's room to manoeuvre.

Some of the gains of the past two decades in abortion, maternity rights and divorce are now being reversed. It's been claimed by Lord Denning, for instance, that in marriage 'the wife is now indeed the spoilt darling of the law'. It has taken women over a century to gain equality with men in the grounds on which we can petition for divorce, in our rights to maintenance and property, and rights to the custody of our children. But the fact that many of these marital rights have been granted at the expense of other rights, such as those as workers is generally ignored. And when equality between men and women gets interpreted as 'unfair discrimination against men', we begin to realise that men will not willingly relinquish privilege.

In matters of divorce, for example, the men's movement has successfully organised itself into groups such as 'The Campaign for Justice in Divorce' and 'Families Need Fathers' to protect their interests in marriage and the family against the rights of women.

Influential men with lawyers and politicians among their members are able to put pressure where it counts. The Law Commission, investigating matrimonial proceedings, reported as early as 1979 that 'We have been told that continuing financial obligations imposed by divorce often cause severe economic hardship for those ordered to pay, normally of course, the husband . . . the obligation to maintain an ex-wife is particularly resented if the husband feels that it is his wife who is really responsible for the breakdown of the marriage . . . For many husbands the effect of divorce may seem to involve not only the end of their marriage but also the loss of home, children and money'.

The upshot of all this has been a concerted effort to prevent these losses from occurring, and women once again become the ones who pay the price for divorce by poverty, homelessness or loss of children.

Although I worked for my husband for over thirty years in the licensed trade, he was by law the only one allowed to hold the licence because he was a man. This was the beginning of my dependency. I received no wages from him and had to be grateful for my keep. All money that was earned during the course of our business life went into his name, or as he preferred to call it, 'the business account'. Although any objection from me always met with 'what's the difference, it's still ours'. That was not so, for I was never allowed any access or suggestion on how it was to be spent.

After many years of extreme cruelty, then later infidelity time and again from him, which I was subjected too because of my dependency on him, my health was beginning to collapse. As if that wasn't enough, he decided we had to part. Because of the circumstances of his job with the brewery, him being the licence holder, I was the one that had to go. My livelihood, home, husband and all that was familiar was taken from me.

My predicament at the moment, financially, is that I have to rely on him sending what he thinks he will weekly. Where he is still living in the lap of luxury, I am almost on a hand to mouth existence.

Because of his lack of co-operation with the solicitors, this situation is becoming intolerable. At the time I'm writing my solicitor is trying to get matters hurried up. But so far it has been months of my husband holding the reigns of power, i.e. all the money.

My work for him over such a long period of time has got him where he is today, financially. Sometimes I feel so strongly about my thirty year investment with him just cast aside.

My doctor says that it was the cause of my deterioration in health. I wish I could bring a case of damages against him as well!

After all it is not unheard of for demands for back-pay and unfair treatment within firms to be heard within the law courts. I'm sure with the information I could supply, and a persistent solicitor who had women's interests at heart I could establish that a great wrong has been inflicted upon me.

After what is agreed I'm entitled to get from the normal divorce settlement and it will no doubt drag on before its done, I'm still going to be in the position of dependency upon my husband, and why? After I've contributed so much the word dependency leaves me speechless!

The publicity surrounding well-known divorce settlements bears no resemblance to the realities of divorce for most of us. The saying that 'every woman is one man away from welfare' is much nearer to the mark.

My husband was a Manager of a well known company. He had worked his way up from an Engineer to top management. We owned our own house, in a good area, had money and clothes and classy colleagues – not really friends but people who were influential – to help him further his career. Now my own situation has changed but not his. He's still middle class and going further up the scale. Whereas myself, I don't exactly know what class I'm in as he left me for good after 22 years of marriage with me helping him to get where he is now. He left me, dumped me and drew all the money out of the bank. He didn't pay the mortgage so the house was repossessed and I was left homeless. I managed to get a privately rented flat which Housing Benefit pays and I'm on Social Security now, which is a pittance – not enough for food, bills and clothes. Its very hard to have to come to this – all the worry that goes with it. Now I'm not sure if I can keep the flat because the landlord is trying to get me out as the rent has been reduced under the Fair Rent Act. If that happens the only thing the council can do is give me bed and breakfast accommodation. How can life be so cruel – I've no money, no clothes, no decent home and hardly any furniture to call my own any more and so much worry about what will happen in the future.

As more and more of us are bringing up children on our own, 'Families Need Fathers' have organised themselves to ensure that the important job of socialising the next generation of recruits isn't taken entirely out of their control. Allies such as Rhodes Boyson attribute 'the wildness of the uncontrolled male young' on the lack of fathers. 'Boys can generally only be civilised by firm and caring fathers.' 'What about Mothers' you might ask, since its usually us who do the work of child care. 'The banishment of the father means that boys take their values from their aggressive and often brutal peer groups and are prepared for a life of violent crime, of football hooliganism, mugging and inner city revolt.' We know a lot of the work we do is invisible, but this is ridiculous.

It seems that men's anxieties about sons in particular – the future recruits for their movement – has caused them to show an uncharacteristic concern to get in on the act of childcare. It's surely the unstated fear that boys might come to see women as heads of households and take their values from 'firm and caring mothers' that has prompted this particular backlash against us. Now many judges refuse to make full child custody orders to women. Custody confers legal rights over a child concerning important decisions such as residence, education and medical care and it seems that these are too important to be left to women alone. What's happening now is that joint orders are increasingly being made in which women may retain the day-to-day care of children but have constantly to refer back to fathers before decisions that affect the child's future can be made. In this way men are able to retain control over both the children and their mother without any responsibility for the hard physical and emotional labour of bringing them up.

> I think that joint custody is a way of controlling mothers on divorce. To quote the judge in my own case 'joint custody is one of the few modern trends of which I wholeheartedly approve. It means that mothers consult with fathers over all the important decisions which have to be made and which will affect the child's future, whereas', here he turned and smiled at me, 'care and control means that you can choose which brand of toothpaste they will use'. Wonderful how all the work, responsibility and emotional energy of bringing up children gets reduced to choosing toothpaste, yet I'm not considered responsible enough to decide which school they'll go to!

Much as we wouldn't want our children to be a battleground for power, it is true that as parents on our own many of us have gained some sense of our own worth from a job well done, in a world which is only too happy to deny us that right elsewhere. The question of men's right to control children doesn't stop at custody controls.

Decisions about reproductive rights, abortion, in vitro fertilisation and embryo implantation start alarm bells ringing in the ears of many of us. Men have tried in the courts to assert their rights over unborn children, to prevent individual women from having abortions, and in hospitals and Parliament to make the decisions about which of us will have babies or not and in what circumstances. It's no wonder that some of us prefer to get on with it ourselves. Although when we do, we are likely to find ourselves impoverished as a result. The 1980s has seen the elimination of maternity grants, the eroding of maternity rights at work and cuts in child benefit. For those wedded to the belief that societies progress, however slowly, to make life better for more people, and all we need is patience, moves like these can make you think. But for those who still have illusions that Britain is the home of fair play, repeated attempts by the European Courts to challenge the British government's reluctance to comply with EEC regulations on sex discrimination and racism and civil liberties might make you despair.

In the area of paid work the picture is no less depressing. Despite the Sex Discrimination Act, the Equal Pay Act, Equal Opportunities documents and frequent interviews in the press with women who've 'made it' in a male occupation, the reality for most women has not changed. We are still the low paid, part-time workers segregated in a ghetto of menial, unskilled work.

In fact, the number of women performing skilled work has declined this century as male workers have increasingly monopolised higher status, skilled work. Although there are now more women working outside the home than ever before, it seems our numbers have done little to improve our bargaining power. In 1984 women earned only 66 per cent of men's earnings. We could write another book about the collusion between male workers, trade unions and employers to resist equal pay. The idea of 'the family wage' earned by the male breadwinner lives on to determine men's wage levels, and to undercut ours, despite the fact that nearly a million of us are single parents and many more of us are the major breadwinners of our families. Even single women have our wage levels determined on the understanding that we are being supported elsewhere by a man.

Government proposals in the 1987 Social Security Act – to change the taxation and benefit systems – includes disincentives for wives who go out to work and reduces our entitlement to state benefits in our own right. The government has done its level best to deter married women with children from registering as unemployed to reduce the unemployment figures, and to confine us in the isolation of the home. Mothers registering for work have to supply proof that our children will not interfere with our availability for work. One woman we know, who doesn't even live with her child, has been prevented from signing on because investigators discovered that she has an extra single bed in her one-bedroomed flat which her fourteen year old daughter uses when she visits at weekends. They have claimed that her childcare responsibilities disqualify her from signing on for work.

This is a far cry from our demands in the Women's Liberation Movement that our role as mothers be recognised by employers. Our demands for work-place creches, flexible hours and retraining facilities now look like pie in the sky.

Although the government boast of exciting new job opportunities, few of the schemes dreamt up by them to provide retraining, or to create jobs, have been designed with women in mind.

At the Women's Education Centre we had money from MSC (Manpower Services Commission) to provide two temporary part-time jobs for creche workers on the Community Programme. [Government Job Creation Programme] Although many women wanted the jobs we had great difficulty filling them because the regulations about who could apply were so stringent that very few women were eligible. For a start, women who'd been out of work for years couldn't apply unless we'd been signing on for the previous 12 months. Given that women are discouraged from signing on this meant that many of us were disqualified straight away. Then, married women with unemployed husbands – although wageless and often poor ourselves – were ineligible because our husbands were getting benefit for us. Thirdly, those of us who were claiming long term benefit found that we would be worse off taking a temporary part-time job and we'd lose our long term benefit when the job came to an end. We tried to get the hours increased so that we could get our money made up by Family Income Supplement [now Family Credit] but the MSC wouldn't wear it. It was yet another version of the poverty trap.

Punitive DHSS regulations often prevent many of us from showing the intiative that gets so much praise in other quarters. Even when we are in a position to help each other and find 'jobs for the girls' the system usually beats us.

We find time and time again that even when we have money to pay tutors or crêche workers at the Women's Education Centre we are unable to employ those women who most need the work because they would lose out on Social [Income Support]. We wanted to offer 4 hours teaching to a woman who'd taught on our course in the past – a really excellent teacher with a lot of experience in Media Studies. At the time she was back on Social and after much consultation with the DHSS she had to turn the work down because they would have taken most of her earnings away from her.

Despite a lot of talk about 'opportunities for women', if we want to get on a government training scheme that isn't typing or clerical work we're likely to have difficulty.

> A woman from MSG came to talk to us on the course about all the new training opportunities for women but when I went to apply for a painting and decorating course it was another story. I was told they only accepted people who already had some grounding in decorating work. That was fine by me. I'd done my own decorating for years and helped a few others out too. But that wasn't good enough, they said I had to have *worked* as a decorator before, What's the bleedin' good of training people who've already got the skill? I know it was just an excuse not to take on a woman.

In a decade of mass employment women have been badly hit and we have lost jobs at a faster rate than men, especially full time jobs. But as employers cash in on a vulnerable labour force weakened by unemployment and government union policies, many part-time jobs have been created for women.

> When the new Hypermarket was built there was the promise of lots of work for the women living on the estates around it. But what they've done is not create real jobs with wages that we can live on but to exploit us even more. They employ very few full time workers – only in management. The rest are shift workers and the length of each shift has been worked out exactly to last just under the length needed to start paying National Insurance, holiday and sick pay – even lunch breaks. They are able to do this because we need the work but the wages, the hours and the conditions stink.

Attacking our education

The general backlash against women which we have described here naturally affects us in every aspect of our lives. For the purposes of this book we need to look particularly at how the messages of hatred, containment and destruction have been directed against the feminist education programme we have been creating for ourselves and what the consequences have been.

In Southampton the Second Chance for Women courses were established in 1979 and the Women's Education centre was created in 1981. Right from the start we met with opposition from patriarcal and male-identified sources.

In 1979 the local authority stepped up its programme of public spending cuts – the services most affected were education and social services. We looked at these policies in detail on Second Chance. It didn't take much perception to realise whose kid's education, whose own education and whose social welfare needs were about to go down the tubes. We decided to make our objections known to our elected representatives in the county council. We wrote numerous letters and joined in a local demonstration against the cuts organised by the Trades Council [Confederation of Trade Union and Labour groups]. Within 2 weeks of the Chairman of the Education Committee receiving our opinions, a full scale enquiry into the politics of our course was ordered. The tutors were accused of socialist bias and we were assumed to be the gullible idiots they had led astray.

A year later a magazine reflecting the writings of some of us on Second Chance was published and began to be used as resource material in the literacy scheme and in other community education projects. Within days of its publication questions were asked at County Hall about 'the desirability of a course in which women are encouraged to swear' because a couple of the pieces of writing in the magazine included four-letter words.

As a working-class woman and mother of 4, who has lived on a council estate all her life, and who's seen more hard times than you've had hot dinners, I am unlikely to let myself be tied to a desk by a university academic and instructed in the art of swearing. 'Fuck' was one of the first words I ever learned as a child and I've been glad to use it on occasions ever since. When those men from the Authority talk about 'bad language' I think they must be referrring to new words I've been learning more recently – like 'freedom' and 'independence' and 'liberation'.

However ludicrious this must seem, the course was again investigated for its alleged bias and 'undesirable outcomes'. Right from the start, then, the pattern was established of assuming that we are stupid and gullible women, and easily led astray by politically motivated agitators. We can't imagine courses for working-class men – trade unionists for example – being investigated for inciting democratic responses to local political issues or for encouraging swearing.

Meanwhile – back at the Women's Education Centre – it took us 2 years to negotiate the use of the building and 5 years to ensure that it was properly heated. The building is old – 19th century probably – but we did it all up inside and established a crèche and fitted it out ourselves.

The only problem was the antiquated heating system – no problem in the summer, useless in the winter. We used to open the oven door and bring in electric fires from home to keep ourselves warm. This led to a running battle for at least 4 winters in which our fires were confiscated, fuses were taken out of our plugs, and gas supplies were cut off.

The local authority, who own the building, and who were busy installing central heating into every other facility on the same site, said they didn't have enough money to heat the Women's Education centre.

The arguments about proper heating for teaching rooms and for the crêche brought matters to a head in a way we hadn't expected.

We were informed by the Local Authority that since we were using a Local Authority building, it was intending to create a 22 strong management committee with representatives from various bodies which would be able to veto our publicity material and even the content of our courses.

Of course we have never thought of having a management structure for obvious reasons, and have organised ourselves quite satisfactorily as a collective, with meetings when we need them to make decisions, and different groups of women taking responsibility for what needs to be done. We have contact with the organisations and agencies that sponsor some of our courses through feminist women workers in those organisations who are also members of our collective.

Luckily for us these plans were dropped eventually, but the episode served to remind us just where the real power lies.

Arguments about heating, access to our building, who should carry keys and whether racist and sexist caretakers should be allowed to shout abuse at women using the centre have all been relatively minor skirmishes compared to the continuing attempts to restrict and control what we actually do in the centre when 'education' is taking place. In this respect the machinations of key men from the University Department of Adult Education have been the most damaging. The university provides the funding for the Second Chance courses and they have brought the department a lot of kudos in terms of 'progressive developments in working class adult education', both in this country and abroad. The disputes between the University and the W E C have been varied but similar.

They have been about alleged bias and contention in our curriculum; about the alleged extremism and undue influence over students of the tutors; about working-class, stroppy and irreverent women making the most of facilities and resources usually reserved for more respectable and respectful adult students.

During the eight years of our existence the Second Chance courses have been investigated twice by the Local Authority, twice by the university, and once by an HMI. Our work has been looked at critically more than any other course in the department. Investigation after investigation of the course reveals countless happy and committed women, quick to come to the defence of Second Chance if any criticism from outside is implied. On one occasion we were told the relationship between tutors and students was 'too good' and was not 'a proper preparation for further study' where such 'favourable relationships' and 'conducive conditions' would not exist. Which is a bit like saying we should be prepared for the worst by being treated badly in anticipation. More often though, the closeness of tutor and student relationships has been one of the main causes for concern.

> Throughout the long and persistent attempt to undermine and control our feminist education programme the underlying reasons for suspicion and hostility have rarely been made explicit, although it has been clear to us that the politics of the programme, and more particularly the personal politics of some of the tutors, have been a major concern. Of course only two of us are lesbian, but it has been assumed over the years – in the well worn tradition of prejudice about the education and conscription capabilities of lesbians – that our influence and power over other 'more reasonable' tutors and all the students must be enormous.

Repeatedly, it seems, the power of known dissidents, deviants and defectors to influence otherwise normal and respectable detainees has been levelled against the collective educational enterprise we are all engaged in.

> In the past part-time tutors working on the Second Chance programme have been required to provide CVs at a time when no other part-time tutors in the university were expected to. To what extent academic qualifications and years of teaching experience and community work compensate for lesbian affiliations we're not altogether sure, but clearly some investigation into credentials of one kind or another was intended by this action.
>
> Attempts have also been made to interfere in the interviewing, counselling and recruitment of students and questions have been asked about whether their sexual orientation influences their chances of being

selected. Of course some students each year are lesbian and others may become so – but given the way the world is, and the enormous degree of belligerence, energy and power that goes into the promotion of heterosexuality as the only conceivable option – the prospect of courses in Southampton filled year after year with gangs of working class lesbians seems almost too good to be true. When those of us who are lesbian are in such a small minority its hard to imagine what damage the defenders of heterosexuality think we might cause.

In the summer of 1986 matters really came to a head with an all out attack on the Second Chance course and the Centre.

Firstly the publicity material for our courses – which we designed to have maximum appeal to working-class women – was changed by staff at the university on the grounds that it ought to appeal to a wider cross section of women. By this they meant middle-class, richer women who would not call themselves feminists and whom they assumed would have a less critical view of the world. For a course like Second Chance, which is well known locally and nationally for its commitment to the poorest and most powerless of working class women, this would have represented a major shift in emphasis, and would have removed already scarce resources away, once again, from those who have least in the first place. The next step was to refuse to allow us to waive fees for poor women. Women who could not afford to pay fees had to write to an administrator at the university who would apply a means test and who also took it upon herself to issue a little lecture on money management. All of this was done without the consent or approval of the tutors responsible for organising and teaching the course for the previous seven years.

The effect was to reduce the numbers of working-class women applying and to cause many others to withdraw once they knew what the financial implications were.

Three weeks into the term, in a course that lasts for a year, we were told that we were overstaffed and at least one tutor would lose her job, and the meagre university wages paid to creche workers would be stopped altogether – immediately. At that point we had 12 children in the creche. The university denied that there was any intention of closing down Second Chance. They merely made it impossible for the usual numbers of women to attend, sacked staff and closed the creche. It was at this point we started to get organised. Our first step was to contact women who'd been on Second Chance in the past, women who were, and had been, part of the WEC, and others we knew would be sympathetic both locally and nationally. Within a few days letters started flooding in to the Centre with messages of support. By the time we'd received 200 we thought it was time to take them to the University's Director of Adult Education, the man responsible for the assault on Second Chance.

We only had about three days to plan the demonstration. A few phone calls and messages passed by word of mouth were all that was needed.

About 60 or 70 women and children gathered at the pre-arranged time and place – all in good humour – some old friends we hadn't seen in years were there – other women had taken time off work to turn up. The kids had little placards and hats saying 'save our creche' and we brought bikes and buggies and little carts to brighten up their journey down the corridors of power.

We walked over to the Adult Education Department in a long line – first time on a demo for most of us but it felt good to be all together. We had this great pile of letters and petitions to give to the Director about the threats to our course.

You have to go up an outside stairway to get to the Adult Education Department – certainly not intended for women in wheelchairs or women with prams. We lifted Gill and her wheelchair in first and then all the kids and buggies. By this time there was a little more jollity and chatter in the ivory tower than is usual. Heads started appearing out of doors and windows – faces looking shocked, angry, affronted. Some little wizened man said if it was adult education we wanted why didn't we join one of their courses. 'We've got a course' we said 'and we'd like to keep it'. His head disappeared ultra quick into his room. We knocked on a few doors asking the way to the professor. Given that all of us were, or had been, students of this department – some of us going on to be degree students – some of us now social workers and teachers and probation officers and nurses – the reception wasn't that friendly. You'd have thought we were a rabble. Admin. staff started locking the doors to their rooms as though they expected us to break in and rifle through their papers – or worse. You'd have thought no one had ever seen a child sucking a lollipop before.

Clearly by the time we reached the professor's room he had been told that we were coming. You'd have thought he'd have been delighted to see such a large demonstration in support of one of his department's courses. Quite the contrary. At first he refused to see us because we hadn't made an appointment. But by then there was no way that we were all just going to go home again. So we started a bit of a chant. That did the trick.

It would have been alright if he'd have been pleasant and polite and said 'Oh how nice to see you. Thank you for coming. Yes I will read all these letters and see what can be done'.

We'd have felt relieved and gone off home and thought our protest had been a success. But of course he wasn't at all like that. He treated us as though we were stupid and rude and as if we didn't know what we were on about.

In the end he agreed to another meeting with us at the Women's Education Centre the following week to talk about all the issues. I suppose it was the most we could expect at that stage.

During the demonstration one of women went to see a self-confessed 'feminist' working in the department, hoping to get her support for Second Chance.

I took copies of the letters we'd received from women, and some men supporters, from all over the country to show her because I couldn't believe she'd want to see Second Chance smashed. I might as well have saved my breath. Within seconds of entering her room she shouted at me to leave and made a complaint to the Director about sexual harassment. Now sexual harassment is a matter feminists take very seriously and is an offence we still struggle to have properly recognised. It's not a term to be used lightly and certainly not in relation to other women trying to have a talk about political betrayal. She knows of course that I'm a lesbian – that I've fought through the courts of this country to keep custody of my children. Given all of this her abuse made me extremely angry. But it also made me realise something about the dangers of anti-lesbian feeling in the Women's Movement. In this case it could make a so-called Sister plead 'professional neutrality' whilst at the same time giving allegiance and yet more ammunition to men.

About the only thing that was heartening about all of this was that our action did cause the Adult Education Department to back down – as they have done before in previous disputes. It's like they persist in believing that one or two mad extremists are up to no good, but when the rest of us turn up as well they are forced to acknowledge our existence.

It would look very bad for them to be seen to be closing down a course and a meeting place that has such support at a time when no-one very much gets passionate about adult education. But that doesn't prevent them from continuing to put pressure on the one or two individuals they can lean on. The Union had to be called in to protect the Women's Studies tutor in the Adult Education Department from disciplinary proceedings because of the demonstration, but it was not long before she was in trouble again, this time for proposing two new courses – in Lesbian Studies and Homophobia Awareness, courses that were being run in many universities in the pre-Section 28 days.

Both courses were regarded as 'highly controversial' and 'extremely sensitive'. If they were to go ahead they had to be 'planned, advertised and conducted with extraordinary care and with an eye to the potential for damaging criticism and hostile comment they embody' i.e. they should be presented in a way that would not offend homophobes and bigots.

A change of title was suggested since homophobia 'is an uncommon word, little known, its etymology being spurious, it is also impossible to guess what it means' 'Queer bashing' might have provided a more marketable title but I suspect it would have been considered less than rigorous in an academic sense.

A great deal of concern about 'academic structure and balance' was expressed and given my views on the matter there was the fear that 'a range of perspectives' would not be put. Presumably courses intended to expose homophobia, prejudice and ignorance about lesbianism should, according to this rationale, also seek to justify homophobia, prejudice and ignorance in an even handed way.

Without wanting to appear conceited, can you imagine any other circumstance in a university in which notions of academic freedom and professional competence are sacrosanct, in which an academic with 20 years teaching experience – who is the author of numerous publications and books and with some small reputation in the area of women's education and adult education – would be subjected to this kind of humiliating interrogation of her academic ability and competence.

Not only this, but a series of three meetings were to be arranged to discuss the proposals in more detail – the second of which was to include an HMI [Her Majesty's Inspector] and the third of which was to include the Vice Chancellor. I would have thought that men of the status of HMI and the significance of Vice Chancellor led fairly busy lives.

I dread to think what discussions went on in the corridors of power to arrange such high level intervention at such short notice. I was informed that the courses couldn't go ahead until the meetings had been completed, but that the brochure in which the course should be advertised would, by then, have gone to press. In other words, if I was able to persuade the powers-that-be to allow the courses to run, they would 'unfortunately' not be able to be advertised.

Of course recent legislation has lent respectability to this kind of repressive behaviour. The backlash has worked. Today we wouldn't even try to get such courses off the ground through the University. After all, there's now government backing for this kind of prejudice.

Nowadays, the University makes no financial contribution to providing a crêche for Second Chance – which it is supposed to fund – and recently opened and confiscated the entire mailing of publicity for the new Woman's Studies courses on the grounds that the letters contained information about non-university provision.

The institutional backlash is of course only part of the problem. We've written in earlier chapters about the response of individual men to women coming to our centre. Their hostility and violence comes from the same threat to their authority over us which also explains attempts by local politicians and educational policy makers to regain control of what we're doing. There's not a lot to choose between an angry husband and an angry Director of Adult Education insisting that we are being indoctrinated by extremists and using the various powers at their disposal to prevent us from continuing.

The effort to keep going, despite continual sniper attacks from the sidelines, takes its toll and uses up valuable energy we should be expending on ourselves. Our centre survives on very little money without the luxury of paid workers or regular grants. Given that we have very few resources and very little power it's amazing to hear ourselves continually referred to as 'a threat'. Except that we are a persistent and vociferous presence – disinclined to give in or go away.

And as a last resort

No one can deny that violence is on the increase, but explanations for this vary. As we've already shown it's our view that male violence, is the direct expression of patriarchal power, the ultimate weapon to control women when all else fails. To many this may sound extreme, but to us there is no other way to adequately explain the extent of sexual abuse, rape, assault and murder of women. Together with sexual harassment and pornography, they are forms of violence which involve the use of force, abuse and degradation of women and also children, and which serve to reinforce the idea of male domination in no uncertain terms.

Clearly not all men commit acts of violence but the problem, from our point of view, is that all men carry the potential to be violent. They can use violence against us if they wish to. If they don't, its because they are deciding not to use that particular feature of their power over women – at least not yet. But the fear and threat of men's violence – used or anticipated – works as one of the main forms of social control and keeps us in our place.

The popular view of this is that feminists are abnormally and obsessively concerned with men's violence, that we are paranoid and unnecessarily fearful. We still have to convince many people that the normal response to the current extent of violence is indeed overwhelming concern, anger and fear.

As part of our preparation for writing this chapter, some of us in the group monitored newspapers for accounts of acts of violence. It was a gruesome task from the start and the cuttings collection we accumulated by the end of a fortnight was distressing for the whole group. We thought we knew the extent of violence from our own experiences and from things we'd read, but the result of monitoring it like this was utterly sickening.

• The family murdered by a man who first battered his 'nagging' mother-in-law to death, then killed his two children and tried to kill his wife – his friend commented 'The police should look no further than John's mother-in-law. If anyone is to blame for this tragedy it is her. She was an evil and demanding woman who made his life a misery'.

• The blind 86 year-old woman who was raped by a youth because he thought 'it was time he lost his virginity'.

• The girl raped by two men and subsequently attempted suicide – one was given a lighter sentence because the judge said that unlike the other 'you restricted yourself to straight intercourse'.

• The woman battered unconscious by her son, and had lived in terror of him throughout his teenage years.

• The woman who was attacked as she pushed her 2 year-old daughter along the canal after which her attacker threw the child into the canal.

• The 13 year-old who was shown porn magazines and raped four times by a 42 year-old who had been released from prison on licence.

• The young American woman who was injected several times with a pain killer then raped in a Wiltshire cornfield before being driven around the country-side and dumped.

• The 18 and 19 year-old young women who were chased down the street by the ex-boyfriend of one of them who then blasted their heads off with a shot gun. Why? 'He felt the girls had been making fun of him'.

• The woman who was murdered by her husband and whose body was chopped into little pieces.

• The 14 year-old girl who had been sexually abused for years by her 34 year-old father.

• The 20 year-old rape victim who had her face 'beaten to a pulp' by a man posing as a taxi driver.

• The 6 year-old girl who was raped by her babysitter.

• The 33 year-old woman who was murdered by her husband because 'she was messing about with other men'.

• The 37 year-old woman who was clubbed to death by her boyfriend because she wouldn't marry him.

And so on and so on.

Don't let anyone tell you that we're extreme or paranoid in our concern over this kind of violence against us. We might feel reassured by the men who claim that they are 'not like this' if they were also as concerned as we are to expose the violence of their sex; if they were spearheading campaigns against male violence and sexual abuse; if they were determined to socialise their own sons differently; and if they were working hard to confront their own sexism and ambivalence towards women. But we see little sign of this happening.

In all the current concern over child abuse we rarely hear it stated that it is men who abuse children. Discussions about sexual abuse or educational programmes aimed at kids rarely make it clear to the children that it is almost certainly men from whom they are in danger. Let us say, once and for all, that it is not women who rape, assault or harass anyone, and that the extent of violence on the part of women is extremely small. A recurring theme running through the issue of male violence, however, is that it's women's responsibility. If children are sexually abused by fathers it must be the mother's fault. If a wife is murdered she must have deserved it. Women and girls by our behaviour or dress are held responsible for rape, child abuse, sexual harassment and murder. We've 'asked for it', 'had it coming to us', have been 'provocative', 'need it', 'wanted it' and even when we've said 'no', 'didn't mean it'.

The messages for men are clear. You can be let off the hook when it comes to any responsibility for your own or any other men's violence. Even if you're convicted of violence, you'll get a reduced sentence if you can lay the blame on women. Women become both the victims and the guilty party. It's enough to make an extremist out of anyone.

Nothing changes

Its not the first time that there has been a backlash against women seeking independence any more than we are the only women who have sussed the patriarchal plot.

We now understand how much male control over us has depended on our silence, and that men have been hard at work silencing women for centuries. We've already shown how men's privileged position in the world has enabled them to omit our experiences from the collective culture. We have many examples of ways in which powerful men have been able to use ideological weapons to manipulate women.

A case in point is the treatment of women workers at the end of the Second World War. Newspapers and newsreels, popular songs and radio all urged women to step up and into the factories to join the war effort. Many women in doing their patriotic duty also found a taste for their own money, a skilled job, state nurseries and public recognition of their value. But the next few years gave them little chance to indulge in it. The return of the conquering heroes also signalled a return to the kitchen sink. The same means of conveying the messages were used, but this time to convince women that it was now their duty to quit the factories and return home. In women's magazines – instead of tips about quick and easy meals – were recipes which took all day to cook, and articles which warned about the dire consequences of maternal deprivation.

One of the achievements of late twentieth century feminism has been the rediscovery and reinterpretation of women's resistance in the past. There's now ample evidence of earlier attempts by women to get out from under, and by men to keep us down. We are not the first wave of feminism – and probably not the second either – but the most recent in a long line of resisters, the earliest of whom we'll probably never know about.

For instance, we know all too little about those women in the past who lived outside the patriarchal household, on their own, or with other women, who were viewed as so threatening – economically, socially and sexually – to patriarchal control, that the result was massive witch hunts in Europe and America in the Sixteenth and Seventeenth Centuries. Diana Gittens in *The Family in Question* describes how women were executed for 'crimes' which included providing 'contraceptive measures, performing abortion, offering drugs to ease the pain of labour'. Fears about numbers of women supporting themselves and living independently of men brought a vicious backlash of persecution and extermination. The modern version of witch hunting is the anti-feminist, and specifically anti-lesbian, attacks we've already described.

We do know quite a lot about the women of the nineteenth and early twentieth century who also called themselves feminists and of the treatment they received at the hands of politicians, newspapers, police and prison warders. The struggle by women to gain the vote has been well documented, and now other campaigns have been researched by contemporary feminists. We now know about the struggles of working-class women for the vote, education, better health care and peace. We also know that many women were involved in campaigns against male violence and male sexual practices which were very similar campaigns to our own and that women writing and campaigning against child prostitution and abuse, rape and male violence were up against similar reactions. Like the judge who urged jurors to be lenient with a man found guilty of incest because it was 'the sort of thing that could happen to any man'.

Sheila Jeffreys, in her excellent book *The Spinster and her Enemies,* shows how relatively large numbers of unmarried women, living independently of men, coincided with a strong, vociferous women's movement, which met with a backlash aimed at discrediting their all–too-uncomfortable analysis in ways which sound very familiar. Spinsters, feminists and lesbians, who resisted the rallying call to sexual intercourse and family life, were accused of being frigid, infantile, abnormal and dangerous, to scare off any other women. 'In the auditorium of every theatre she sits the pale guardian . . . she haunts every library . . . In the schools she takes the little children and day by day they breathe in the atmosphere of her violated spirit.'

Male historians have paid little attention to these campaigns except to call the campaigners prudes and puritans. It's good to have a feminist interpretation of their work and to reclaim them as pioneers of an analysis which points the finger at patriarchy. The debates in which they were engaged and the backlash they experienced are uncannily like our own experiences. One MP speaking in a parliamentary debate in 1921 claimed that lesbians would destroy civilisation. 'These moral weaknesses date back to the very origin of history and when they grow and become prevalent in any country it is the beginning of the nation's downfall.'

Writing about sex education 55 years later another MP, Rhodes Boyson, claimed: 'The positive bringing out of images of lesbianism and homosexuality as if they were equivalent forms of life could bring death in one generation . . . there is no future in it. It is the end of creation.'

Some things never change.

What is to be done

Unless we're vigilant the backlash will hit home. Those of us treated as defectors – independent women, feminists and lesbians – don't enjoy being blamed and isolated and are beginning to feel the cold. While we have no intention of selling out, or giving up on our principles, in an effort to 're-enter the fold', it's tempting to take refuge in purely personal solutions that can make life seem more bearable. We can even build walls around our lives which protect us from a hostile world, behind which we do what we want. But they're walls which also confine us and keep us quiet.

For women without much of a stake in the future except, perhaps, our kids, it's tempting to keep our heads down, not to cause trouble and devote ourselves to the home front. Some of us have little choice. Ferreting through second hand clothes shops, walking to save the bus fare and queueing up for the Social doesn't leave much time for changing the world.

> Living on Supplementary
> is a very exhausting existence
> We use up so much energy
> There isn't much left for resistance.
> We're in the kitchen most of the time
> Baking or washing the clothes
> It's those time-consuming basics
> like hanging out nappies in rows.
> At times its not where we want to be
> but that's not the point, don't you see.
> We bake what we eat or we're out in the street.
> If you says its not right, we agree.
> It's a mile to the oven for women like us
> With no freezer, no wages, no car.
> It's a walk into town and much longer back
> We don't like it, but that's where we are.
> We're not sitting at home by the telephone
> Reading this week's Woman's Groan
> We're stretching the stew at the end of the queue
> Buying flour and spuds by the stone.

But at home in our nuclear family bunkers, with the acid rain of propaganda homing in on us, we are isolated and vulnerable. We get caught in the crossfire between our fragile sense of self and our all too keen sense of guilt for wanting something better. At the very least, the danger is that we'll give up the struggle to be independent women as well as good homemakers, mothers or wives. But worse – we'll be made to feel there's something wrong with us and what we need is treatment.

They tell us not to leave our children when they're young – so I tried to get a job where I could take my daughter with me. It was impossible. They tell us to get a job to get out of the poverty trap but won't let us sign on for work if we've got young children. We were living – well barely living – on £30 per week. I was at my wits end so I went to see the doctor. He said he could either prescribe tranquillisers or arrange for me to have therapy at the psychiatric clinic. But I don't want either – I want a job and enough money to live on. Now they've said I'm ill, I do feel ill and depressed and desperate. But I also feel angry . . .

Women in Britain eat our way through more tranquillisers and anti-depressant drugs than anyone else in the world. This is usually because it's all we're offered in the place of independence, decent jobs and homes, or any control over our own lives. 'Drugging us up to the eyeballs' keeps us quiet and gets us back on our feet – after a fashion – at little financial cost to society and with no need to think of changing that society.

We know of a woman whose refusal to wash up or clean the house was taken as a sign of mental illness. Another who couldn't cope with the demeaning and brutalising sexual demands of her husband and was labelled mentally unstable. Both women – and many others for all we know – were hospitalised against their will. Today's mental hospitals and psychiatric clinics admit working-class and black women at a much higher rate than any other group in the population. Women are sectioned and drugged and given ECT [Electro-Convulsive Therapy] in ways that are as horrifying as they are pointless. Women returned to the situation of poverty, hopelessness, abuse and dependency that create these problems in the first place might have our senses dulled by drugs, our anger quietened by incarceration and our memories destroyed by ECT. But since we weren't 'ill' in the first place, neither are we 'cured'. Back home our situations haven't changed. Of course all of this is a tried and tested remedy for dealing with difficult 'cases'. It silences objectors, serves as a warning to others and keeps the 'problem' under control.

> Every so often
> Susan goes skating
> a woman on ice
> a windmill rotating.
> She goes on her own
> with a handful of change

not batting an eye
when they look at her strange.
Her eyes are wide open
she knows what they say
a no hoper head-case
out for the day.
She stays for the session
turning around
slowly at first
till sure of her ground.
Then faster and faster
at home on this slide
where no one can catch her
or capture her pride
peacefully gliding
deciding the pace
her out of touch clothing
floating in space.
She knows they are calling
all clear the ice
waits till there's no one
doesn't think twice
Untying her laces
her mind on the block
where every so often
the treatment is shock.
Holding her skates
like two broken wings
swaps them for shoes
she bought for two rings.
Short cut through the woods
back over the fence
where high price surroundings
are small recompense.
She tore down the curtains
her husband had sworn
had kept going to pieces
had stayed out till dawn.
A difficult patient
they write in their words
lacks dedication
watches the birds.

In terms of race and class the backlash presents women with
additional dangers. The attempt to divide the nation socially and
economically, means that all too often the contact between black
and white, working-class and middle-class women is reduced to a

minimum. Or else our paths only cross in fraught client/
professsional relationships when we are often forced on to opposite
sides. Since we've been writing this book we've observed how the
distancè between us seems to be getting wider and we sense that
some middle-class feminists are rather more optimistic than we are.
Perhaps they are just more cushioned from the economic fallout.
Perhaps this is understandable. If you've got a decent job with equal
opportunities, if you're self-supporting and have more bargaining
power in your personal relationships, it might seem as though
'things are getting better' for women.

In this atmosphere, surrounded by women's books and feminist
journals and friends with similar lifestyles perhaps even discussions
about post-feminism seem appropriate. But beware the backlash.
Middle-class feminists might have found a voice, and have funded
the means to air it in publishing, on television and in films, but all
around black and working-class women are still shouting to the
wind. Unless we get the chance to say what our experiences are,
they will continue to be ignored.

Many middle-class feminists have moved into the growing equal
opportunities bureaucracies. While we're all for improvements in
the working situations of women, the brand of organisational
feminism that seems to be emerging from these endeavours is not an
end in itself. Setting up, and sitting on, endless committees can
drain your energies and cloud your vision – there is more to
liberation than this. The femocratisation of women's political
energies follows a male model and can divert attention from where
it's really needed. It certainly doesn't change anything for those of
us on the outside of these organisations.

To those women 'working from within' men's organisations –
whether it's the Labour Party, Local Authorities or University
Departments – we ask you to remember that your constituency is
women. You owe your allegiances to women and these are more
important than the loyalties demanded of 'the chaps' within
patriarchal institutions. The strategies you use, and the ways in
which you do your work, must seek to transform men's
organisations and prevent them from remaining as the clubs and
outposts of an empire run by men. Their rules were made to
preserve male power and you must learn to break them.

Be irreverent – expose their stupidity and pomposity.
Be disloyal – tell the truth about their corruption and hypocrisy.

Be obtrusive – tell your own truth and take delight in its emotion and
passion and partiality.
If talking to them doesn't change them – stop talking.
If their meetings are fixed against you – don't go to them.
Ignore threats about promotion and references – if you're not prepared
to be compromised or smashed, careerism isn't an option anyway.
Once you stop wasting your energy on writing out proposals, attending
pointless meetings, hoping the boys will like you, and surviving the flack,
you'll find you liberate a lot more useful energy to spend on doing more
important things.
Things like re-distributing their resources to women wherever possible.
Asset stripping their buildings – of space and facilities – for women.
Getting on with things they'd never agree to if you asked first. Refusing
to do things which are a distraction from making women a priority.
Working with women who give out energy rather than men who take and
crush it.

Which is not to underestimate the courage and perserverance it
takes to practise daily disobedience to the fathers. And it's certainly
not to minimise the severity of the backlash unleashed on women
who step boldly and with deliberation out of line. But it does mean
that – if you are brave enough and irreverent enough – there is a way
through all the restrictions and reprisals for some kind of positive
resistance and to a growing sense of women taking control of our
own affairs.

For those in the business of women's education it's still very easy
to get diverted along pathways which lead to the sticks rather than
towards the light of liberation. We've seen that efforts to get
women's needs recognised within education have met with some
success where organisers have seen it as an opportunity to boost
falling sales and get more 'bums on seats'. What's on 'offer' isn't
always in our interests.

The popularising of a safe and sanitised brand of women's
education – courses in 'coffee and confidence' or 'assertiveness
training' to improve on 'small talk' aren't going to get us any further
than 'hostess cookery' or 'basket-weaving for beginners' did in the
past – and is a view of women's education which sees us only in need
of confidence and company and will do little to lead us towards
independence or autonomy. Likewise women's education couched
in the theory and practice of therapy and counselling – which
emphasises personal development through the interaction between
the teacher/counsellor and student/client – re-emphasises a class
view of education and has nothing to offer us in the way of women's
liberation.

These are just some of the dangers of the backlash. If we are to survive it, and avoid getting smashed or diverted, we must hang on to what we know is true. We haven't made the analysis of our oppression glibly or painlessly. We know that our position today is the product of centuries of patriarchal rule and that men have institutionally and personally asserted their power over us and restricted our own. We shouldn't forget that or begin to doubt it. But with this analysis there also goes a vision of the future in which things will be different, where we will be freed from the constraints that men place upon us and where we will be safe to pursue our lives without the fear of male violence. We want a future in which men can be equal but not privileged, strong but not dominant, and in which their own power and esteem does not depend on our submission and humiliation. We look to a future in which women will no longer be exploited and abused but valued and empowered and able to change the course of a world which has been run by and for men for too long. If we are to work towards this vision, we need not only to survive the backlash but to find the strength and strategies to resist it both individually and collectively.

Looked at from the trenches, where most of us have few resources and little power anyway, messages that tell us to 'make the best of it' or 'do our duty' are more likely to hit home than those telling some of us we can 'make it if we try'. Either way, in the war of words, we must beware of the ideology associated with the backlash. When so much of what we see, read and hear around us – from politicians, in the press, on television, down the pub and in the pulpit – are ploys intended to manipulate our ideas and to control our behaviour, it's important to know what is being attempted. Recognising these lies for what they are is the first line of defence against them. We can't afford either individually or collectively, to lose the battle against false ideologies or to let our truths be buried.

Next, we can refuse to co-operate. We know enough about how women have been silenced in the past, and how 'divide and rule' tactics have been used to separate us from each other. We won't collude in baiting or disowning those who live their lives differently – those of us who are labelled 'extremists', 'scroungers' or 'perverts'. Nor will we collude in, or let pass anti-woman sentiments – from the pin-ups in the tabloids to the crude and tasteless humour of so-called comedians – which we are supposed to find harmless or amusing. They are neither. If we did the same kind of things, in the same relentless fashion, to men, there might be some justification for accusing us of being man-haters. In fact, they are assaults which reflect women-hatred on a massive scale, which diminish our freedom and which we must not let pass unchallenged.

> The comic loves a nagging wife
> he knows the golden rule
> shut 'em up
> by any means
> and his is ridicule
> He also loves a mother-in-law
> her knowledge is a threat
> so he lets her know how far to go
> just in case she should forget.
> He follows a tradition
> women are his game
> a stitch in time
> a laugh a line
> the jokes are all the same.
> He never lets the side down
> he's never at a loss
> give 'em an inch
> they'll take a yard
> let 'em know who's boss.
> He's confident and cocky
> quite blatant with his blows
> he's got a licence
> for his mouth
> keep 'em on their toes.
> Not you luv, is the message,
> It's her just up the road
> so clap on cue
> it isn't you
> control them is the code.
> He lives on dubious laughter
> confusion is the key
> Make 'em laugh
> Make 'em cry
> Make 'em anything but free.

Nor will we co-operate with the relentless pressure on us to devote ourselves entirely to others. It's not good for them and its disastrous for us. 'Changing the system' by 'working from within' takes on a whole new meaning when we refuse or forget to service those who are fit, able and old enough to do it for themselves. We're always being told that our influence over the next generation is enormous – so lets make sure it is, and that the enormous energy we put into bringing up our kids is spent in ways that challenge the patriarchal order. It means learning not to let anything pass, to point out all the time to our children that there are alternative and better ways of running the world. The battle for the hearts and minds of our children is another one we can't afford to lose or give up through exhaustion.

Next, we need to disobey the messages that tell us what we can and can't do. This includes the whole battery of contraints, customs and prohibitions that prevent us from taking up space in the world, everywhere from the working men's club to the labour market. We need to challenge the rules that keep us out, confront the warnings that deny us access and become the thin end of a wedge that one day will force the doors open.

Faced with 2000 years plus of patriarchal power and 99 per cent of the world's resources monopolised by men, the prospect of any of us, or even the woman next door changing the world single-handed is, of course, ludicrous. Changing men's institutions from within is also largely impossible when the systems we're tied up in are part-time shitwork, the family, psychiatric clinics, Social Security and Social Service. 'Making our voices heard' here, 'breaking the rules' and indulging in a spot of 'asset stripping' are more than likely to end us up in hospital or prison. In circumstances like these, we have desperate need of each other, and of alternative sources of support and understanding. When all around us women are being brutalised, abused, taken for granted and put down, including us, we need to learn to love ourselves and to value each other.

Together we can refuse to listen to the voices that tell us that 'the time's not right', 'the recession is too deep', 'resources are too scarce'. We can make up our minds to put our collective energies into creating more women-centred groups like the ones that grew from women's energies in the 1960s and 1970s. Creating Women's Aid and Rape Crisis Lines, women in the Women's Liberation Movement made our concerns and vulnerabilities a priority when no-one else would, and in doing so created not only safe, women-only spaces for us to use when we needed them, but also the inspiration to see what can be achieved when we work together. Our Women's Education Centre is just one example of what we mean.

Of course, working together to set up independent organisations that meet our needs, and running them according to our own rules, takes enormous energy, but it's a positive energy that strengthens and empowers us rather than drags us down. In the 1980s and 1990s we can still make good use of alternative action to reduce our financial vulnerability and to help secure our economic independence. We need more women's workers co-operatives, childcare collectives, welfare rights centres, women's education and training centres and women's housing co-operatives. The kind of women-centred, women-positive developments that give us more chance of making ourselves economically independent and in control of our lives. We're also desperately in need of women-centred, women-controlled alternatives to Social Services to help us withstand the stress that prolonged deprivation, isolation and abuse place upon us in the home.

Whatever difficulties and constraints Social Service Departments and social workers feel they experience, they are nothing compared to the stress we face when we turn to them for help. For too many of us, social workers have become the not-so-soft police, granted a license by the state to scrutinise and interfere in our lives in ways that are totally unacceptable in a so-called free society, without the resources to do very much to improve the circumstances in which we're forced to live.

The strength of the Women's Movement has always been in its alternative, grass roots, locally-based response to women's immediate concerns and grievances. The recognition that these concerns affect us all has put groups of us in touch with each other across countries and continents. In the early days of its re-emergence the Women's Movement paid great attention to the politics of everyday life and to the recognition that family life and women's economic dependency on men is a major source of our oppression. There was the recognition that any woman – every woman – is the potential victim of male violence, and in setting up rape crisis lines, incest survivors groups and women's refuges, we accepted the conviction that 'no woman is safe until we are all safe'. But somewhere along the line we seem to have lost sight of those principles.

The backlash against feminism in recent years; a decade of Thatcherism; internal disagreements within the movement about how to deal with the legacy of race, class and sexual divisiveness we have inherited from men; the complacency of some and the exhaustion of others has left a disparate and dispirited movement. Now, as the backlash rolls relentlessly on and many of us are getting poorer, we need to recreate the general sense of outrage about what is happening to us. We need all women, especially those cushioned from the worst effects of the backlash by good jobs, social class and relatively independent lives, to recognise that their personal prosperity is not an indication that things are getting better for women generally. They are getting worse.

Those of us at the sharp end of poverty, racism, male sexual abuse and oppression need support from other women if we are to take effective collective action. One woman's poverty, abuse or socially induced mental illness is not 'her problem'. It's a problem that touches us all. As long as any woman can be smashed by fear or force or prejudice or hatred, we can all be smashed. We are all being smashed. What strikes some of us down today will strike others down tomorrow. Unless we get ourselves together. The resistance we can make on our own against false ideologies, the dangerous indoctrination of our children and the limitations placed on our freedom to take up space in the world, are nothing compared to what we can do together. If we can re-group, re-kindle the outrage we feel on behalf of each other and remember that there are better ways to run the world, we have more of a chance. Our options are clear. If we don't take control of our own lives, we shall remain in the control of others.

In terms of women's education, which has been the focus of this book, which, by the way, we've now proved we can write despite the odds, of course we realise that education on its own won't change the world. However, a critical, empowering, women-centred education that links 'what we know' with 'what we need to do' is an important tool in our collective struggle for personal and political freedom. Not 'men's education' or 'men's education for women', but education in which we make the knowledge, we are the teachers and we are in control, can help all of us women, whoever we are, to learn together in ways that will inspire and strengthen us in our continuing struggle for women's liberation.